HANDS-ON
SOCIAL
MARKETING

SECOND EDITION

For Gil, Ariel, and Leora, who changed me for good

HANDS-ON
SOCIAL
MARKETING

A Step-by-Step Guide to Designing Change for Good

SECOND EDITION

Nedra Kline Weinreich

Weinreich Communications

Los Angeles | London | New Delhi
Singapore | Washington DC

For information:

SAGE Publications, Inc.
2455 Teller Road
Thousand Oaks, California 91320
E-mail: order@sagepub.com

SAGE Publications India Pvt. Ltd.
B 1/I 1 Mohan Cooperative Industrial Area
Mathura Road, New Delhi 110 044
India

SAGE Publications Ltd.
1 Oliver's Yard
55 City Road
London EC1Y 1SP
United Kingdom

SAGE Publications Asia-Pacific Pte Ltd
33 Pekin Street #02-01
Far East Square
Singapore 048763

Printed in the United States of America

Library of Congress Cataloging-in-Publication Data

Weinreich, Nedra Kline.
Hands-on social marketing : a step-by-step guide to designing change for good/Nedra Kline Weinreich. — 2nd ed.
    p. cm.
Includes index.
ISBN 978-1-4129-5369-6 (pbk. : acid-free paper)
1. Social marketing. I. Title.

HF5414.W44 2011
658.8—dc22   2010017528

This book is printed on acid-free paper.

10   11   12   13   14   10   9   8   7   6   5   4   3   2   1

Acquisitions Editor:	Lisa Cuevas Shaw
Editorial Assistant:	MaryAnn Vail
Production Editor:	Catherine M. Chilton
Copy Editor:	Gillian Dickens
Typesetter:	C&M Digitals (P) Ltd.
Proofreader:	Annette R. Van Deusen
Indexer:	Diggs Publication Services
Cover Designer:	Gail Buschman
Marketing Manager:	Helen Salmon
Permissions:	Karen Ehrmann

Brief Contents

Detailed Contents

Foreword

When applied correctly and comprehensively, social marketing can be an effective tool for health promotion, environmental protection, economic development, policy advocacy, and other positive social and behavioral changes among individuals and communities. When applied incorrectly, often by using a few selected techniques or strategies instead of the entire social marketing process, social marketing programs are less effective and essentially mislabeled as "social marketing." By following the step-by-step program presented in this book and using its thoughtful worksheets, you can develop scientifically sound social marketing programs that are likely to be effective for your program goals and intended audiences.

As Director of the National Center for Health Marketing at the U.S. Centers for Disease Control and Prevention from 2005 to 2010, I supported the effective application of social marketing to major domestic and global challenges, including efforts to prevent HIV, increase physical activity, promote influenza vaccine, and increase awareness and action on climate change. In these and other cases, the effectiveness of the program is often predicted by its comprehensive use of social marketing and the extent to which information from and about the target audience informs its development and implementation, sometimes known as its "customer centricity." This book provides excellent strategies and examples for formative research and audience engagement, which are absolutely critical for developing effective social marketing programs.

In the decade that has passed since the release of the first edition of *Hands-On Social Marketing*, there have been enormous changes in marketing and communication with profound implications for social marketing, now and in the future. The proliferation of the Internet and social media has changed when and how people share information in their networks and how they make decisions in their lives. The rapid diffusion of mobile technology domestically and especially globally has created opportunities for empowerment and intervention where they never before existed. The introduction of principles from design and behavioral economics offers great potential for increasing the customer centricity and impact of our programs. These topics are well addressed in this new, second edition of *Hands-On Social Marketing* and will help social marketing professionals incorporate these important developments into their work.

I believe this book is well grounded in the science and research of social marketing and its related disciplines yet presents practical information, advice, and strategies in an easy-to-read and easy-to-use manner that will be useful for students as well as novice and experienced social marketers. Following its principles consistently and comprehensively will help you develop more effective social marketing programs. It is a valuable resource that I keep handy on my own bookshelf.

Jay M. Bernhardt, PhD, MPH

Professor and Chair
Department of Health Education and Behavior
Director, Center for Digital Health and Wellness
University of Florida
Gainesville, FL, USA

Preface

The world of social marketing is a much different one than when the first edition of this book was published in 1999. Over the course of a decade, social marketing has pushed its way into widespread recognition as an effective approach for changing individual and social behavior. While still not a common household term, the professionals in fields such as public health, social services, and environmental protection who need to know about it are at least aware of its existence. Institutions such as the National Center for Health Marketing at the U.S. Centers for Disease Control and Prevention and the United Kingdom's National Social Marketing Centre have done an excellent job of promoting the strategic social marketing process to both policymakers and program planners. And a panoply of conferences and books on all aspects of social marketing leads students and professionals alike in learning both theory and practice.

In addition to evolution in the field of social marketing itself, much has changed in the practice of all types of marketing. While the Internet had already been around for a while when the first edition came out, since then, social media have revolutionized the capabilities and expectations of how people gather and communicate online. The tools continue to grow and change, but the underlying philosophy of bringing "power to the people" and easily connecting with others with similar interests has meant that we have to change how we think about marketing. This paradigm shift means we can no longer just communicate to our audience but must engage with them as well.

Another strand of marketing that this book develops more fully is how to apply the design approach to behavior change so that we do not need to rely on communication or engagement for people to make the optimal choice. Building in this angle and looking at the social marketing process more broadly has resulted in modifications to the steps as originally laid out in the previous edition, as well as additional chapters.

While many things have changed in this new edition, what has not changed is the book's focus on helping those both in the field and in the classroom learn how to develop social marketing programs through a step-by-step process of strategic planning and design. *Hands-On Social Marketing* was written for practitioners who want to apply the concepts of social marketing in the "real world." Organizations at the community level might not have at their fingertips the benefit of extensive resources and expert assistance that often are found in state and national social marketing programs. Each chapter takes into account the challenges faced by organizations with small budgets and little experience with developing and implementing this type of program. Despite this orientation, the information in this book is equally applicable to those working at the state, national, and international levels.

The beauty of social marketing is that it provides a clearly defined process for program development. This book explains that process and provides detailed advice on how to successfully accomplish each stage. Moreover, the book is designed to be user-friendly and functional—a tool as much as a teacher. By using the many accompanying worksheets in your planning, you will have a ready-made "consultant" asking you all the right questions as you go along. For best results, read the whole book through *before* starting to plan your program.

The main message I hope you get from this book is that you *can* do social marketing yourself. You do not need to hire a high-priced advertising agency or spend large sums of money to put these ideas into practice. This book emphasizes low-cost research methods and tells how to stretch a small budget without sacrificing quality. The biggest investment you will need to make is mental, not material; it is simply to develop the understanding needed to begin thinking from a social marketing perspective.

ACKNOWLEDGMENTS

I would like to thank Lisa Shaw, my editor at Sage Publications, who has been enormously patient as I sometimes unsuccessfully balanced working on this new edition of the book with all my other projects. Thank you as well to everyone else at Sage who assisted in the production of this book, including MaryAnn Vail, Catherine Chilton, and Gillian Dickens. A special thanks goes to my husband, Gil, and my children, Ariel and Leora, who are so loving and supportive of everything I do.

SAGE Publications would like to thank the following reviewers:

Martin L. Wood
Ball State University

Karin Gwinn Wilkins
University of Texas at Austin

Michele Vancour
Southern Connecticut State University

Benjamin Tyson
Central Connecticut State University

Ted Schlie
Lehigh University

Michael Peterson
University of Delaware

Beth Offenbacker
Waterford, Inc.

James Kiwanuka-Tondo
North Carolina State University

Susan Roberts-Dobie
University of Northern Iowa

Section I

What Is Social Marketing?

SECTION OVERVIEW

Before jumping into creating your social marketing program, it is essential to understand the fundamentals of social marketing and how best to use it. In Section I, you will learn these fundamentals in the following four chapters:

- Chapter 1: Social Marketing Basics
- Chapter 2: Not Just Business as Usual
- Chapter 3: The Social Marketing Mix
- Chapter 4: The Social Marketing Process

Social Marketing Basics

What is it about Starbucks that keeps people coming back to spend over $4.00 each time? Ask who goes to Starbucks, and most people will answer things like "yuppies," "coffee connoisseurs," or "people with money." Starbucks is not just about coffee—it offers branded music collections, comfy chairs to sit in to chat with friends, Wi-Fi for your office away from home, social and environmental initiatives, and its own language (what is a "venti double half-caf skinny mochaccino" anyway?). The company has created an aspirational lifestyle that people can join just by walking around with a Starbucks cup.

What if we could create a brand for health or social behaviors that people kept returning to over and over? It would be a product that they aspired to "own" and wanted to make sure other people knew they liked. The product would be fun and easy to use, aligned with their values, and its communications would be tailored to feel like the brand was talking directly to them. The behavior would simply become the obvious choice, without having to make a conscious decision to do it. In fact, we can create this kind of brand using the tools and techniques of social marketing.

As organizations and government agencies search for solutions to bring about positive change on many of the most intractable problems in society, they are increasingly turning to the field of social marketing for answers. Whether it's motivating kids to get active to prevent obesity, making recycling an automatic behavior, or tackling a massive issue such as poverty, professionals and policymakers are finding that social marketing offers an approach that brings together the most effective thinking from many different fields in a systematic process.

Traditionally, when organizations or government agencies have wanted to influence people's behaviors on a mass scale, they have used either an educational or policy approach. The educational approach presumes that if you just give people the facts, they will make the rational decision to take action; all they need is information. With some topics, this approach works well; we've done a good job of teaching people the 911 phone number to call for emergency services. Unfortunately, education is necessary but may not be sufficient to bring about behavior change on more complex or emotion-based behaviors. Decades of showing kids pictures of smokers' diseased lungs were not enough to keep teens from smoking in droves.

Policies that legislate a particular behavior under threat of jail or a fine, or increase the costs through taxation, can be very effective. These coercive methods make sense for behaviors that can hurt other people or are basic life-saving actions, such as preventing drinking and driving, wearing seatbelts, or not smoking in a public place. But do we want to live in a world where all

3

our health or social behaviors are regulated? Diminishing liberty and free choice should only be done as a last resort when other methods have not worked.

DEFINING SOCIAL MARKETING

Since the early 1970s, social marketing has emerged as an effective way of persuading people to voluntarily adopt healthy and prosocial behaviors for issues that may require more than just laying out the facts. Simply put, social marketing is the use of commercial marketing principles and techniques to promote the adoption of a behavior that will improve the health or well-being of the target audience or of society as a whole. These are the same methods that a company such as Coca-Cola uses to sell its soft drinks—a focus on its consumers, market research, and a systematic process for developing a marketing program. The key characteristic that distinguishes social marketing from commercial marketing is its purpose; that is, the benefits accrue to the individual or society rather than to the marketer's organization. In addition, the cross-pollination of disciplines with marketing, including anthropology, social psychology, design, public health, behavioral economics, and persuasive technology, keeps the field dynamic and brings the best thinking about behavior change together in a cohesive process.

Who Uses Social Marketing?

This is just a sample of the many types of organizations that use social marketing in their education and prevention efforts:

- Centers for Disease Control and Prevention
- National Cancer Institute
- National Heart, Lung, and Blood Institute
- U.S. Environmental Protection Agency
- U.S. Department of Agriculture
- U.S. Agency for International Development
- International health ministries
- State/provincial health departments
- Local health departments
- Community-based organizations
- National nonprofit organizations
- Universities
- Environmental agencies/nonprofits
- Social service agencies/nonprofits
- Private foundations
- Community coalitions
- Corporations

WHAT SOCIAL MARKETING IS NOT

All too often, the well-intentioned nonprofit director who uses marketing techniques to raise funds for the director's organization, or the health educator who creates a television commercial without even talking to the people the educator is trying to reach, believes that he or she is practicing social marketing. Conducting a focus group, creating an awareness campaign, designing communications for a nonprofit—all of these may or may not be part of a social marketing program; it depends on whether they are done systematically—following the social marketing process.

Use of the term to mean many different things has led to confusion about what social marketing is. In addition to misunderstanding what social marketing means in a health and social issue context, a growing number of people from outside the field have co-opted the term to refer to social media marketing. Since the emergence of social media in the mid-2000s, a large contingent of Internet-focused marketers have managed inadvertently to sow extensive confusion as they took over "social marketing" for their own purposes and shifted the balance of online references to the term over to their definition. Although a feisty contingent of (real) social marketers works hard to combat the semantic takeover, there are more of them than us, and the field of social marketing needs to do a better job of marketing "social marketing."

STRENGTHS AND LIMITATIONS

As with any tool, social marketing cannot be expected to solve every type of health and social problem. Social marketing is at its best when used to effect and sustain healthful or socially beneficial behavior change, increase program use, or build customer satisfaction with existing services. The same techniques can be used to move from a focus on individual-based changes to working more broadly for changes at the community level, including policymakers, media, and other community institutions.

A social marketing program would not be effective for certain issues such as complex problems with many contributing or confounding factors, problems not under individual control (e.g., genetic flaws), and addictive disorders. You also would be ill advised to undertake a social marketing approach if you are unwilling or unable to commit the resources needed to do it well.

What Issues Have Been Addressed With Social Marketing?

- HIV/AIDS
- Breast cancer
- Family planning
- Immunization
- High blood pressure
- Cholesterol
- Radon
- Nutrition
- Panic disorder
- Asthma
- Breastfeeding
- Drug abuse
- Energy conservation
- Smoking
- Oral rehydration therapy
- Volunteerism
- Child abuse
- Osteoporosis
- Physical activity
- Recycling
- Animal protection
- School enrollment
- Bicycle helmets
- Depression
- Educational opportunity
- Voting/civic engagement
- Pollution prevention

In some cases, an organization might be better off using its funds to add staff or capacity to its current services rather than to develop a social marketing project.

CHAPTER 2

Not Just Business as Usual

The social marketing approach differs greatly from how health and human service organizations typically go about developing programs or materials. Often, professionals in these organizations think they know what people's problems are, what services they require, and what they need to know. These professionals believe that if they could only get all the information out to the general public, then the people they are trying to help would see that they are at risk and change their behavior. Unfortunately, this common approach often is ineffective.

FOCUS ON BEHAVIOR CHANGE

The endless barrage of "awareness campaigns" on various topics has conditioned people to think that the best cure for any problem is to offer up all the facts about an issue and assume that people will do the right thing. Once they understand the problem exists, surely they will see the light! Unfortunately, the number of health professionals who smoke or are overweight attests to the fact that knowledge does not always lead to action. Knowledge may be necessary, but it's usually not sufficient.

When you create a social marketing program, you will need to be very clear about what behavior you want people to adopt. Changing awareness, attitudes, and beliefs are all important steps on the path toward behavior change, but true success does not occur until someone takes action. An organization promoting the integration of people with disabilities into the workforce may be thrilled if employers have increased positive attitudes as a result of the campaign, but if they never actually hire a qualified person with a disability when the opportunity presents itself, can the organization say it truly met its goal? Just like companies ultimately judge their success by the amount of profit they bring in, the bottom line for social marketers is behavior change.

TARGETING AND SEGMENTING YOUR AUDIENCE

The first lesson of any kind of marketing is that there is no such thing as targeting the general public; social marketing is no exception. Like an extra large T-shirt, a one-size-fits-all strategy doesn't fit most people particularly well. To be most effective, specify the audience for your program as precisely as possible. Think about all the different groups you want to involve in your social marketing program. They might include the following:

- Your clients or the people you want to reach
- People who influence your primary audience such as parents, spouses, teachers, physicians, and peers
- Policymakers
- Media professionals
- Your supervisors or board of directors
- Your employees, co-workers, and volunteers

These all are quite distinct groups, each of which requires different types of communications and strategies for the social marketing program to work.

Even within each of the preceding categories, there are many different types of people. For example, a program to prevent sexually transmitted diseases among teenagers might take different approaches for males and females, for younger and older adolescents, for those who do not believe they are at risk and those who do but need help convincing their partners to use condoms, or for those who get regular Pap smears and those who do not. Some teens read at a 12th-grade level, and others require pictures to understand the messages. Clearly, the same approach will not work for all of these subgroups.

The objectives of your program will guide you in identifying the appropriate audience, and research will help you tailor your approach to that audience. The social marketing method of segmentation advocates dividing your audience into different subgroups and developing strategies specifically for one or more of these groups.

RESEARCHING YOUR AUDIENCE

Too often, the typical approach to program development is that program administrators base messages and strategies on what they think the target audience needs to know. They develop multifaceted programs with expensive audiovisual presentations, four-color brochures, and newspaper advertisements. Staff think that the program is great, but they cannot understand why no one shows up for their services.

What is wrong with this picture? Did they ever ask the people they are trying to reach what types of programs or services they need? Maybe if they asked, they would find out that people in the target audience would like to have come but could not for any of the following reasons:

- They could not afford babysitters.
- They would rather be connected with a job service or drug rehab center than take health education classes.
- The program was scheduled during the day, while everyone was working.
- They do not read the newspaper and so missed the advertisement.

■ They did not think the program was for people like them.

Social marketers know that to create effective programs, they must talk (and listen) to the people in their target audience to find out what they want and need as well as what would have the greatest effect on changing their behavior. Research forms the cornerstone of social marketing and makes program development a bottom-up process with guidance coming from the target audience rather than the usual top-down approach.

BUILDING A COMPREHENSIVE STRATEGY

When people think about social marketing, they naturally focus on the most visible element of the strategy, which is the communications piece. But the most effective programs are like an iceberg—only a small part of the strategy is visible, with the bulk of the hard work that went into it only clear once you dive deeper into the campaign development. Creating a program that starts and ends with messages and materials is not true social marketing. As will be discussed in Chapter 3, a social marketing strategy—the social marketing mix—comprises a set of decision points that ensure the "marketing" piece of social marketing remains front and center.

A strategic social marketing approach is based on research and includes thinking through elements like what the product is and its most salient benefits to the target audience, price considerations and how to reduce perceived costs, how to make the product available at the times and places the audience will be most receptive, which promotional tools should carry the messages, and more. Perhaps you will find that your issue can be addressed by making some environmental design-based changes that do not even require the target audience to be persuaded to change their behavior. If, after mapping out a comprehensive strategy, it makes the most sense to focus on communications as your primary approach, that's one thing. But don't go straight to developing materials without putting in the strategic forethought.

FOLLOWING A SYSTEMATIC PROCESS

The following situation might sound familiar.

The Springfield Blister Council just realized that National Blister Prevention Week is coming up in a couple of months. Every year, the council scrambles to put together a campaign and to get the word out through the media. An online fact sheet is cobbled together, posters are designed from an idea the intern came up with, and press releases are sent to the main

What Is a Target Audience?

You will see the term *target audience* used frequently throughout the book. The target audience is the people whose behavior you wish to affect. Your target audience might be those your organization already serves as clients or members, or it could be a new group of people you want to reach who do not yet know about you. You can think of the target audience as your potential customers or as consumers who are considering whether to adopt your "product" over that of the competition. Often, they will be the people most at risk for the problem you are addressing. You may direct your social marketing campaign to the target audience, or you might decide that others, such as their key influencers or policymakers, are the most important to address to increase the chances of bringing about change. Note that the term *audience* is not meant to imply that they are passive recipients of information, as the best campaigns involve participation and engagement beyond just seeing or hearing messages.

Listening to Your Audience

The American Legacy Foundation's Truth Campaign[2] moved away from the usual approaches to keeping kids from starting to smoke by conducting research on the reasons why teens smoke in the first place. The program creators dug deeper to look at the universal teenage values that make smoking appealing—a desire to rebel against authority, the drive toward independence and self-expression while at the same time wanting to be part of a group. Rather than the then-common approach of showing pictures of diseased lungs and focusing on the long-term health effects of smoking, the campaign took a different tack by redirecting those teenage values in positive directions.

The Truth Campaign deflected adolescent rebellion away from parents and teachers and toward the tobacco industry by focusing on how cigarette marketers lie and manipulate people to start and continue to smoke. The campaign cultivated a teen movement to take on the tobacco industry and held events around the country to provide opportunities for teens to come together and express themselves. Teens were directly involved in the design of the campaign and encouraged to spread the message from peer to peer.

Evaluation results showed that this strategy of listening to the target audience about what would be most appealing and effective paid off. Between 1999 and 2002, the Truth Campaign was credited with preventing approximately 300,000 youth from smoking, with the prevalence rate 1.5 percentage points lower than it would have been in the absence of the campaign.[3]

newspaper and television stations. Somehow, the campaign does not seem to have much effect, particularly among the people at highest risk for blisters. Council staff have resolved that this year they will start earlier and send press releases to a greater number of media outlets.

Not surprisingly, if this is all the Blister Council staff are changing, then the campaign is unlikely to be any more effective than it has in the past. No matter how far in advance the staff begin work, haphazard planning results in a disjointed campaign. Without information on how best to reach the people most likely to get blisters, which messages are most effective in motivating behavior change, and results of evaluations of past campaigns, the council might not be doing much more than making its staff feel good.

Social marketing provides a systematic process to follow that ensures that programs are based on research rather than on one person's idea of what looks good. Ideally, a campaign like this one would be part of the organization's long-term social marketing strategy rather than a one-shot blip on the blister prevention radar screen. By developing a comprehensive strategy based on research, the Blister Council staff would already know the key messages they need to convey to the target audience and which media would be most effective in reaching it as they prepare for National Blister Prevention Week.

DEVELOPING A SOCIAL MARKETING MIND-SET

Social marketing involves more than just blindly following a step-by-step process. Successful practitioners adopt a social marketing mind-set that affects their perception of every aspect of their programs, similar to the customer-centered mind-set described by Alan Andreasen.[1] In other words, they see the world through social marketing–colored lenses.

---

[1]Andreasen, A. (1995). *Marketing social change.* San Francisco: Jossey-Bass.

[2]Evans, W. D., Wasserman, J., Bertolotti, E., & Martino, S. (2002). Branding behavior: The strategy behind the Truth (SM) campaign. *Social Marketing Quarterly, 8*(3), 17–29.

[3]Farrelly, M. C., Davis, K. C., Haviland, M. L., Messeri, P., & Healton, C. G. (2005). Evidence of a dose-response relationship between "truth" antismoking ads and youth smoking prevalence. *American Journal of Public Health, 95,* 425–431.

Just as Copernicus radically altered how people thought about the world by showing that the earth revolves around the sun, social marketing has moved clients, constituents, and citizens into the center of the universe for the professionals serving them. An effective social marketing program focuses on the consumer; all of its elements are based on the wants and needs of its target audience rather than on what the organization happens to be selling.

Once you adopt a social marketing mind-set, you might look at your organization in a different way. Rather than providing services or designing materials the way in which the program director likes them best, social marketers ask their clients what they need to adopt a particular behavior. In all decisions, they look at the issue from the consumers' point of view, asking themselves, "How can we best serve our clients?" instead of "How can we make life easier for ourselves?" And as in commercial marketing, they keep their eyes on the bottom line—not sales but rather behavior change.

Social marketing concepts are extremely versatile. You can use these techniques for many different purposes:

- To develop a communication campaign

- To create specific promotional or educational materials

- To improve the services your organization provides

- To design the environment to make it easier for people to adopt a behavior change

- To create new programs

Whatever your final objective, the guiding principles remain the same.

In a famous tale, the Jewish sage Hillel was asked by a non-Jew to define the essence of his religion while standing on one foot. Hillel responded, "What is hateful unto you do not do unto your neighbor. The rest is commentary; now go and study."[4] Likewise, the essence of social marketing (one-footed or otherwise) is that you must target and research your audience to create a strategic, consumer-centered program. The rest is commentary; now keep reading the book.

---

[4]From the Talmud, as recounted in Telushkin, J. (1991). *Jewish literacy.* New York: Morrow.

CHAPTER 3

The Social Marketing Mix

As you design a social marketing program, you will need to think through various strategic factors to create an approach that is most likely to appeal to your audience and meet its needs. To develop a comprehensive strategy, social marketing borrows an idea from traditional marketing practice called the "marketing mix." In the planning process, research with the target audience assists in making programmatic decisions about the following:

- Product
- Price
- Place
- Promotion

These often are called the "four Ps" of marketing. They have been adapted to fit social marketing practice and are used somewhat differently from how they are used in commercial marketing.

Social marketing also adds some Ps of its own:

- Publics
- Partnership
- Policy
- Purse strings

Considering each of these strategic elements as you develop the social marketing mix increases the likelihood of a successful program. A common misstep is to focus only on the promotion piece, ignoring the rest of the Ps, thereby creating a communications—and not a social marketing—campaign. This is like thinking you have solved the whole jigsaw puzzle because you put a piece on the table.

PRODUCT

If motivating people to change their health or social behavior were as easy as convincing them to switch brands of toothpaste, there would be no need for the subfield of social marketing. But trying to affect complex and often emotion-based decisions is rather different from selling a tangible product. The social marketing "product" is the behavior you want the target audience to adopt. The product may fall anywhere along a continuum ranging from physical products (e.g., smoke detectors), to services (e.g., medical examinations), to practices (e.g., breastfeeding, eating a heart-healthy diet), to more intangible ideas (e.g., environmental protection).

The first step in defining your product is to be very clear about the behavior you are seeking to encourage; it should be something that can actually be observed. Ask yourself, "What would it look like if someone successfully completed the behavior?" Rather than your product being "ending prejudice against people with developmental disabilities," identify the specific behaviors that you want people to do or avoid. Perhaps the behavior would be providing employment opportunities, avoiding hurtful language, or engaging someone in a friendly conversation. You would need to decide which behaviors will have the most impact on the problem and are appropriate for your target audience.

To have a viable product, people must first feel that they have a genuine problem and that the product offered is a good solution to that problem. If your target audience members do not see themselves as being at risk or in an improvable situation, then they are unlikely to take measures to protect or better themselves. You might need to build awareness or provide the necessary skills before going about promoting behavior change.

You also might find that you need to refine the product you are offering to make it more effective in reducing the problem, easier to use, or more attractive to the target audience. A family planning clinic with inconvenient hours, rude staff, and a waiting room with big windows that allow passersby to see who is inside probably needs to focus on fixing its product before looking at other elements of the marketing mix.

Positioning Your Product

Your product must be designed to appeal to the target audience and be presented in a way that highlights its attractive features. Show how your product is different and better by creating a niche for it (i.e., promoting it for specific types of people or to solve a particular problem) or by identifying the benefits that make it more appealing than the competition. This is called "positioning" your product. Answer the consumer's question, "What's in it for me?"

Identify the attributes and benefits that can help position the product in the minds of the target audience. An attribute is an objective fact describing the product, whereas a benefit tells you the value that the consumer gets from the attribute. For example, a car might have a convertible top as an attribute, but the benefit for some consumers is that they can have the wind whistling through their hair as they drive, making them feel young and free. The car might have leather seats, with the resulting benefits that its owners can feel wrapped in luxury and that other people can see they are persons of means.

To identify benefits, ask your audience members "So what?" to determine why an attribute might be valuable to them. You can create a "ladder" that links various attributes to their associated benefits. For example, in the hypothetical benefits ladder in Table 3.1, some attributes of physical activity are that it increases the heart rate and helps to burn fat and increase metabolism. The immediate benefit of these attributes, as identified by the target audience, is that they result in weight loss. The benefits associated by the target audience with losing weight are improved appearance and self-image. Laddering these benefits even further yields the

TABLE 3.1   Benefit Ladder: What Are the Attributes and Benefits of Physical Activity (the product) That We Can Use to Appeal to the Target Audience?

Attribute	Benefit	Benefit	Benefit
Increases heart rate Helps to burn fat and increase metabolism	Lose weight	Look better Feel better about yourself	Be sexier
Increases high-density lipoproteins/Decreases blood pressure	Lowers cholesterol level Lowers risk of heart disease Lowers risk of stroke	Live a longer and healthier life	Watch your grandchildren and great-grandchildren grow up
Produces endorphins	Reduce your stress levels	Feel more energetic	Feel more in control of your life Get more done in your day
Builds muscle strength	Become stronger	Be more independent in your daily activities	Have more freedom
Can be done with other people	Spend time with your family and friends	It is an opportunity to socialize	Have fun
Can be done alone	Spend time for yourself	Get away from it all	You deserve to have private time
Many people do it	Join the trend toward exercise	You will fit in	People will approve of you

information that looking good and feeling good about one's own body makes a person sexier. By probing what your target audience members truly deem important (at the end of the benefits ladder), you can uncover more effective ways of appealing to them.

Position the product by showing its key benefits relative to the competition. In social marketing, the competition can be other behaviors or simply nonadoption of the target behavior. For example, if the behavior you are promoting is breastfeeding, then the competition would be feeding the baby formula from a bottle. If you are trying to encourage people to eat more fresh fruits and vegetables, then the competition would depend on the positioning you chose. As a snack food, the competition might be potato chips or cookies; promoting fruit as a dessert, the competition could be ice cream or low-fat diet desserts; and for vegetables as a side dish to a meal, the competition might be instant mashed potatoes, garlic bread, or no side dish at all.

To illustrate how the social marketing mix works, let's look at a real-world example and how the program designed each of the Ps. The U.S. Centers for Disease Control and Prevention (CDC) created the VERB Campaign to increase and maintain physical activity among "tweens"—youth ages 9 to 14.[1] In addition to a comprehensive literature review, campaign organizers conducted extensive formative research with tweens and their parents, including focus groups, interviews, and ethnographic research, which they used to design the program.

(Continued)

[1]Wong, F., Huhman, M., Asbury, L., Bretthauer-Mueller, R., McCarthy, S., Londe, P., & Heitzler, C. (2004). VERB™—a social marketing campaign to increase physical activity among youth. *Preventing Chronic Disease, 1*(3), A10. Available from: URL: http://www.cdc.gov/pcd/issues/2004/jul/04_0043.htm

(Continued)

In the case of the VERB campaign, the product is physical activity. The campaign used its research to identify the benefits that would be most attractive to its audience of tweens and what they value: spending time with friends, playing, having fun, being active with parents, and gaining recognition for their efforts. A big focus of the campaign was giving tweens the opportunity to explore and discover their world—another key value—through various games and activities centered on exercise. The VERB campaign positioned itself to tweens as "their brand for having fun," and the developers were careful to avoid any sense of physical activity as something that kids "have to do." The VERB campaign's product—physical activity as a fun, cool way of life—inspired kids to adopt this lifestyle.

Though tweens have many activities in their lives that compete with physical activity, the campaign focused on sedentary activities such as television, video games, and computer time as the main competitors. Getting parents involved in encouraging kids to choose alternate activities was a key piece of the strategy to overcome that competition.

PRICE

Price refers to what the target audience has to give up to adopt the behavior. The price could be monetary, but more often in social marketing, it involves intangibles such as time, effort, and old habits. Emotional costs can be part of the price as well; in the use of condoms by young men, for example, the price might include feelings of embarrassment when buying the condoms, the possibility of rejection by partners who do not want to use condoms, or giving up the pleasure of unprotected sex. By determining through research what the target audience considers to be the price of performing the behavior, the marketing mix can be designed to minimize the costs so that they do not outweigh the perceived benefits. If the costs outweigh the benefits for an individual, then the product will not be as attractive, and the likelihood of adoption will be low. But if the benefits are perceived as greater than their costs, then chances of trial and adoption of the product are much greater.

Setting a monetary price, particularly for a physical product such as bicycle helmets or energy-efficient light bulbs, can be tricky. If the product is priced too low or is provided free of charge, then consumers might perceive it as being less valuable. If the price is too high, then some will not be able to afford it. Social marketers must balance these considerations and often end up charging at least a nominal fee to increase perceptions of value and affordability. If your program is able to provide services or products for free, you can determine how the target audience will respond through your research.

By conducting research with our target audience, we can find out which are the biggest barriers and which positioning statements are most believable and convincing.

In the VERB campaign, the price that tweens identified for physical activity include financial costs (e.g., for classes or equipment), psychological costs (e.g., not feeling "good enough" to participate in a particular sport), environmental costs (e.g., no safe places to play in the neighborhood), or time-related costs (e.g., parents are not available to supervise or drive tweens to activities). The campaign emphasized the benefits to show that they far outweigh the price.

To get around the barriers that tweens identified as standing in the way of engaging in physical activity, the campaign incorporated various approaches:

- ■ To show tweens that physical activity is for everyone, they included kids of various shapes and sizes, ability levels, and ethnicities in the campaign visuals.

- To keep tweens from dismissing all physical activity because they don't like certain sports, the campaign emphasized finding their own "verb"—what they enjoy doing most.

- To demonstrate that physical activity does not just mean team sports and expensive equipment, the campaign included backyard-centered activities as well.

- To help ensure that tweens are supported when they seek out physical activity opportunities, the campaign focused on their parents as a secondary target audience.

PLACE

In commercial marketing, *place* generally refers to the distribution channels; that is, where and how are the customers going to get the product? Because in most social marketing programs, the product is a behavior rather than a physical item, the question then becomes, "Where is the behavior available to the target audience?" This helps to determine where to expose the target audience members to the program's messages or to put systems in place that facilitate adopting the behavior.

You need to make it very easy for your target audience members to perform the behavior or to encounter the messages you want them to think about; they will not go out of their way to find your campaign. Ideally, your campaign should reach people in a time and place where they are already thinking about or making decisions related to the behavior. This is the concept of "aperture"[2]; just like a camera's lens opens and shuts very quickly to let in the light when you take a picture, you have only a small window of opportunity to get your message through to the target audience at a time and place they can act on it. They will be much more receptive if you try to nudge them toward the desirable behavior at the appropriate time, rather than when it's far from their minds.

To get people to spay or neuter their pets, reach them at the pet store with an onsite clinic or when they are reading their favorite pet fancier magazine and thinking about how to take care of their pets. If you want to reach busy professionals with messages about nutritious snacking, then put your message where and when people are thinking about snacking on the way home from work (drive-time radio or billboards) or at the grocery store.

Another element of place is ensuring that the product is accessible to those you want to reach and maintaining the quality of delivery of the message. If your campaign urges the target audience to see doctors for screenings or information, then two pieces must be in place. First, target audience members must have access to doctors. Second, the doctors should be prepared to do what the campaign says they will do. Otherwise, individuals might act on the campaign messages but without the desired outcome. By determining the activities and habits of the target audience, as well as its level of access to the delivery system, you can pinpoint the best place for your product.

Think about the mechanics of how the product will be delivered. Will you have a "sales force" of community members who will promote the product within their social networks? If so, how will they receive and provide the product? How will you integrate partner organizations or businesses into your distribution network? Are there other existing product delivery systems that

---

[2]Media Research Department, DDB Needham. (1990, May). *Opening up aperture: A study of commercial environment.* Chicago: DDB Needham.

you could "piggyback" on to get yours to the audience? Consider less conventional product distribution methods beyond just media-based approaches.

> The VERB campaign defined place as a location "where tweens can be physically active in a safe environment." Without a suitable and accessible site to exercise, the campaign's efforts to convince kids to get active would be for naught. These places could include backyards, schools, parks, churches, sports organizations, youth or other community organizations, or any other place that had appropriate facilities where tweens could get active and have fun. These places also needed to be considered "cool" by the tweens to make them desirable.
>
> As a place that tweens spend a lot of time, schools were a key part of the outreach strategy. Teachers received media and materials to share with their students as well as ideas for ways to incorporate physical activity in a fun way during the day. In addition, tweens could get involved at community-based events such as cultural festivals where the VERB campaign set up "activity zones" to try out different physical activities. In targeted communities, "street teams" of college-aged adults challenged tweens to get active at events and tween hangouts and rewarded them with fun VERB-branded promotional items.

PROMOTION

Because of its visibility, promotion is what many people think of when they hear about social marketing. Although it is just one part of an integrated strategy, it is a very important one. Promotion deals with how you get your message about the product out to the target audience. The focus is on motivating people to try and then to continue performing the behavior.

Promotion can involve many different methods of conveying the message, including the following:

- Advertising (e.g., television or radio commercials, billboards, posters)

- Public relations (e.g., press releases, letters to the editor, appearances on talk shows)

- Social media (e.g., blogs, social networks, Twitter)

- Promotions (e.g., coupons, contests, in-store displays)

- Media advocacy (e.g., press events designed to encourage policy change)

- Personal selling (e.g., one-on-one counseling, peer educators)

- Special events (e.g., health fairs, concerts)

- Entertainment (e.g., dramatic presentations, songs, television shows)

Research will tell you which are the most effective and efficient ways of reaching a particular target audience. Find out the following: What media does it watch? Where does it get its information? What spokespeople are most credible to the group?

The VERB campaign used many different types of promotional methods to reach its audience:

- Paid media advertising on television and radio in general market and ethnic media channels
- Print advertising in youth and parent magazines, as well as ethnic newspapers
- Media partnerships that resulted in public service announcements run during primetime and children's programming
- Activity promotions such as "The Longest Day of Play" on the summer solstice and "Extra Hour for Extra Action" when clocks were set back from daylight savings to standard time
- Custom-developed materials distributed through schools in youth publications such as *Weekly Reader* and *TIME for Kids* and Primedia's Channel One school-based video news. Other promotions via schools included book covers, day planners, and customized lesson plans.
- Community-based events and grassroots marketing, such as cultural festivals with a VERB-hosted "activity zone" for kids to try out different physical activities. They also used college-aged "street teams" to engage tweens in being physically active in their communities and create buzz about the VERB brand.
- Viral marketing through programs such as the VERB Yellowball, in which 500,000 yellow rubber balls were distributed to tweens to play with and pass along to a friend, along with documenting online what they did with the ball and tracking it from person to person
- Contests and sweepstakes centered on getting kids to move, such as a pedometer-focused contest among schools to accumulate the most number of steps
- Public relations, particularly focused on youth- and parent-centered news outlets
- Community partnerships with organizations across the country to provide opportunities to tweens to get active and to reach parents or influence the environment to support tweens in their activities
- Partnerships with corporations and sports teams to reinforce the campaign's messages
- Websites for tweens, their parents, and partners for further engagement with the VERB campaign

Beyond the four Ps of traditional marketing—product, price, place, and promotion—social marketing must add four more Ps to take into account its unique nature, as discussed in the following sections.

PUBLICS

As mentioned earlier, social marketers often have many different audiences that their program must address to be successful. *Publics* refers to both the external and internal groups involved in the program. The most important external public certainly is the target audience, those people whose behaviors and attitudes you want to affect. Beyond the primary audience, there might be several secondary audiences whose members influence the decisions of the target audience members (e.g., friends, family members, teachers, physicians, bloggers). Another external public could be policymakers who have the ability to create an environment conducive to behavior change or maintenance. Also, those who act as "gatekeepers" in controlling the messages that your target audience receives from the program, such as media professionals and business owners, might need to be convinced that your issue is important and worthy of their attention.

In addition to the many external audiences you might face, addressing your internal publics from the beginning can be the most critical to the success of the program. Often, staff and supervisors must "buy in" to the concept and planned execution of a campaign before it is ever shown to a target audience member. If the head of your organization does not understand what social marketing is and why you need to do things differently from standard operating procedures, the program might never get off the ground. Or, if your campaign provides a phone number and the receptionist does not know how to respond to the callers, then all the hard work that brought the target audience to that point is lost. Educating your staff and supervisors about social marketing, as well as keeping everyone informed about the specifics of the campaign and their roles in it, is crucial.

The VERB Campaign had many different publics it needed to reach out to in order to make the program a success:

External Publics

- Tweens
- Parents of tweens
- Schools—teachers and administrators
- Community-based organization staff
- Corporations
- Public service directors at radio and television stations
- Local reporters in various media
- State and local governments (particularly health departments and parks and recreation departments)

Internal Publics

- Centers for Disease Control and Prevention Project Team
- Department of Health and Human Services Staff
- Project subcontractors, such as advertising agencies and evaluators
- Policymakers in the U.S. Congress (funders)

PARTNERSHIP

Social and health issues often are so complex that one organization cannot make a dent by itself. By teaming up with other groups in the community, your organization can extend its resources as well as its access to members of the target audience. Figure out which organizations have similar audiences or goals as yours—although not necessarily the same goals—and identify ways in which you can work together so that both can benefit.

Some examples of the partners that the VERB Campaign worked with on this project include the following:[3]

- National Recreation and Park Association
- Girl Scouts of America
- Girls, Inc.
- National Association for Sport and Physical Education
- County health departments and community coalitions
- Media networks such as Viacom, Disney, Primedia, and AOL
- YMCA
- Boys and Girls Clubs
- National sports leagues and individual athletes
- Musicians
- Sporting goods manufacturers and retailers
- Schools

POLICY

Social marketing programs can do well in motivating individual behavior change, but that is difficult to sustain unless the environment surrounding the target audience supports that change for the long run. In many cases, policy change has been very effective in providing that type of support. For example, as it has become more difficult for smokers to light up in the workplace and other public places because of policies at various levels (from organizational to federal), many people have decided that smoking is not worth the hassle. Providing recycling containers to each resident will increase the likelihood that they will separate the recyclables from their garbage. Media advocacy techniques, which influence or put pressure on policymakers or an industry through the generation of media attention, and other legislative advocacy such as lobbying can be effective components of a social marketing program.

The VERB Campaign encouraged families to advocate for changes in their communities that would facilitate kids' physical activity. This included taking actions such as the following:

- Writing letters to school administrators and board members to support daily physical education and recess time
- Contacting parks and recreation officials to ask for more opportunities for children to get active
- Encouraging local officials to install park equipment, bike paths, or other resources for physical activity

[3]Bretthauer-Mueller, R., Berkowitz, J. M., Thomas, M., McCarthy, S., Green, L. A., Melancon, H., et al. (2008). Catalyzing community action within a national campaign: VERB™ community and national partnerships. *American Journal of Preventive Medicine, 34*(Suppl.), S210–S221. http://www.ajpm-online.net/article/PIIS0749379708002596/fulltext

PURSE STRINGS

Finally, social marketing generally differs from commercial marketing in the sources of its funding. A company selling a product for its own profit generally will use money for its marketing efforts from start-up capital put down by its owners or from the revenue the company earns. Most organizations that develop social marketing programs operate through funds provided by sources such as foundations, governmental grants, and donations. This adds another dimension to the strategy development—namely, where will you get the money to create your program? You might already have funding at this point, or you might be considering seeking money for a specific project. This book may assist in developing a funding proposal by helping you think through the key elements of your proposed program and your budget needs. You also might consider selling a tangible product as part of your program to keep it self-sustaining.

> The VERB Campaign was funded by the CDC's budget, which is determined annually by Congress. The program also leveraged in-kind donations from media partners, such as ad time and space from media outlets on top of the ads that the campaign purchased. The campaign's many other partners also donated resources to help spread the program throughout the country. Unfortunately, after five years, Congress failed to renew funding to continue the program, and the campaign ended.

CHAPTER 4

The Social Marketing Process

Although the prospect of creating a social marketing program might be daunting, following the common advice of breaking a large task into smaller ones will help. Social marketing provides a straightforward framework for program development that, if followed, ensures that each critical piece occurs at the proper time. The process involves research at every stage, with constant reevaluation to assess whether the program is on track. In practice, social marketing is not necessarily a clear series of linear steps but rather a process of feedback and adjustment that might require revisiting past stages to make changes based on new information. For the purposes of this book, however, we discuss these steps in sequence.

STAGES IN THE SOCIAL MARKETING PROCESS

The social marketing process consists of six general stages, each of which involves several different types of activities:

- Analysis
- Strategy development
- Program and communication design
- Pretesting
- Implementation
- Evaluation and feedback

The process can be visually depicted as the pyramid shown in Figure 4.1.

Step 1. To create an effective social marketing program, you must understand the problem you are addressing, the audiences you are targeting, and the environment in which the program will operate. The analysis phase uses research to understand and focus on those factors that are likely to play the biggest role in improving the issue.

Step 2. The strategy phase, based on what you learn in the analysis phase, forms the foundation on which the rest of the program is built. The research results are used to develop a workable strategy for effecting behavior change.

FIGURE 4.1   The Social Marketing Process

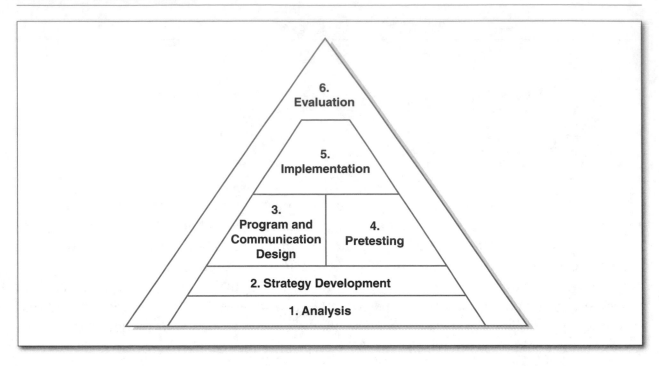

Step 3. The program and communication design phase follows the guidelines laid out in the strategy to design the program's overall approach, as well as messages to be conveyed and the materials that will carry the messages to the target audience.

Step 4. The pretesting phase involves using various methods to test messages and materials with the target audience members to determine what works best to accomplish the program's objectives. It is not uncommon to go back and forth several times between design and pretesting as you make necessary changes in the messages, materials, or overall strategy and explore whether the new approach works.

Step 5. In the implementation phase, the program is introduced to the target audience. Preparation is essential for success, and implementation must be monitored to ensure that every element proceeds as planned.

Step 6. Finally, the evaluation and feedback phase assesses the effects of the program as a whole as well as the individual elements of the strategy. Evaluation occurs throughout the process of program development, not just at the end, and feedback is used at each stage to improve the program.

Each of the following chapters explains the steps of the social marketing process in detail.

ETHICAL CONSIDERATIONS IN THE SOCIAL MARKETING PROCESS

Social marketing can be used to either good or ill effect. Beyond just good intentions, its purveyors have a societal duty to carry out their mission in an ethical manner. This means looking at each aspect of your program as you plan and implement it to consider whether it has the potential to do harm in any way. Behavior change is serious business, and it is preferable to do nothing rather than to implement a program that makes matters worse. For example, manipulating or deceiving people to bring about a positive health or social outcome never can be justified. Neither can coercion in any form, even if the actual behavior change is voluntary. Offering an impoverished woman a large sum of money in exchange for her becoming sterilized might force her to make a choice she really does not want to make.

Not all ethical issues are so cut-and-dried. A program that promises more than the product can deliver, or that omits information about the risks of adopting a particular behavior, also might be ethically suspect. In some instances, placing the entire responsibility for change on the individual rather than on the social institutions that created a problem in the first place (e.g., polluting factories causing respiratory problems in a community) might be not only ineffective but also an injustice to its victims.

Thinking a program through to its next logical step might help to avoid problems arising as an unintended consequence of your efforts. This will preclude situations such as the woman who has just learned of a potential tumor through a social marketing–based mammography screening program but does not receive a referral for additional testing. Another example is the man who responds to a smoking cessation promotion, only to find that all of the classes are booked for the next 4 months and therefore loses the motivation brought about by the social marketing campaign. Look at your program from all sides, particularly at the point where it ends, to identify any potentially harmful effects or ethically questionable components.

Section II

Step 1
Analysis

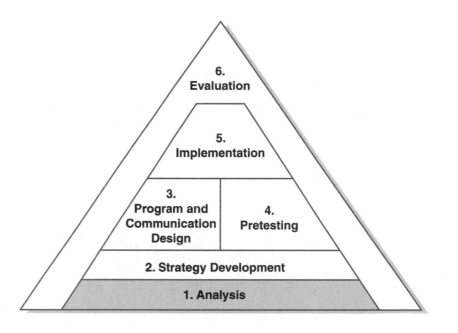

SECTION OVERVIEW

Before you jump into designing your social marketing program, you need to take a deep breath and just look around. Research plays an important role in the development of your program, and the first step is to gather all the information you can about the problem you are addressing, the environment in which it occurs, who it affects, and how it impacts their lives. In addition, your available resources will dictate the scope of the project. This section consists of the following chapters:

■ Chapter 5: Research in the Social Marketing Process

■ Chapter 6: Analysis

■ Chapter 7: Conducting Formative Research

Research in the Social Marketing Process

Research plays a key role throughout the social marketing process—in understanding the issue and audience to develop an effective strategy, in tracking the implementation of the program, and in assessing the success of your efforts. If the word *research* is too daunting for you, think of it as gathering information from many different sources.

Each type of research is used at different points during the process:

- Formative research aids in the development of the strategy and includes the problem and environmental analysis, target audience research, and pretesting of messages and materials.

- Process evaluation research refers to the monitoring systems you put in place before and during implementation to track what is happening in the program and how people are responding in real time.

- Summative evaluation research helps you determine the effects of your program on reaching your goals and objectives, particularly in whether you brought about changes in factors such as knowledge, attitudes, and behaviors.

This section will focus on formative research as you start to build your program.

FORMATIVE RESEARCH

The role of formative research in social marketing is to guide the initial development of the program. It helps to answer questions such as the following:

- What is the problem you are addressing?
- What is the context in which the problem exists?
- Who will be your target audience?
- How does your target audience think and behave as related to the problem?
- What product can you offer that will appeal to your target audience?

■ What are the main barriers keeping your target audience from taking action?

■ How can you best reach your target audience?

■ Which messages and materials work best?

■ What is the best social marketing mix?

Formative research occurs throughout the first four steps of the process: analysis, strategy development, program and communication design, and pretesting.

Before you start any research, know why you are collecting that information. Andreasen suggests a process called "backward research" in which you first identify the key decision points of the program and then determine the information needed to make those decisions.[1] From there, ascertain the best way in which to secure that information. Someone else might have already done the work for you by conducting research on that topic, or you might need to collect the data yourself. For example, to decide how best to reach your target audience with your message, you will need to find data on the types of media it pays attention to and where it gets its information on your issue, not just the standard knowledge, attitudes, and behaviors statistics. By thinking through the exact type of data needed, you can decide whether to use primary or secondary research and quantitative or qualitative approaches.

PRIMARY AND SECONDARY RESEARCH

Generally, the most efficient way in which to gather information is through secondary research data from studies already conducted by other researchers or organizations. Secondary research includes sources such as journal articles, books, census data, marketing databases, and unpublished studies. The advantage is that your organization does not require on-staff expertise (beyond understanding and interpreting the research) or the additional expense of conducting its own research. It is rare, however, to find secondary research that answers all of your questions or addresses your specific target audience. You most likely will need to use a combination of secondary and primary research (i.e., data you collect yourself).

Primary research has the benefit of being tailored to the specific needs of your program. By using the process of backward research, you will know the questions to ask to get the information you need for strategic decision making. And you will be conducting research with precisely the people for whom the program is being developed.

In the pretesting stage, primary research is unavoidable; you must test your messages and materials with your own target audience. Such research also is necessary to assess the effects of the social marketing program once it has been implemented. As you will learn, primary research does not have to be difficult or expensive. You can conduct your own research, and your organization will be better off for it.

---

[1]Andreasen, A. (1988). *Cheap but good marketing research*. Homewood, IL: Business One Irwin.

QUANTITATIVE AND QUALITATIVE RESEARCH

Another research concept that you need to know is the distinction between quantitative and qualitative research methods. When you think of the word *research*, what comes to mind? Things like statistics, experiments, and precision? The type of research most of us are familiar with involves quantitative methods such as standardized surveys, random samples, and statistical analysis. The results of quantitative research help you to understand how many people believe or behave a certain way, which characteristics are related to each other, and the probability that any behavior change was related to exposure to your program. In the quantitative world, things are black and white; they are either statistically significant or not. The only answers you obtain are those for which you thought to ask questions.

On the other hand, qualitative research methods help you to understand the "why" of an issue, bringing you beneath the surface of an answer. Many of these methods, such as focus groups, in-depth interviews, and observational studies, come from anthropology as well as commercial marketing. Qualitative research helps you to understand the issue from the target audience members' points of view and enables you to find out why they think or do something the way they do. Responses are placed in context, and something as complex as human behavior is not reduced to a multiple-choice question.

Using both quantitative and qualitative research provides different perspectives on the same situation. There are times when one type of data is more appropriate than the other, but by integrating research methods throughout the program development process, your overall understanding of the issue will be much deeper.

CHAPTER 6

Analysis

Social marketers must know as much about the market they are entering as someone considering opening a new pizza delivery service in a particular community. Is there a demand for pizza delivery? Who are the potential customers? Who is the main competition? Why have previous companies failed or succeeded? What are the start-up costs? Before investing money and effort in starting the company, a good businessperson would investigate these issues thoroughly.

Similarly, social marketers must analyze several major issues when beginning to plan a social marketing program, including the following:

- The problem to be addressed

- The environment in which the program will be implemented

- Resources available for the program

By understanding the problem and environment, you will be better able to identify potential opportunities and stumbling blocks for the program. A realistic assessment of your available resources will help to narrow the scope of the program or may highlight the need for participation from other groups.

ANALYZING THE PROBLEM

If you are planning a social marketing program, then you probably are already familiar with the topic you will be addressing. If not, then you might need to learn more about the issue before proceeding. Either way, research will help determine the approach the program should take. Secondary research is the best place to start to find the information you need. Once you have more narrowly defined the target audience and scope of the project, you also should conduct your own primary research.

Conducting a Literature Review

A literature review reveals the research information that already exists on your issue and helps you apply that knowledge to your own program. The process consists of the following steps:

1. Start with an Internet search to find freely available resources on your topic online.

   - Have an idea of the type of information you need to learn about your issue, such as biological or psychosocial aspects, epidemiology, and previous interventions that have been attempted.

   - You may be able to find excellent reports and articles, as well as data sets, that provide both broad and specific insights into your issue and audience.

   (Continued)

(Continued)

- Try different variations of keywords in your search to help you find everything that might be out there. Include social media and news sites in your search as well.

- Follow links on the sites you find most useful to discover new sources of information that may not have shown up on your search.

2. Search the academic databases for the most valid research in peer-reviewed journals.

- If you have access to a university library, you may be able to search its databases such as MEDLINE, PsychINFO, and POPLINE online or on site. You can also search Google Scholar for references to academic articles, books, and other publications.

- Once you have references and abstracts, identify which articles are most likely to yield the types of information you need. If you are at the library, you can look for each article in the journals carried by the library and make copies of the most relevant ones. Many full-text articles are also available for purchase online by the journal publishers.

- Look at the references listed at the end of relevant articles to see whether there are others you should look up as well.

3. Contact organizations that work to address your topic (e.g., federal agencies, national nonprofits).

- Ask whether they offer publications with the information and data that you need (there might be a fee involved).

- Speak with individuals involved in projects similar to yours to learn more about their programs and to obtain their insights.

4. Integrate all the material you find into a useful reference.

- Group the information from each source by subject, and write it up into a coherent summary. Keep track of where each piece of information came from in case you need to refer back to its source (i.e., create references or footnotes).

- Clearly highlight key information and provide recommendations for developing your own program based on what you learned from the literature review.

The questions you can answer using secondary research include the following:

What aspect of the problem will you address? There are many ways in which to approach a problem. For example, a social marketing program addressing child abuse might try to convince abusive parents to stop hitting their children. It could make it easier for teachers or community members who suspect abuse to make reports to the authorities. It could teach abused children to ask trusted adults for help. It might promote preventive behaviors to parents who have not yet abused their children but are at high risk. Or, it could help adult victims of child abuse get needed treatment. Each of these angles is a way in which to address the issue of child abuse, and further research might steer you toward the more effective approaches. The angle you choose will help narrow the target audience options.

What is the epidemiology of the problem? Epidemiology describes how a disease or problem is distributed in a population. Ideally, you should try to find data for your specific community or the geographic area of the program. How common is the problem (its prevalence)? How quickly are new cases occurring (its incidence)? Who is most at risk of acquiring the disease or social problem? Is the problem more severe among certain groups of people? For example, although the prevalence of HIV infection is relatively high among older gay White men, its incidence rate has slowed in comparison to other groups such as women and young minority men. Those who are at highest risk or who suffer the most serious consequences are good candidates to be your target audience.

What can be done to prevent the problem from occurring or spreading? By understanding the causes of the disease or problem, you can identify the key preventive behaviors to promote.

Skin cancer, for example, is associated with exposure to the ultraviolet rays of the sun. Preventive behaviors would include using sunscreen, wearing a wide-brimmed hat, covering exposed skin, and staying out of the sun during peak sunlight hours. Regular skin screenings can catch potential precancerous or cancerous moles from growing and becoming deadly. Depending on your program's goals and the target audience you choose, you might decide to promote one specific preventive behavior or all such behaviors.

What are the consequences of the problem? Visualization of the potential negative consequences of an action often is effective in averting an unhealthy behavior. As a result of efforts by Mothers Against Drunk Driving (MADD) to highlight the devastating effects of drunk driving through its media campaigns, people who have been drinking might think twice before getting behind the wheel. Older smokers often quit when they realize that they might not be around to see their grandchildren grow up. As you design your program, you can test various consequences to see whether any of them "hit home" with the target audience.

What knowledge, attitudes, and behaviors are related to the problem? Determine whether members of the potential target audiences are even aware of the issue and consider themselves at risk. How many of them think that the disease or condition is serious or that they can do something to prevent it? How many are actually practicing preventive behaviors? Are there differences between certain groups such as men and women or younger and older teens? For example, if girls are more likely to engage in aerobic exercise and boys prefer weight training, then a school-based exercise

Expert Interviews

You can quickly learn a lot about how to develop your program by speaking with people who have been there before. In all likelihood, you are not the first to address the problem or target audience, so why not benefit from the experience of others? Expert interviews are a way of learning the lessons of other programs, whether they were successful or not.

Locate appropriate people to interview by first checking the literature to find published descriptions of programs addressing your issue and then contacting those projects' directors. They might not have exactly the same angle or target audience, but there may be enough commonality that you can gain some valuable insights for your own program. Ask as many people as possible who work in the field whether they know of any current or past programs similar to yours. Your interviewees probably will be able to steer you to additional people to interview. Relevant federal clearinghouses also might be able to give you a list of government-funded projects related to your issue around the country. Tell your participants as much as you can about your project so that they can speak to the particular issues you might need to consider. The following questions could be helpful to use in your interviews:

- Could you describe the project? The goal? Messages? Media? What did the campaign ask people to do?

- Who was your target audience? How did you go about choosing it? How narrowly did you segment its members?

- Did you conduct any research with the target audience to help in developing the campaign?

- What did you learn from the research that might be applicable to other campaigns?

- Did you evaluate the campaign? What did you use to measure success?

- Do you have any experience developing programs for our population? What types of messages, media, or approaches do you think would be most effective for them?

- Is there anything you wish you had done differently with your campaign that might be useful for us to watch out for as we develop ours?

- Was there anything that you found worked particularly well?

curriculum might need to encourage boys to incorporate more cardiovascular activity into their routines.

How successful have previous attempts been to address the problem? If you are not aware of what has already been tried, you might indeed be condemned to repeat the past, including making the same mistakes as others. Rather than reinventing the wheel, learn which interventions have been effective. Search the literature for other programs that have addressed the same issue, and contact the sponsoring organizations for more information. You can conduct expert interviews with people who have worked on similar projects around the country. Ask them what worked and what they would do differently next time. Many people are willing to give their advice, and you might find the time it takes well worth it.

ANALYZING THE ENVIRONMENT

Having learned as much about the problem as possible, particularly as it relates to your community or area, turn your attention now to the environment that will surround the social marketing program. Nothing occurs in a vacuum, and your program is no exception. Your campaign will be just one of many messages that people receive in the course of their days. Knowing what you are competing with will help you break through the clutter.

The environment can be either a help or a hindrance, presenting opportunities or barriers. To create sustained behavior change, the environment must be conducive to the actions you are promoting. After analyzing the situation, you might realize that the program should devote resources to creating a supportive context for your target audience's behavior change efforts. For example, a program promoting good eating habits to inner-city residents without stores that sell produce or other fresh foods could remove that obstacle by establishing a farmer's market or working with neighborhood stores to stock healthful foods. Making recycling bins ubiquitous will make it easier for people to avoid adding their bottles and cans to the landfill.

Your environmental analysis should consider the following questions as they relate to your issue:

What social, economic, or demographic factors might be at work in the community? Find out the trends that might be affecting the lives of your target audience members. Social issues such as poverty, crime, and homelessness have obvious and not so obvious effects on what people may be willing or able to do. If a large factory has just closed in a small city, then people might need to find new jobs before they can make other changes in their lives. Other factors such as a predominant religion (e.g., Mormonism in Utah) or a large gay community (e.g., in San Francisco) might be relevant to how you develop your program.

What is the political climate in relation to the topic or target audiences you are addressing? Although not true for many issues, some topics have become so politicized that social marketers must be aware of potential conflicts as they develop their programs. Topics such as AIDS prevention, climate change, tobacco, alcohol, and guns have active proponents and opponents who have very different ideas about the subject. Determine who your potential allies and adversaries may be and forge strategic alliances whenever possible. You also might find it more effective to deal delicately with controversial subjects that are at odds with community norms.

What current policies or pending legislation might affect your target audience's response to the social marketing program? Often, one of the most effective things your program can do is to get your hands dirty in the sausage making of legislation. Policies at the organizational, local, state, and federal levels—whichever are appropriate—can go a long way toward promoting an environment that supports behavior change. For example, stricter laws regarding selling alcohol or cigarettes to minors reduce access to these substances by young people. Or, if Medicaid or private insurance companies do not cover an important preventive procedure, you might need to work to change that policy before urging people to ask for it from their doctors.

What other organizations currently are addressing the issue in your community? Before you plan your own program, investigate whether other organizations are working toward similar goals so that you can avoid duplication of efforts. There might be programs at the local, state, or national level addressing the same issue or target audience in your own community. One option is to join forces with those organizations and either complement or expand their efforts. Otherwise, you can decide whether to reinforce existing campaigns, approach the issue from a different angle, or target a different audience.

What messages will be competing with your program for attention? On average, your target audience members may be exposed to 3,000 or more marketing messages daily,[1] so you need to make sure that your messages get noticed. Competing messages may come from the constant buzz of commercial advertising, from social media, from opponents of your cause, or even from within your own field. You can conduct a media audit and monitor social media to assess the messages out there about your issue. You might find rampant misinformation, suggesting that your program needs to educate media professionals and other audiences. You also might find that the "competition" uses certain channels in a particularly effective manner. For example, if you are working to keep young people from smoking, then determining which local events are sponsored by tobacco companies will be useful in focusing your efforts.

> ### Auditing Media Messages
>
> If you will be employing media strategies in your program, you should have an idea of the types of messages that are already out there. Your target audience might gain much of its knowledge and form its opinions on your issue based on what it sees and hears in the traditional and online media. To be most effective as you prepare to develop your program, conduct a media audit to identify whether and how your issue is covered. You also might wish to monitor the activities of your opponents as well; for example, an underage drinking prevention campaign should be aware of the latest promotional strategies employed by the alcohol industry.
>
> *(Continued)*

[1]Shenk, D. (1997). *Data smog: Surviving the information glut.* New York: HarperEdge.

(Continued)

Cover traditional media, including news programs, television shows, and advertising messages on TV, billboards, and transit ads, in your audit, if appropriate. You also may include movies, popular music, music videos, and other entertainment media such as magazines and tabloid newspapers. And don't forget about social media such as blogs, social networking/microsharing sites, message boards, and other types of websites or online advertising. A guide to monitoring social media can be found in Chapter 19.

The media audit can last for a set amount of time (e.g., 2 weeks, 1 month) or can be ongoing throughout the life of your program, which would be the ideal. The scope of the audit will depend on the number of media outlets and types you decide to include and the amount of staff time you have available to devote to monitoring activities. You might wish to limit the traditional media audit to the major local newspaper/news site, top-rated local television newscasts, or most popular television shows in your media market if you cannot cover all the media in your community.

To assess the news coverage of your issue, you can set up an RSS feed to collect mentions of your issue, organization, or campaign from online news sources (see Chapter 19 for guidance). You can also skim each section of the newspaper every day and clip any stories that are related to your issue in some way. Similarly, watch television newscasts or listen to the radio news each day (you might find it easier to record these to review at a later time). If you are not able to spend the time doing this yourself, then you can contract with a media monitoring service, which will scan the media outlets you designate and provide you with the actual newspaper clippings or audiovisual program transcripts of all stories that contain references to your topic or organization. Some well-known national services are BurrellesLuce (www.burrellesluce.com), Cision (www.cision.com) and Vocus (www.vocus.com). They also can analyze the content of the stories, providing you with a comprehensive report that shows which topics are covered by each outlet and the biases of reporters covering your issue. You can do a content analysis yourself, using a short checklist such as the Content Data Form and tabulating the results.

What channels are available in the community to promote your message? In every community, many different resources are available through which you can get your message out to the target audience. Assess your options so that you can keep them in mind during the planning process. These resources may include the following:

- Media outlets (e.g., newspapers, television and radio stations, websites)

- Community events (e.g., annual parade, local festivals)

- Popular activities (e.g., high school sports, attending the movies)

- High-visibility or high-traffic areas (e.g., main street, public restrooms)

- Local businesses frequented by the target audience

What opportunities exist to redesign the environment to support the behaviors you are working toward? Look for the physical decision points that people reach that determine whether they take the desired course of action or not. These might be things like the location of stairs versus elevators; the accessibility of safe, aesthetic walking paths in a community; the ease of locating and turning off lights in unused offices; or the degree of privacy afforded by voting booths in various configurations.

As you conduct research, keep your eyes and ears open for clues about ways in which to reach your target audience. Be creative and go beyond the standard media channels.

ANALYZING YOUR RESOURCES

Before you get too excited about everything you would like to tackle through your social marketing program, come back down to earth. Realistically assess your available resources before proceeding

Content Data Form

News Media/Blogs

Date/time:

Medium: ❑ Newspaper   ❑ Television   ❑ Radio   ❑ Website

Name of outlet:

Name of reporter/
blogger:

Wire service or syndicate
(if applicable):

Type of story: ❑ Hard news   ❑ Feature   ❑ Column   ❑ Opinion   ❑ Other

Topic of story/headline:

Issues/items included   ❑ Epidemiology   ❑ Prevention   ❑ Treatment   ❑ Consequences
(customize checklist for
your issue):   ❑ Opposition   ❑ New research   ❑ Policy   ❑ Our
organization

Editorial slant: ❑ Positive   ❑ Negative   ❑ Neutral

Entertainment Media

Date/time:

Medium: ❑ Television
show   ❑ Music/music
video   ❑ Movie   ❑ Publication   ❑ Other

Name of production/
publication:

How issue arose: ❑ Portrayed
desirable
behavior   ❑ Portrayed
competing
behavior   ❑ Mentioned
issue   ❑ Other

Describe the
scene/context:

Overall depiction of issue: ❑ Positive   ❑ Negative   ❑ Neutral

Approximate number of relevant seconds/minutes or paragraphs:

Advertising Messages

Date/time:

Medium: ❑ Newspaper   ❑ Television   ❑ Radio   ❑ Web

Name of outlet/site:

Name of advertiser/product:

Probable target audience:

Benefits promoted:

Other messages included:

TABLE 6.1   Budget, Research, and Production

Sample Programs With Various Resource Levels

This table gives you examples of what programs with various-sized budgets might expect to accomplish in terms of research and production. Keep in mind that this is a very rough guide; it does not take into account any pro bono (free) services that you might be able to obtain to stretch your budget, the size of the population you are trying to reach, or other factors that are unique to your strategy or program. As the budget becomes larger, items may be added to those included in the previous lists.

	Small Budget (Less Than $100,000)	Moderate Budget ($100,000–$1,000,000)	Large Budget (More Than $1,000,000)
Steps 1 and 2: Analysis and strategy development	■ Literature review ■ Informal target audience research	■ Additional secondary research ■ Focus groups	■ Knowledge, attitudes, and behaviors survey ■ Market segmentation database analysis
Step 3: Program and communication design	■ Print materials ■ Website ■ Word of mouth ■ Social media ■ Online video ■ Environmental design	■ Radio spots ■ Print ads ■ Comprehensive online campaign ■ Search engine ads	■ Television spots ■ Billboards
Step 4: Pretesting	■ Informal target audience research ■ Self-administered questionnaires ■ Readability testing	■ Focus groups ■ Expert/gatekeeper review	■ Intercept interviews ■ Theater testing ■ Multiple rounds of pretesting
Step 5: Implementation	■ Partnering ■ Public relations ■ Online community building	■ Kickoff media event ■ Paid media placement	■ Additional media buys
Step 6: Evaluation and feedback	*Process:* ■ Recordkeeping *Outcome:* ■ Secondary data ■ Data from existing records ■ Social media evaluation	*Process:* ■ Formal media monitoring *Outcome:* ■ Systematic observations ■ Qualitative methods	*Process:* ■ Management effectiveness/ efficiency analysis *Outcome:* ■ Knowledge, attitudes, and behaviors survey

Note: Dollar figures are approximate and in 2010 terms. Hiring outside contractors will add to the cost.

any further. Your strategy will look much different if you have $25,000 to work with instead of $2,500,000, and this is the point at which to think about your budget.

Your Internal Resources

A program needs more than money to succeed; it takes skilled personnel, adequate office facilities, access to the target audience, and (not least of all) time. Some questions to ask yourself before moving forward include the following:

■ What is the total budget you can afford for the social marketing program?

- How much of the budget comes from grants or other outside funding, and how much will be paid by your organization?

- Does the organization have staff with the ability to plan and carry out each step of the social marketing process, including research and production?

- If not, do you have funds to hire a consultant or advertising/public relations agency?

- Do you and your staff have the necessary time to devote to developing, implementing, and monitoring a social marketing program?

- Does your organization have adequate office facilities and equipment?

- Does your organization have access to the target audience members?

- Do you currently have any partner agencies with the skills or access that your organization lacks? Are there any other organizations with whom you could team up?

- Do you need to seek additional funding before proceeding?

- Given your answers to the preceding questions, is it feasible for your organization to develop a social marketing program at this time?

If you find that your current resources are not adequate for the type of program you had envisioned, then you have two choices: Either narrow the parameters of the project or find more funding. This might mean sending out more grant proposals or expanding project resources through partnerships with other organizations.

Should You Use an Outside Agency?

Although you are an expert in the work that you do, you might not have the same level of expertise in every field it takes to create a social marketing program. If you feel confident that you already possess those skills, that is great. If you feel you need some outside assistance for all or part of the program development, that is okay too. The Resource Analysis Worksheet (Worksheet 3) at the end of this chapter will help you to assess the areas where your staff have sufficient expertise and where you might wish to receive additional training. Following are some questions to consider in making a decision about hiring a contractor to work with you on the campaign:

What type of agency or consultant should you use? Advertising, public relations, marketing—how do you choose which type of agency you need? They often have similar capabilities, but each has a different focus. A marketing firm generally looks at the big picture, starting with a strategy based on research and determining the most appropriate activities within the larger context of the marketing mix. Advertising agencies and public relations firms focus on the narrower disciplines within marketing, with ad agencies usually creating and producing advertisements and public relations firms using other promotional strategies to get their clients' messages out. Ideally, look for a company that specializes in social marketing or at least has some experience in the area.

With which aspects of the program do you need assistance? You might already have research expertise in your organization or a freelance graphic artist with whom you always work but need help with placing your ads in the media. Or, you might want to develop the script for a television spot yourself but require assistance with the technicalities of production. Carefully consider whether you want someone to create your program from start to finish or to take on selected activities such as research, creative services, production, media planning and distribution, partnership development, and/or public relations.

(Continued)

(Continued)

What type of budget do you have? Even if you have only a small budget, do not hesitate to contact agencies for assistance if you need it. They might be willing to provide services at a reduced rate or might even take on your organization as a pro bono (free) client. If not, prioritize the activities you need help with and do the lower priority items in-house; it will be a learning experience. Some types of firms, such as media planning services, are compensated by the media outlets with which they place your ads and technically work at no cost to you (although you can save money by doing it yourself [see Chapter 18]). You might wish to consider hiring a social marketing consultant or freelancers rather than a full-service firm to save money.

How will you find agencies to choose from? Select a firm to do social marketing for you the same way in which you would select any other type of outside consultant. Ask for recommendations from people and organizations you trust. Look for examples of campaigns or programs that you particularly like, and find out who produced them. Local chapters of organizations, such as the American Association of Advertising Agencies and the Public Relations Society of America, also might be able to provide lists of firms in your area, although it is not necessary to work with someone local. Contact the most promising candidates and set up meetings to discuss your needs, or send out a request for proposals to solicit bids to produce your campaign.

What criteria will you use to select the contractor? Determine what skills and expertise you feel are most important to your program and find an organization that matches those criteria. If the firm has not done social marketing before, does it have experience with any health or social issues or with your target audience? Is the work that it has done for other clients effective and of high quality? Do you feel that the staff with whom you will be working understand your needs and will listen to you? Do not expect an agency you are considering to create a sample campaign before you have signed a contract, but an agency should be willing to discuss its overall strategic approach to developing your program.

How will you work together? Remember that you are the expert on your issue. It is up to you to provide the agency or consultants with the information needed to create your program. Share any research you have conducted, as well as your preliminary social marketing strategy, to ensure that you have similar expectations from the beginning. Make clear what you do and do not like about the ideas the agency or consultants offer, and communicate regularly throughout the development process.

Working With Partners

As mentioned in Chapter 3, partnership is one of the "Ps" in the social marketing mix. Even if you have sufficient funds, consider inviting others to join the project to expand the reach of your program. Build connections with key people and organizations that have the potential to bring attention and credibility. By pooling resources and promoting the campaign through many organizations working toward the same goal, you can produce a synergistic effect greater than each could achieve on its own. Just as the power of a choir derives from its union of many voices, a powerful campaign requires groups throughout the community to come together in a coordinated effort.

Depending on their resources and interests, partners might wish to participate in many different ways. You can specify what they will do or allow them to decide the type of role they would prefer. Some possibilities include the following:

- Distributing your program materials and spreading the word about your campaign to their clients/customers/constituents

- Referring members of the target audience to your program

- Including your product or messages in their own program or materials

- Adapting your materials to include their contact information

- Co-branding your promotional efforts together, particularly in for-profit and nonprofit partnerships

- Offering use of their staff or volunteers to the program

- Writing letters of support for your program

- Providing a well-known spokesperson for the program

- Being involved in media interviews and press conferences

- Assisting in research and evaluation activities

- Providing financial support or "in-kind" contributions (e.g., printing, media time, use of their conference facilities)

Despite the benefits of working with partners, whenever you bring in additional organizations, you expose the program to new and different types of challenges. Too many partners also can make the program an administrative nightmare. It is up to you to decide the balance you need between expanding the program and letting go of control over parts of the process. Communication is essential to preventing potential problems before they start.

Some typical issues you might encounter and possible solutions include the following:

You feel a loss of ownership of the project. With many organizations participating, you might end up compromising on some aspects of the program or letting go of some control over the project's direction. Giving your "baby" over to others can be a difficult thing, especially when

Picking Partners

Think carefully about who would be good partners before approaching other groups. Just because an organization has expressed interest in being involved in the campaign does not mean that it is the best partner for your program. Be strategic in building alliances. Some criteria for choosing a campaign partner are whether the organization has the following attributes:

- Provides access to members of the target audience

- Has credibility or influence with the target audience

- Has resources (e.g., staff, financial) and/or skills (e.g., media relations) that it is willing to make available to the campaign

- Has qualifications appropriate to the topic of the campaign

- Has a preexisting relationship with you or your organization

- Is enthusiastic about the social marketing program

Some types of organizations to consider as partners include the following:

- Health departments
- Social service agencies
- Voluntary organizations (e.g., American Cancer Society, American Heart Association)
- Nonprofit community organizations
- State or national organizations
- Professional associations
- Corporations or local businesses
- Educational institutions
- Religious institutions
- Media outlets
- Public safety agencies
- Hospitals and health care agencies
- Service organizations (e.g., Elks, Rotary Club)
- Youth organizations (e.g., Girl Scouts, 4-H Clubs)
- Foundations
- Insurance companies and health maintenance organizations
- Political officials

they take the credit for its success. Try to avoid power struggles, and keep focused on the reasons you brought in the partners in the first place.

Partners do not participate as agreed. There is nothing more frustrating than thinking that your partners are carrying out their tasks when the organizations have not even begun taking the necessary actions. Find out why they have not started. Do they have the materials? Do they know what to do? Do they need additional assistance from you? Help them to live up to their commitments without doing the work for them.

Partners go "off strategy." Your partners might take the plan and materials you give them and use them in a way that was not intended. It may be fine for them to adapt the materials and program to fit their situations, but make sure that the use still fits with your original strategy.

Partnership becomes time-consuming. By its nature, working with other organizations takes time and effort. This includes helping them to understand the project, determining areas of mutual benefit, meeting to work out logistics, and engaging in ongoing communications. Try to build enough time into your plan to allow for the extra effort and to give your partners advance notice of upcoming needs as well.

Your partners are getting bored with the project. Just as your staff eventually might tire of the campaign, your partners occasionally will require a dose of motivation. Set long- and short-term goals for them to strive to meet. Have contests to see who can make the most referrals or bring in the most Facebook fans, with prizes awarded at the end. Share success stories with them so they can see that what they are doing is making a difference.

Corporate partnerships offer different types of opportunities for a social marketing program. If a company manufactures or sells a product or service that is related to the behavior you are promoting, or if their primary customers are your main target audience, see if you can work with them to mutual benefit. For example, the SIDS Foundation partnered with Pampers to print a "Back to Sleep" reminder for parents directly on the diapers that babies should sleep on their backs. The U.S. Environmental Protection Agency's Energy Star program is another example of partners working together toward a shared behavioral goal—to persuade consumers to buy energy-saving appliances. Beyond contributing money to your social marketing program or promoting your campaign or organization in their own marketing, look for where you might be able to influence product design, distribution, pricing, or promotion to match your own strategy more closely.

WORKSHEET 1: PROBLEM ANALYSIS WORKSHEET

1. What is the problem or issue your social marketing program will address?

_____

_____

2. What are the possible angles you could take in addressing the problem or issue?

_____

_____

3. From your secondary research, what is the epidemiology of the problem in your population?

   a. Prevalence (how often it occurs): _____

   b. Incidence (rate of new cases): ❑ Rising ❑ Staying the same ❑ Decreasing

   c. Characteristics of people most at risk of having the problem:

   _____

   _____

   _____

   _____

   d. Are there groups in which the consequences of the problem are most severe?

   _____

   _____

   _____

4. What are the main ways in which the problem can be prevented?

_____

_____

_____

5. What are the most common or most serious consequences of the problem?

_____

_____

_____

(Continued)

(Continued)

6. What knowledge, attitudes, and behaviors are related to the problem? How widespread are they among your population?

Approximate Percentage of Population

a. Knowledge:

_____   _____
_____   _____
_____   _____
_____   _____

b. Attitudes:

_____   _____
_____   _____
_____   _____
_____   _____

c. Behaviors:

_____   _____
_____   _____
_____   _____
_____   _____

7. What approaches have been used to address the problem by other organizations?

_____
_____
_____
_____

8. Who are potential experts for you to interview?

Name	*Organization*	*Phone Number/E-mail*
_____	_____	_____
_____	_____	_____
_____	_____	_____
_____	_____	_____

WORKSHEET 2: ENVIRONMENTAL ANALYSIS WORKSHEET

1. What are the geographic boundaries in which your program will take place (e.g., neighborhood, city, state)?

   _____

   _____

2. What trends or other factors might affect the environment in which your program will take place?

   a. Social:

   _____

   _____

   _____

   b. Economic:

   _____

   _____

   _____

   c. Demographic:

   _____

   _____

   _____

   d. Political:

   _____

   _____

   _____

3. Which groups, community leaders, or other individuals do you foresee opposing your program?

   _____

   _____

   _____

4. Which groups, community leaders, or other individuals should you actively seek support from as allies?

   _____

   _____

   _____

(Continued)

(Continued)

5. Are there any policies, laws, or pending legislation that might affect how your target audience responds to the social marketing program? If so, do you want to try to address these issues in your program?

	Policy Change/Lobbying Necessary?	
Policy/Legislation	*Yes*	*No*
_____	_____	_____
_____	_____	_____
_____	_____	_____

6. What other organizations currently are addressing the issue in your community?

Organization	*Services Provided*	*Populations Served*
_____	_____	_____
_____	_____	_____
_____	_____	_____
_____	_____	_____

7. What are the main messages that will be competing with your program for attention?
   a. General advertising related to topic:

   _____

   _____

   _____

   b. Messages by opponents to your cause:

   _____

   _____

   _____

   c. Messages by allies to your cause:

   _____

   _____

   _____

8. What channels are available in the community to promote your message? Check all that apply:

- ❏ Television
- ❏ Radio
- ❏ Daily newspapers
- ❏ Weekly newspapers
- ❏ Community- or issue-specific websites/blogs
- ❏ Billboards
- ❏ Transit advertising
- ❏ Community events
- ❏ Sports events
- ❏ Movie theaters
- ❏ Local businesses
- ❏ Health or social service agencies
- ❏ Professional groups
- ❏ Other _____
- ❏ Other _____
- ❏ Other _____

WORKSHEET 3: RESOURCE ANALYSIS WORKSHEET

1. What is your total budget available for the social marketing program? $ _____

2. Where is the funding coming from?

   a. _____ $ _____

   b. _____ $ _____

   c. _____ $ _____

3. In which of the following areas related to social marketing do you or other staff members have skills or expertise? (check all that apply)

   ❑ Literature review

   ❑ Quantitative research (e.g., surveys)

   ❑ Qualitative research (e.g., focus groups, interviewing)

   ❑ Partnership development

   ❑ Message development

   ❑ Materials development

   ❑ Website design

   ❑ Social media/online marketing

   ❑ Graphic design/print production

   ❑ Audiovisual production

   ❑ Public relations

   ❑ Media planning/buying

   ❑ Evaluation

   ❑ Program planning and management

4. Do you need to hire an outside agency to assist with any of the above activities?

   ❑ Yes ❑ No

   If yes, list the activities in order of priority:

   _____

   _____

   _____

   _____

5. How much time do you and other staff members have to devote to the social marketing program?

Staff Member	Hours per Week	Total Hours

6. Do you have any additional space or equipment needs for the social marketing program?

   _____

   _____

   _____

   _____

7. What level of access does your organization have to target audience members?

   ❑ Low: We would have to work hard to find them

   ❑ Moderate: We have some dealings with them

   ❑ High: They are the primary population that we serve

8. What are the organizations you should consider partnering with for the social marketing program? Do you already have relationships with any of them?

Organization	Relationship Established?

(Continued)

(Continued)

9. Preliminary Social Marketing Program Budget
   Use this as a rough estimate for now, and refine it as you develop your strategy:
   a. Personnel:

   _____ $ _____

   _____ $ _____

   _____ $ _____

   b. Research:
      (1) Formative research .... $ _____
      (2) Process evaluation .... $ _____
      (3) Outcome/impact evaluation .... $ _____
   c. Materials/website production .... $ _____
   d. Media buys .... $ _____
   e. Mailing/distribution .... $ _____
   f. Other expenses

   _____ $ _____

   _____ $ _____

   _____ $ _____

   Subtotal $ _____
   g. Contingencies (add at least 10%) $ _____
   Total $ _____

10. Do you need to seek additional funding before proceeding with the program?

   ❑ Yes ❑ No

11. Is a social marketing program feasible to develop and implement at this time?

   ❑ Yes ❑ No

CHAPTER 7

Conducting Formative Research

RESEARCHING THE SEGMENTS

Now that you know exactly which segments you are targeting, build on the information you have already gathered from secondary research. To determine the best way in which to reach the people in each segment, go directly to the experts—members of the segments themselves. Words that come straight from the horse's mouth often are more useful in helping you to develop appropriate messages than are preprocessed secondary data. The key at this stage is to learn as much as possible about the world and worldview of each target audience segment.

The questions to ask through primary research are similar to those in the secondary research collection process, but with additional depth and detail. Your aim is to get a clear and complete picture of how best to reach each segment of your target audience. The research questions fall into the following generic categories, which you must customize for your program:

- Knowledge
  - Are the target audience members aware of the problem?
  - Do they know the key facts about the problem?
  - Do they have any misconceptions about the problem?
  - Do they know how to prevent or control the problem?
  - Where do they get their information about the problem?

- Attitudes and beliefs
  - Do target audience members believe they are at risk?
  - How important do they feel the problem is, compared to other issues they face in their lives?
  - What other issues are associated with the problem in their minds?
  - How do they feel about the behavior you will ask them to perform?
  - What are the benefits and barriers they see to performing the behavior?
  - Do they think that they can perform the new behavior?
  - Do they think that the people in their social network will provide positive support for the behavior? What are the perceived social norms related to the behavior?
  - Who or what has the most influence on the attitudes and beliefs of the target audience? Who do they look up to?

53

- Behaviors

    - What are the current behaviors of the target audience related to the problem?
    - At what stage of behavior change are they (precontemplation, contemplation, preparation, action, or maintenance)?
    - Have they tried the new behavior? If so, why have they not adopted it?
    - In what circumstances do they perform the behavior currently?
    - What would make it easier to perform the new behavior?
    - Do they need new skills to help them perform the behavior?

- Communication channels

    - Which media channels does the target audience pay the most attention to (e.g., television, radio, newspaper, online)?
    - Which types of vehicles in each channel are preferred by the target audience (e.g., television shows, radio stations, newspaper sections, websites, social networks)?
    - At what times and places does the target audience view or listen to these media?
    - What does the target audience do in its leisure time?
    - What organizations do the target audience members belong to?
    - What words do they use when talking about the problem?
    - Who do they see as a credible spokesperson about the problem?

Social marketers use a variety of research techniques to gather this information and learn more about how each target audience segment thinks about and deals with the problem. Ideally, both qualitative and quantitative methods should be used together for a more complete picture. Each type of research provides a different type of insight into your target audience members' lives. These research techniques include the following:

Qualitative Methods

- *Focus groups* bring together small groups of individuals with similar characteristics for a focused conversation about a particular topic. A moderator leads the discussion and probes how people think and their reasons for doing things. By conducting several focus groups with each segment, you might be able to identify the most effective messages or approaches to use. Step-by-step guidance in how to conduct focus groups yourself can be found later in this chapter.

- *In-depth interviews* with one person at a time let you explore more sensitive issues that people might be uncomfortable speaking about in front of a group. The objective and types of questions are the same as in focus groups, but the intimate nature of this method leads to more detail than you might get in a group setting. Analysis of the interviews looks at both individual responses and the aggregation of all the interview data.

- *Case studies (ethnography)* focus on one person's or one organization's experience and the context in which it occurs. This is a way of gaining an in-depth understanding of the situation and its meaning for those involved while highlighting important lessons for program development.

- *Observational studies* involve watching members of the target audience engage in an activity relevant to the program to determine whether they perform the desired behavior correctly or at all. They might know that they are being observed if asked to demonstrate how they do something, or they might not be aware if the researcher watches unobtrusively. Observations must be planned and recorded systematically, with a specific purpose, and can be done quantitatively as well.

Quantitative Methods

- *Knowledge, attitudes, and behaviors (KAB) surveys* tell you how many people in the population are thinking or doing something. Although this can be an expensive and time-consuming undertaking, this type of survey can be very useful for identifying and understanding the audience's demographics, psychographics, and behaviors. A KAB survey conducted in the planning stage is most effective as baseline data, particularly if the same survey is repeated once the campaign has been implemented (see Appendix B for a sample KAB survey).

- *Intercept surveys* find their respondents by going to locations frequented by the target audience such as shopping malls and supermarkets. Interviewers systematically screen passersby to find target audience members who are willing to respond to an interview. Questionnaires typically are short and closed-ended to encourage participation, although they can include open-ended questions. Intercept surveys are commonly used to pretest program materials.

- *Marketing databases* typically are compiled by commercial firms and provide information about a target audience's lifestyle, psychographics, media habits, and consumer spending activities. This information can be expensive, however, and might not include data for lower income populations.

If you do not have access to the expertise needed for more formal research methods, then informal information gathering also can provide helpful insights. Go out and find members of your target audience. Talk to them, but more important, listen to them. You can bring people together over pizza to talk about their thoughts regarding the problem, what would motivate them to change their behavior, and what their lives are like. Go to the Laundromat and talk to people while they wait for their clothes, survey students on a college campus between classes, or chat with a group of teenagers hanging out at the local mall. If you do nothing else, at least invest some time in speaking directly with target audience members.

Even if you have very little money for research, there are low- to no-cost ways of gathering valid research data about your target audience:

- Public health or marketing students at a local university could do the research as a class project or an internship.

- An advertising or public relations firm might be willing to provide research or other services on a pro bono (free) basis or at a greatly reduced price if it is convinced of the value of the project.

- You might be able to "piggyback" on research that your partners or other organizations are conducting by adding some questions or expanding the research population.

- Receive training and then train your staff or volunteers to moderate focus groups or conduct interviews so that you will not need to hire an outside firm.

- Use social media monitoring tools to collect a sample of posts to analyze what people are saying about the issue or your organization.

- Observational studies often provide useful information without requiring more than the cost of staff or volunteer time. If, for example, you want to know whether people compare food nutrition labels, observe people as they shop at the supermarket and take notes on what you see.

Collecting useful information might take some resourcefulness and creativity, but the end product will be invaluable in helping you as you design the social marketing program.

The data you gather at this stage of the process can serve as a baseline from which to identify any changes occurring as a result of your program. Start thinking about your evaluation now so that you can build into your research the types of methods and questions that will identify meaningful transformations that took place in the target audience. For example, you might wish to conduct a KAB survey during the planning phase, both to provide information for formative research and to compare to the results of a postcampaign survey for evaluation purposes later. Section VII provides additional details about planning survey and other quantitative research to help you put an evaluation plan in place from the beginning.

FOCUS ON FOCUS GROUPS

Focus groups are the research method most often associated with social marketing programs. They are used to obtain insights into people's perceptions, beliefs, and language related to a particular issue. Focus groups can be used at several points in the social marketing process—to conduct preliminary research for strategy development, to test messages and concepts, to pretest draft executions, and to evaluate the target audience's response to the social marketing program. This section provides in-depth information on how to set up and conduct focus groups yourself.

Participants

Focus groups generally involve 8 to 10 participants but may be as small as 5 or 6 people when you want more in-depth participation or if the subject is very sensitive. With groups larger than 10 people, not everyone may get a chance to talk, or getting through the questions might take too long. Do not have more people than you can comfortably fit around the table you will use.

To be most effective, each focus group should comprise people who are similar to each other in ways that correspond with your audience segmentation criteria. By separating each segment of your target audience into its own focus group, you can identify any differences that might exist among subgroups. Putting similar people together also will help them feel more comfortable speaking candidly. For this reason, avoid putting people of different social or professional status in the same group (e.g., labor and management, physicians and laypeople). If appropriate, you might want to do focus groups with your program's secondary target audiences as well.

The participants should not know each other too well, although they do not need to be strangers. Preformed groups or sets of friends might have their own way of communicating with each other that an outside observer might not pick up on, leading to misinterpretation or missing pieces of information. You also should exclude people who work in marketing or advertising or who work on the issue under investigation in some way. Focus groups should have some spontaneity to them, and people who know what to expect might not respond candidly or be truly representative of your audience.

To ensure that the participants are fairly representative, conduct at least two or three focus groups with people from each segment. When you start hearing the same ideas over and over with no new insights emerging, you have achieved saturation with that segment. You probably will not gain much by doing more than three or four focus groups per segment.

If you were developing a program to promote mammography, for example, you might conduct a set of focus groups with three different categories of women over 50 years of age: those who receive mammograms every year, those who have had at least one mammogram but not on an annual basis, and those who never have had a mammogram. You could divide those segments still further by age, by family history of breast cancer, by socioeconomic status, or by whatever attributes are important to your program. But be careful not to subdivide the segments too much because each new characteristic multiplies the number of focus groups you must do and might not make a big difference.

Recruitment

Where will you find the people to participate in your focus groups? You have several options:

- Get them to contact you. Use communication channels, such as an announcement on your blog, a newspaper ad, or flyers in waiting rooms, to get the word out about the focus groups. Use a financial incentive or the promise of an opportunity for people to voice their opinions as the reason for potential participants to call you to sign up. Using this method, however, will primarily bring in people who have strong feelings on the issue or who are more outgoing.

- Contact them directly. Recruit target audience members proactively by approaching people in a shopping mall, purchasing a commercial marketing list, or using random telephone screening.

- Get referrals. Perhaps a community organization or health clinic can refer people to you. You also can use a technique called "snowballing" by asking the people you recruit to give you names of other friends or acquaintances in the target audience who might be interested in participating.

Create a short questionnaire that you can use to screen interested potential participants as they contact you. Make sure that they fall into the right categories for the target audience and the particular segments you are researching. You also can find out when they would be available for the focus groups and either assign them to a group on the spot or wait to select a time that works for most people in that segment and call them back. Appendix C provides a sample focus group recruitment questionnaire.

Because 8 to 10 people generally is the right number for each focus group, recruit at least 10 people to make up for the inevitable no-shows. Recruit people about a week in advance of the focus group sessions. If you have enough time, send each person a letter or e-mail confirming the date and time of the focus group along with directions to the facility. Call participants the day before to remind them and to confirm their attendance.

Participants should not know too much about what they will be discussing in advance. You can tell them something like, "You will be participating in a group discussion about health issues" or "We want your opinion on some advertisements we've developed for a new campaign." If you get too specific, they might think of what they want to say in advance, inhibiting the spontaneity of the group. Do not be too evasive, however, or else they might think you are hiding something for a nefarious reason.

Focus groups should last between 1 and 2 hours but no longer than that (or else the quality of responses will decline). When you sign up the participants, tell them the focus group will last for 2 hours and plan to use only 1½ hours. You will then have the extra time if you need it, or the participants will be pleasantly surprised to get out early.

Depending on how you are gaining access to your participants, you most likely will need to provide an incentive to get people to participate. If you are working with a captive audience such as at a workplace or in a school, then you might not need to "bribe" them to attend. But if your participants have a choice whether to attend or not, then you should offer an incentive as an indication that you know their time is valuable. This can be in the form of cash (usually at least $40) or another item of value to the target audience members such as dinner, a gift certificate to a local store, movie tickets, or something else that appeals to them. Appropriate incentives may vary among audiences; a physician might feel that his or her time is worth more than a "paltry" $100, whereas teenagers might be thrilled with a pizza party. You also might need to consider basics such as offering child care during the focus group and providing transportation for people to get there.

Environment

Many communities have special facilities designed specifically for conducting focus groups that are rented out to market research firms. These are conference rooms, often located in shopping malls, that have one-way mirrors behind which researchers can observe the group and videotape the proceedings. You most likely will not need to go to these lengths for your research if you have an appropriate location to hold the focus groups.

The focus groups should be held in a neutral and comfortable setting such as a conference room or a community center. Use a room that has minimal distractions (e.g., ringing phones, people walking through) and has a door you can close for the privacy of the participants. Set up the room with a round table or U-shaped seating so that the focus group moderator can have eye contact with everyone.

Record the session to allow the moderator to focus on the group without taking notes on what is being said. Audio recording is less obtrusive and threatening than use of a video camera. You will need a good recorder with a table microphone to pick up voices from all directions. The moderator should explain to the group why the session is being recorded and how the recording will be used—to ensure participants of their privacy.

You might wish to have someone serve as the assistant moderator to help check people in, monitor the audio recorder, and coordinate logistics. This allows the moderator to focus his or her attention on the group itself. Others working on the project who wish to observe the focus groups can take turns serving as the assistant moderator. Having additional observers in the room can make the participants feel self-conscious and undermine the informal character of the group.

Make the room as comfortable and friendly as possible. You can offer refreshments, such as soda and coffee, but avoid crunchy foods that can drown out the voices on the recording. As people come in, have them make name cards for themselves (by folding a piece of card stock in half) and put them on the table in front of their seats.

Questions

As simple as a focus group might seem to an outside observer, in reality it is the result of hours of preparation. The process begins with the development of a topic guide—a sort of "road map" for the moderator to follow. The topic guide provides an outline of the topics to be covered, which helps to keep the discussion on track and makes sure nothing is left out. See Appendix D for a sample focus group topic guide.

The questioning approach generally flows from general issues to the more specific or sensitive questions. The questions do not necessarily need to be followed in the original order if the discussion naturally leads to a different topic, but everything should be covered eventually. With a good topic guide, key issues will emerge naturally, without the moderator bringing them up. You might need to design different topic guides for each focus group segment; not all questions might make sense in each group.

Focus groups generally start with an introduction by the moderator explaining what will happen and laying down some general rules. The goal is to create an open, comfortable atmosphere and to let the participants know that they can trust the moderator.

Assistant Moderator Duties

■ Take responsibility for all equipment and supplies:

 □ Audio recorder, microphone, tapes/memory, batteries, extension cords

 □ Name cards, markers, pens, handouts

 □ Honoraria

 □ Refreshments

■ Arrange the room before participants arrive.

■ Sign people in as they arrive. Take care of latecomers unobtrusively.

■ During the focus group, sit off to the side, out of the sight lines of the participants. If possible, sit at a different table with the audio recorder.

■ Take notes during the discussion, including main points and well-said quotes, as close to word for word as possible. Also note nonverbal activity such as nods, laughs, and agreement or disagreement among participants.

■ Make a sketch of the seating arrangement to help the moderator remember participants' names afterward and to assist the transcriber.

■ Monitor the recording equipment. Know how it works; make sure that the correct buttons are pushed, make sure that the microphone is turned on, and check periodically that it is recording. Label the files with identifying information.

■ Do not participate in the discussion unless invited to do so by the moderator. Save questions or responses to the participants' discussion until the end. The moderator may ask the assistant to summarize the main points that came up or to refer back to the notes for clarification.

■ Hand out the honoraria at the end, and have participants sign that they received the money or incentive.

■ Debrief with the moderator afterward.

Tell the participants why you have brought them together and why what they are doing is important. Although you still might not want to "show all your cards," you can give them general information about what they will be discussing. If knowing the organization sponsoring the focus groups would bias people's responses, then you can use other honest subterfuges. If your program is, for example, the county's Drug Abuse Prevention Project for High-Risk Youth, then you can say you are with the county health department. A well-known provider such as Planned Parenthood could call itself a women's health organization. Or, you can hire an independent moderator who will use his or her own company's name without giving an indication of who the research is for.

The ground rules should cover the following issues:

■ Confidentiality (use first names only)

■ What you will do with the results

■ Who will hear the recordings

■ Importance of one person speaking at a time within the group discussion

■ Encouragement of different points of view

■ Desirability of both positive and negative comments

■ Neutrality of moderator (feelings not hurt by negative comments)

■ Duration of focus group and when "honoraria" or incentives will be received

To begin, have the participants go around the table and introduce themselves. Ask them to provide their first names and any other relevant information that will establish them as peers of the other participants and might help in interpreting their later comments. This may include their ages, whether they are married, whether they have any children, where they live, and/or the types of work they do. You also can ask them to answer an easy question to get everyone talking. The question should be relevant to the purpose of the focus group but not necessarily "on topic" (e.g., what they do in their free time, their favorite radio station or television show, their health-related goals, their pet peeves about doctors).

Designing effective questions for the main section of the focus group takes strategic thinking. The questions you ask will depend on your purpose; exploratory focus groups will be very different from pretesting focus groups. Separate the questions that are nice to know from the ones that you need to know. Make sure that you have a purpose behind every question you ask. Use the idea of "backward research" to identify all the information you need to make decisions in your program. Design questions to get that information in the most effective way.

Although your inclination might be to get as much information from your participants as possible, do not try to fit too much into the time you have available. Asking too many questions on different topics can make the participants bored or fatigued. As a rule of thumb, you probably can fit about 8 to 12 main questions (with several follow-up questions each) into 2 hours. If necessary, you can have the participants fill out a short written survey at the end to collect demographic information, quantitative responses to very specific questions, and/or information that might not be appropriate to ask during the focus group. During the focus group, you also can have participants provide anonymous written responses to key questions that they might not be comfortable revealing to others.

Moderating Skills

The person who serves as moderator ideally should be trained in conducting focus groups or experienced in group facilitation. This does not mean that you cannot moderate your own focus groups if you do not have these skills. Many organizations offer training in focus group moderation, or you can refer to one of the books listed in Appendix A for assistance. Moderating focus groups well is a skill that is learned and developed through practice.

Consider training target audience members or people from the same community to moderate the groups. They might be able to elicit more honest or extensive responses than would a moderator who is noticeably different from the target audience members. Using more than one person to moderate a series of focus groups has advantages and disadvantages; with more people, you can complete more groups in a short period of time, but you might not be able to easily compare the results from each group because of differences in style and questioning techniques.

Prior to the first focus group, if you will be the moderator, memorize the topic guide. Knowing the questions in advance helps you to lead from one question to the next when the time is right without having to refer to the guide. You should be alert and focused, so take some quiet time alone before the group starts. As participants arrive, greet them and engage in small talk to make them comfortable.

The moderator's role during the focus group is that of a neutral referee, keeping the discussion on track without doing much of the talking. Participants should be encouraged to talk to each other rather than solely to you. In addition, avoid showing any personal reactions to what the participants say; they should perceive you as being completely nonjudgmental. That includes both verbal and nonverbal responses—head nodding, raising eyebrows, saying "That's right" or "Hmmm."

Focus Group Questioning Strategies

- Start with more general questions and funnel down to more important specifics.
  - What issues related to your health have been on your mind the most lately?
  - What does the term *heart disease* mean to you?
  - What is the first thing you think of when I say "water"?
  - What do you like most about recycling?
- Use open-ended questions, not yes-or-no questions. These can be discussion stoppers.
- Do not ask too many "why" questions. They make people feel like they have to be able to defend their answers. Instead, ask what features they like or what influenced them to do something.
- Have preprepared "probes" to find out more information about people's answers to a particular question (e.g., "What are you basing that on?" "Which is most important?" "What do you think is ideal?").
- Ground people by using questions about their past experiences rather than asking about future intentions (e.g., "Think back to the last time you were driving in heavy traffic. What feelings were you experiencing?").
- Other types of questions you can use include the following:
  - Role-play. "Pretend I'm a friend of yours who has been having sex without birth control. What advice would you give me?"
  - Project traits onto other people. "How would you describe a person who carries a gun?"
  - Hypothetical situations. "In what types of situations would you bring your child to the doctor?"
  - Meaning of the obvious. "What does confidentiality mean to you?"
  - Chain of questions. "Why is that important to you?"
  - Sentence completion. "The best thing about this product is. . . ."

As the moderator, you will need to actively listen and ask questions about what the participants say. You can ask for clarification, probe for more information, or point out contradictions to explore what participants really mean to say. Make sure that you bring back the discussion if it wanders too far afield, although letting it digress briefly can be useful; you might learn things you would not have thought to ask about.

If you have problems getting the discussion going, or if certain people appear reticent, you can encourage them to talk through nonverbal cues. Eye contact can help bring people into the group and make them feel comfortable speaking. You also can use silence as a tool to facilitate participation. After asking a question, or after someone else has spoken, wait for at least 5 seconds before continuing. Although it doesn't sound like much, that silent pause can feel like a long time and it gives the participants a chance to think about what was said and to respond. If you move on to the next item without leaving any lag time, then you risk missing a thought that has begun to percolate. Finally, be sensitive to the group's receptiveness to discussing the topic. If you encounter resistance, then you might need to adjust the topic guide accordingly or perhaps consider conducting one-on-one interviews instead.

Try not to become an authority figure in the group by answering questions if they come up. Ideally, wait until the end of the group to answer questions or to correct information that is wrong or harmful. Often, other people in the focus group will provide answers. This also lets you see how well they understand the topic.

At the end of the focus group, thank everyone for their participation and give them their promised incentive. Afterward, go over the discussion with the assistant moderator to identify the "big ideas" that emerged and to confirm that your understandings of what transpired correspond. You might wish to make notes of your immediate impressions while they still are fresh in your mind. If necessary, make changes to the topic guide based on spontaneous discussions that you found useful during the session.

Focus Group Moderator Qualities

A good focus group moderator should have the following qualities:

- Experienced in doing focus groups (or at least have some training)
- Familiar with the topic
- Similar to the participants or at least comfortable interacting with them
- Able to put others at ease
- A good listener
- Nonjudgmental
- Able to ask questions in a way that will not bias the answers
- Able to think on his or her feet
- Flexible

Analysis

Interpreting focus groups involves several levels of analysis. Within each focus group, look at the words spoken by individuals as well as the key points made by the group as a whole. Also, compare the main ideas that emerged across all the focus groups to identify similarities and differences in the findings.

Before beginning the analysis phase, have transcripts made from the recordings of the focus group proceedings. Although it is not always necessary, ideally a word-for-word transcript of each group would be provided by a professional with experience transcribing focus groups. This ensures that you will not lose potentially valuable information—in the form of an idea, the words that are used, or the context of a given remark. But this method can be expensive if you are doing a large number of focus groups.

In the more common approach, you can listen to the audio yourself and transcribe all of the contents or just key sections, or you can rely on the notes taken by the assistant moderator and fill in missing information as you listen. This also can serve the purpose of refreshing your memory about what happened in each session before you start your analysis. The main advantage of having a professional transcribe the recordings is that it will save you time; every hour of focus group time can take about 3 hours to transcribe.

Begin by reading over all the transcripts and any notes you and your assistant moderator took during each session. As you read, look for trends and strongly or frequently held opinions. Go through question by question and note the main points emerging across the groups. Also, make a note of any quotes that support the points you see emerging.

Keep the following points in mind:

- Do not take responses out of context. Remember that respondents were reacting to a particular question or a comment from another person.

- Note the words that people use to talk about the issue, particularly if they tend to use different words than you do (e.g., *protection* vs. *contraception*).

- Do not quantify the responses you receive or generalize them to a larger population.

- Try to remember as you read the transcripts whether there were sounds of agreement or disagreement from the rest of group that did not get written down. Only one person might have said an important quote, but if everyone agreed nonverbally at the same time, then it might have been missed in the transcription.

- Comments that are specific and based on someone's own experiences should be given more weight than those that are general and impersonal.

- There is no one right way in which to analyze qualitative data, but there are wrong ways.

Before preparing a report of your findings, determine who will be reading the report and how it will be used. A more informal report would include a short summary of key findings, perhaps in a bulleted list. If you need to create a more formal report, then provide a point-by-point analysis with selected quotes to back up your findings.

Analysis Case Study: The Fifth Guy Campaign

As the Florida Department of Health considered how to help its population prepare for a possible influenza pandemic at some point in the future, it had to take into account the fact that the majority of residents of the state did not feel at risk for contracting any kind of pandemic virus and did not intend to take any action to prepare for that possibility.[1] Public health leaders, on the other hand, with guidance and funding from the Centers for Disease Control and Prevention (CDC), considered an influenza pandemic—most likely an avian flu variety—to be a genuine possibility. Polls showed that 65% of adults were slightly familiar with the idea of a pandemic, from news reports and other media, and 68% reported being concerned about the issue. Despite this, 64% did not believe that an avian flu pandemic would threaten the United States, which resulted in a lack of action taken for preparation.

The department decided to narrow the focus of the social marketing campaign to creating citizen awareness, without causing panic. Statewide focus groups explored the knowledge, attitudes, and behaviors of the adult population about pandemic flu. Four focus group sessions in each of the three most prevalent population segments (general population [Caucasian and African American], Hispanic/Latino, and Haitian) each had eight participants who were 21 years of age or older. The groups demonstrated that participants did not know very much about pandemics or how the influenza virus was spread. Because they did not feel it was an imminent threat, they did not see the benefit to preparing for it early.

On the positive side, most people knew about preventive measures that could be taken to prevent the spread of seasonal flu, such as hand washing, staying home when sick, and covering coughs. One theme that emerged was the concern for being socially ostracized for behaviors seen as being out of the norm.

A quantitative survey provided more information about the hygienic and preventive practices of the target audience. They also asked about respondents' perceptions of what other people do, related to hygienic behaviors. In all cases, their self-report of behaviors was higher than their perception of others' behaviors, particularly in hand washing (94% reported washing every time they used the restroom but thought only 48.7% of other people did so). This idea that the social norm of hygienic behaviors was relatively high but had room for improvement became the focus of the campaign. Observational research by other health organizations had determined that 80% of people (four out of five) wash their hands after using the restroom. The Fifth Guy campaign was based on the idea that people should try not to be that fifth person who does not wash his or her hands. Depiction of social norms and "fitting in" played a strong role in the campaign.

The campaign personified the "fifth guy" as a character named Ben Mitchell who, through his clueless and obnoxious disregard for hygienic standards, disgusted everyone he came across. They made the setting the workplace, which many people identified with, and had Ben's co-workers react strongly against his flouting of the social norms of hand washing, covering sneezes and coughs, and staying home when sick. The humorous tone of the ads grabbed people's attention and emphasized the idea, "Don't be the Fifth Guy."

The campaign included television and radio spots, billboards, posters, and stickers. Materials were translated into Spanish and Creole. Spots ran on both English and Spanish network and cable television stations. A popular Florida grocery store chain placed ads on its grocery carts. Print ads ran in local newspapers, and public relations efforts earned media coverage as well. The actor who played the role of "Ben Mitchell" went on a media tour of the state, giving radio and television interviews while carrying the urinal featured in the television ads. Online, a website (www.5thguy.com) provided information and interactive activities, and Ben maintained a MySpace page as the character showing himself touring the state (www.myspace.com/5thguy).

---

[1]Plourde, C., Cook, L., Mitchell, P., & Jennings, C. (2008). Talk to the fifth guy: A lesson in social marketing. *Cases in Public Health Communication & Marketing, 2,* 11–38. www.casesjournal.org/volume2

WORKSHEET 4: AUDIENCE RESEARCH WORKSHEET

1. What methods will you use to research your key target audience segments?

Qualitative Methods	*Quantitative Methods*
❑ Focus groups	❑ Knowledge, attitudes, and behaviors survey
❑ In-depth interviews	❑ Intercept survey
❑ Observational studies	❑ Marketing databases
❑ Informal information gathering	❑ Other data sources
❑ Other _____	❑ Other _____

2. Do you or your staff members have the necessary skills to conduct and analyze the research methods you have chosen?

   ❑ Yes. We have the expertise on staff.

   ❑ Possibly. We need some additional training.

   ❑ No. We need to hire outside assistance.

   If more training or outside **assistance** is needed.

   a. What is your available budget? $_____

   b. What type(s) of research or training do you need assistance with?

   _____

   _____

   _____

   c. From which companies or consultants will you solicit bids?

   _____

   _____

   _____

   If research will be done in-house:

3. What is your available budget? $_____

4. Who will be responsible for coordinating the research activities? _____

(Continued)

(Continued)

5. Who will assist in the research activities?

Name	*Role*
_____	_____
_____	_____
_____	_____
_____	_____

6. Where will you find target audience members to participate in your research?

_____

_____

_____

7. How will you contact potential research participants?

❑ In person

❑ Telephone

❑ Mail

❑ E-mail

❑ Advertisement

❑ Website/social network site

❑ Partner organization: _____

❑ Other: _____

8. Research timeline:

Activity	*Date to Be Completed*
Put research team in place	_____
Design research plan	_____
Develop questionnaires or other research instruments	_____
Test and finalize research instruments	_____
Train people who will be conducting the research	_____
Recruit research participants	_____
Conduct research	_____
Input or organize data	_____
Analyze data	_____
Create final report	_____

Section III

Step 2
Strategy Development

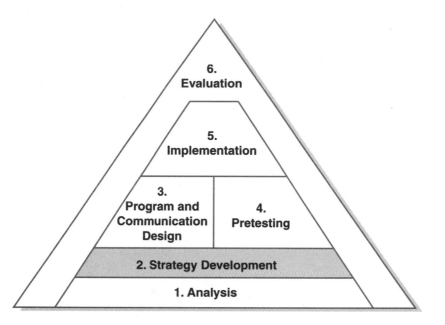

SECTION OVERVIEW

With the research complete, it's time to take all the information you have gathered and apply it to creating a comprehensive strategy. First, you will need to refine which segments of your target audience you will target in your program and to determine whether you will use different approaches with various groups or focus on one main segment of the audience. Then, you will create the social marketing mix for your audience and design a plan for how to put it into action. This section consists of the following chapters:

- Chapter 8: Segmenting the Target Audience
- Chapter 9: Building the Social Marketing Strategy

Segmenting the Target Audience

Through the secondary research you did in the analysis phase, you probably have some ideas about who your primary target audience(s) will be. Although your initial inclination might be to create an all-inclusive campaign, segmentation will help you to be more strategic in developing your program. Even if you feel that the issue is one that affects people across the population (e.g., energy conservation, dental health), narrowing down the audience allows you to tailor the message to specific needs of particular groups. "Targeting" the general public is like using scattershot ammunition to try to hit a bull's-eye; it is possible but not very efficient.

WHY SEGMENT?

Target audience segmentation is one of the central features of social marketing borrowed from commercial practice. Companies such as McDonald's know their consumers inside and out and create advertising aimed at particular segments of the population. For example, one campaign might be created for working mothers who are too busy to cook dinner but want to feed their children wholesome meals. Another might target fathers who interact with their children mainly on weekends and want to make that time special. And free toys linked to the latest Disney movie are designed to make young children clamor for a "Happy Meal." The same product—a meal at McDonald's—is being promoted, but different benefits are touted to each consumer segment.

Similarly, social marketers can use segmentation to identify the groups most reachable by a social marketing campaign and to position their product for each segment. Segmentation helps you to develop an audience-centered program by getting to know and understand the various subgroups that might be in your target audience. Creating a profile of the people in each segment can focus your thinking and keep you on track as you go through the planning process.

In addition to aiding in understanding the audience, segmentation can help you to spend resources more efficiently. The segments you choose to address through your program will depend on the characteristics of each segment and your own resources. If certain subgroups of the target audience are at higher risk for the problem you are addressing ("targets of risk"), then you might consider concentrating the program on those groups. In addition, you might identify some segments as being easier to reach or ready to make a behavior change ("targets of opportunity"). Where these two factors meet is likely to be the most efficient and effective use of your funds.

WHAT IS A SEGMENT?

The goal of segmentation is to identify distinct groups of people who are like each other in key ways and, therefore, are liable to respond to particular messages similarly. Think of a segment as a horizontal slice of a pyramid that represents the whole population. Slices taken from near the base of the pyramid will let you reach more people, but your program will not be as "personalized" as if you took a slice from near the top. The balancing act lies in choosing between segments that are not very different from the population as a whole versus being so specific that only a small number of people fall into the segment.

Segments may be based on many factors[1] such as the following:

- *Geographic:* size of city/county, residential density, climate

- *Demographic:* age, gender, income, occupation, education, number of children, race/ethnicity, immigrant generation, language, literacy

- *Physical/medical:* medical history, family history, health status, illnesses or disorders, risk factors

- *Psychographic:* lifestyle, personality characteristics, values, conceptions of social norms

- *Attitudinal:* attitudes, opinions, beliefs, judgments about product, benefits sought or barriers avoided, stage of behavior change

- *Behavioral:* product user status, frequency of behavior, occasion for use, other health-related activities, media habits, Internet use

In social marketing, it often is more useful to go beyond simple demographics such as gender and race—although these also might be quite important—to attitudes and behaviors. People who smoke might be more similar to each other (for the purposes of a social marketing program) in their attitudes than in their demographics. A possible segmentation scheme for a program to encourage current smokers to quit might use the following factors as segmentation variables:

- *Smoking status:* current smoker/not current smoker

- *Desire to quit:* yes/ambivalent/no

- *Ever tried to quit:* yes/no

- *Self-efficacy about quitting:* high/medium/low

- *Attitude about smoking's effects:* worried/fatalistic/invincible

- *Age:* teenager/young adult/middle-aged adult/older adult

---

[1]Adapted from Table 1 in Albrecht, T., & Bryant, C. (1996). Advances in segmentation modeling for health communication and social marketing campaigns. *Journal of Health Communication, 1,* 65–80.

One possible segment for this program would be older adult smokers who want to quit, have tried to do so unsuccessfully, do not think they can do it, and are worried about the effects of smoking. Another segment would be teenage smokers who are not certain about quitting, have not yet tried to quit, believe they have the ability to do so, and have a fatalistic attitude. Additional research also might reveal whether there are other important segmentation criteria such as reasons for smoking, barriers to quitting, and demographic characteristics.

In this example, there are hundreds of possible combinations of attributes for each segment. If the population you are addressing is fairly homogeneous to begin with, then extensive segmentation might not be necessary. But if you are dealing with a diverse population, or if your program has a national or state scope, segmentation can help make sense of the complexity.

TARGETING THE SEGMENTS

To determine the most important segmentation criteria, consider which are the most important factors that determine whether a target audience member adopts the relevant behavior. Think about the geographic, demographic, physical/medical, psychographic, attitudinal, and behavioral characteristics that might define subgroups of the target audience that would respond differently to your program.

Identify the "targets of risk," that is, the segments that would be more likely to have the problem because of their behaviors, attitudes, or other factors. Targeting the people in these segments would have the biggest payoff if they were to adopt the desired behavior. These might be groups that have the highest prevalence of the problem, that

Stages of Behavior Change

As much as social marketers might wish it were true, complex behavior change does not occur instantaneously. The stages of change model (or transtheoretical model) describes a process of five stages that people must go through to change their behavior.[a] By knowing which stage most of your target audience members are in, you can craft appropriate messages to move them along to the next stage (this is discussed further in Chapter 11). These five stages provide you with ready-made segments you can use to help define your target audience:

1. *Precontemplation:* Individuals are not aware that they are at risk or have a problem, so they have no intention of changing their behavior in the foreseeable future.
2. *Contemplation:* Individuals are aware that there is a problem and begin to consider whether to take any action.
3. *Preparation:* Individuals intend to take action soon and make plans to do so.
4. *Action:* Individuals modify their behavior or take other related steps to address the problem.
5. *Maintenance:* Individuals continue the changes made in the action stage for as long as necessary if the behavior requires more than a one-time action.

In your research, you can assess which stage someone is in through the use of a question in the following format:[b]
Do you currently volunteer at least once a month at a nonprofit organization?

a. No, and I do not intend to start doing so within the next 6 months. (*Precontemplation*)
b. No, but I intend to start doing so within the next 6 months. (*Contemplation*)
c. No, but I intend to start doing so within the next 30 days. (*Preparation*)
d. Yes, I have been doing so for less than 6 months. (*Action*)
e. Yes, I have been doing so for more than 6 months. (*Maintenance*)

a. Prochaska, J., & DiClemente, C. C. (1983). Stages and process of self-change of smoking: Toward an integrative model of change. *Journal of Consulting and Clinical Psychology, 51*, 390–395.

b. Grimley, D., Riley, G., Bellis, J., & Prochaska, J. (1993). Assessing the stages of change and decision-making for contraceptive use for the prevention of pregnancy, sexually transmitted diseases, and acquired immunodeficiency syndrome. *Health Education Quarterly, 20*, 455–470.

know the least about prevention, or whose members' lifestyles make it more likely that they will be affected by the problem.

In addition to thinking about risk factors, consider the "targets of opportunity," that is, the segments that are easier to reach or change. It is only natural, especially in health and social programs, to want to change everyone at once or even to start with the hardest to reach groups first. But the advantage of targeting the people who are ready to change or are more easily reachable is that you will see results right away, and those people can then help you reach out to others. These segments might be at the preparation stage of behavior change, just needing your program to give them that extra nudge to take action. Or, they could be the people already using your services who have positive attitudes about making healthful changes in their lives.

Rank the segmentation criteria that you think are most important. If you target all of these factors, how many people will you actually be addressing in each segment? Is it a large enough number to make it worth your while? If not, consider going back up the list until the size of the segments justifies the allocation of resources. Although the targeting will be less specific, you should create only as many segments as you can handle efficiently. If you feel that your segments are too large but you do not have enough information to identify further criteria, then the next step is to conduct additional research with each segment to see whether it is fairly homogeneous or whether there are subgroups you can detect.

Allocating Resources

When you have determined the segmentation categories, you must decide how you will approach resource allocation within the program. Choose from among three basic strategies:

- Allocating equal amounts of resources to all relevant segments
- Allocating different amounts of resources to each segment
- Allocating all resources to only one or a small number of key segments

Generally, programs of moderate size can realistically address from one to three segments. Those with less resources should focus on one segment at a time for best results.

Andreasen offers a set of nine criteria to consider in creating segments and allocating resources.[2] Approaches to each segment may differ because of the distinctive needs of some groups, differing responsiveness of segments, or the degree of efficiency in using separate strategies for each segment.

The nine factors are the following:

- *Segment size.* Are there enough people in a segment to comprise a useful market?
- *Problem incidence.* Are there higher rates of the problem or risky behaviors in some segments?

---

[2]Andreasen, A. (1995). *Marketing social change.* San Francisco: Jossey-Bass.

- *Problem severity.* Are the consequences of the problem (e.g., deaths) more severe in some segments?

- *Defenselessness.* Are the members of the segment able to take care of the problem themselves, or do they need outside help?

- *Reachability.* Are some segments harder to reach because they are more difficult to find or require more costly methods?

- *General responsiveness.* Are some segments more ready, willing, and able to respond to the social marketing program than are others?

- *Incremental costs.* How much more will it cost in money and effort to reach additional segments? Is it worth it?

- *Responsiveness to marketing mix.* Will some segments respond differently to particular marketing mix elements and require different strategies?

- *Organizational capability.* Does your organization have the expertise to create and deliver differentiated strategies?

Segmenting Secondary Audiences

Once you have identified the likeliest primary target audience segments, consider whether there are any secondary target audiences that you might need to enlist as part of your social marketing program. Think about them in relation to the questions you have already asked yourself about the primary audience segments, for they should be segmented as well. Addressing them in addition to the primary target audience will involve extra costs in research, development of a secondary marketing mix, and materials but could be the best way in which to reach the primary audience.

Additional questions to ask yourself about secondary target audience segments include the following:

- What groups or individuals have the most influence over the behavior of the primary audience?

- How do they exert that influence?

- What benefits would the secondary audience receive from serving as a program intermediary?

- What might be the barriers to involving them in the program?

- What are the secondary audiences' own knowledge, attitudes, and behaviors related to the problem?

As with the primary target audience, the next step after identifying the likely segments within the secondary audience is to conduct your own research directly with the people in each key segment. This serves to refine the preliminary segmentation and to expand your knowledge about the people in these very specific groups.

The Healthstyles Segmentation System

Commercial marketers often use databases of information on consumers' buying habits, demographics, psychographics, and leisure activities to identify the most appropriate audience segments to target. One public relations firm, Porter Novelli, combined such a database with additional data collected from the same respondents regarding their health-related beliefs, attitudes, and behaviors to create the American Healthstyles Audience Segmentation Project.

Rather than just looking at an audience's lifestyles, the Healthstyles system provides insight into the psychological and social factors that affect the presence or absence of certain health behaviors. Porter Novelli gathered information on five indicator behaviors that are more likely than others to reflect an audience's orientation to health: smoking, exercise, nutrition, weight control, and alcohol use. Analyses of the resulting database identified seven Healthstyles audience segments, which are briefly described here:

- *Decent Dolittles* (24% of the adult population). They are one of the less health-oriented groups. Although less likely to smoke or drink, they also are less likely to exercise, eat nutritiously, and work to stay at their ideal weights. Decent Dolittles know that they should be performing these behaviors to improve their health, but they do not feel that they have the ability. Their friends and family tend to avoid these behaviors as well. They describe themselves as "religious," "conservative", and "clean."

- *Active Attractives* (13%). They place a high emphasis on looking good and partying. Active Attractives are relatively youthful and moderately health oriented. They tend not to smoke and limit their fat intake more than do other groups. They are highly motivated, intending to exercise and keep their weight down, but they do not always succeed at this. Alcohol consumption is an important part of their lifestyle, and Active Attractives often are sensation seekers, constantly looking for adventure. They describe themselves as "romantic," "dynamic," "youthful," and "vain."

- *Hard-Living Hedonists* (6%). They are not very interested in health and tend to smoke and drink alcohol more heavily and frequently than do other groups. They also enjoy eating high-fat foods and do not care about limiting their fat intake. Despite this, they tend not to be overweight and are moderately physically active. Although they are the group least satisfied with their lives, they have no desire to make any health-related changes. Hard-Living Hedonists also are more likely to use stimulants and illicit drugs than are other segments. They describe themselves as "daring," "moody," "rugged," "independent," and "exciting."

- *Tense but Trying* (10%). They are similar to the more health-oriented segments except that they tend to smoke cigarettes. They are average in the amount of exercise they get and in their efforts to control their fat intake and weight. They have a moderate desire to exercise more, eat better, and control their weight more effectively as well. The Tense but Trying tend to be more anxious than other groups, with the highest rate of ulcers and use of sedatives and a higher number of visits to mental health counselors. They describe themselves as "tense," "high-strung," "sensitive," and "serious."

- *Noninterested Nihilists* (7%). They are the least health oriented and do not feel that people should take steps to improve their health. Accordingly, they smoke heavily, actively dislike exercise, eat high-fat diets, and make no effort to control their weight. Despite this, they tend to drink alcohol only moderately. Of all the groups, Noninterested Nihilists have the highest level of physical impairment, the most sick days in bed, and the most medical care visits related to an illness. They describe themselves as being "depressed," "moody," and "homebodies."

- *Physical Fantastics* (24%). They are the most health-oriented group, leading a consistently health-promoting lifestyle. They are above average in not smoking or drinking, exercising routinely, eating nutritiously, and making efforts to control their weight. They tend to be in their middle or latter adult years and have a relatively large number of chronic health conditions. Physical Fantastics follow their physicians' advice to modify their diets and routinely discuss health-related topics with others.

- *Passively Healthy* (15%). They are in excellent health, although they are somewhat indifferent to living healthfully. They do not smoke or drink heavily and are one of the most active segments. Although they eat a high amount of dietary fat, they are the trimmest of all the groups. The Passively Healthy do not place much value on good health and physical fitness and are not motivated to make any changes in their behaviors.

Source: Maibach, E., Maxfield, A., Ladin, K., & Slater, M. (1996). Translating health psychology into effective health communication: The American Healthstyles Audience Segmentation Project. *Journal of Health Psychology, 1*, 261–277.

Sources of Market Segmentation Data

Nielsen-Claritas, Inc.

(866) 273-5418
http://www.claritas.com

The PRIZM lifestyle segmentation system provides detailed data combining demographics with product, media, and lifestyle preference information, sorted by ZIP code.

Mediamark Research, Inc. (MRI)

(212) 884-9200 or (800) 310-3305
http://www.mediamark.com

MRI offers comprehensive demographic, lifestyle, product use, and media data collected annually from more than 25,000 consumers throughout the continental United States. Psychographic segments include health and medical, eating/cooking/food, green, civic/political engagement, financial behavior and more.

Porter Novelli

(212) 601-8000
http://www.porternovelli.com

The Healthstyles audience database includes information on health practices and attitudes for American adults combined with more general lifestyle information such as media use, attitudes, self-perceptions, activities, and shopping patterns.

Experian Simmons

(212) 471-2850
http://www.smrb.com

The Simmons National Consumer Study collects over 60,000 variables from more than 25,000 American consumers. They offer specialized studies of Hispanic consumers, teens, gay/lesbian/bisexual/transgender consumers, and local information for 210 American media markets.

Strategic Business Insights

(650) 859-4600
http://www.strategicbusinessinsights.com/vals

VALS (Values and Lifestyles) categorizes U.S. adult consumers into distinct groups based on their psychology and key demographics. Using factors such as self-orientation and resources, VALS defines eight consumer segments by their attitudes, behavior, and decision-making patterns.

WORKSHEET 5: SEGMENTATION WORKSHEET

Using the secondary research you have gathered, answer the following questions as best you can:

1. What geographic characteristics define separate segments within your population?

   _____

   _____

   _____

2. What demographic characteristics that are most relevant to the problem define separate segments within your population?

   _____

   _____

   _____

3. What physical or medical characteristics define separate segments within your population?

   _____

   _____

   _____

4. What psychographic characteristics, such as lifestyle, personality, values, and social norms, define separate segments within your population?

   _____

   _____

   _____

5. What behaviors put people most at risk of the problem?

   (a) _____

   (b) _____

   (c) _____

6. What behaviors help to reduce the risk or prevent the problem from occurring?

   (a) _____

   (b) _____

   (c) _____

7. How can you best segment the target audience on the basis of the key behaviors listed in Question 5 and/or Question 6 above (e.g., users/nonusers, frequency of use, reason for use)?

(5a) _____

(5b) _____

(5c) _____

(6a) _____

(6b) _____

(6c) _____

8. What attitudes or beliefs related to the problem or relevant behaviors listed above define separate segments within your population?

_____

_____

_____

9. Are there any segments you definitely will not target in your program because, for example, it is not feasible or there are already programs in place addressing those groups?

_____

_____

_____

10. Look over the possible segmentation criteria you have noted above and write down the five that you think are most important, in order:

(1) _____

(2) _____

(3) _____

(4) _____

(5) _____

11. For Question 10, put a star next to the segment(s) most at risk of having the problem you are addressing in your program (targets of risk).

12. For Question 10, put a circle next to the segment(s) you think would be most easily reachable or changeable through your program (targets of opportunity).

13. How will you allocate resources to the segments you will address through your program?

 ❑ Allocate equal resources to all segments

 ❑ Allocate different amounts of resources to each segment

 ❑ Allocate all resources to only ___ [number] segment(s)

14. Are there any secondary audiences who influence the target audience that you should consider addressing in your program? Identify the most important segments:

_____

_____

_____

CHAPTER 9

Building the Social Marketing Strategy

On the basis of the results of the research you have conducted, you can start to build a program strategy. This strategy might need to be modified as you do more research, but it will serve as a reference point throughout the program development process. In the strategy, you will set goals and measurable objectives, consider the elements of the marketing mix as they relate to your program, and create a work plan for program development.

SETTING GOALS AND OBJECTIVES

With the data you have gathered about the problem and the target audience, you can now set reasonable goals and objectives for the social marketing program. Having measurable objectives from the outset is a way in which to assess the success of the program. Without having a destination in sight, you might steer in the wrong direction, never knowing you have lost your way. You must be careful, however, to be realistic when setting goals. It is not very likely that you will reduce heart disease by 30% after a 6-month campaign, but maybe you can increase by 30% the number of people who are aware that eating high-cholesterol foods is related to heart attack risk.

The goal of the program refers to the overall change in the health or social problem your program will strive to reach, for example, "to decrease the incidence rate of HIV infection in the target population by 10%" or "to reduce household water use by 15%." A program may have a single goal or several distinct goals. Ask yourself, "How will the world look different if we achieve the goal?"

Objectives describe the intermediate steps that must be taken to reach each goal. They are not the activities you will use to get there but rather the steps that have to happen to lead to attainment of the goal. The objectives may relate to changes in knowledge, attitudes, skills, or behaviors of the primary or secondary target audiences; changes in the environment or policy; or project milestones (e.g., attaining a certain number of project partners).

Avoid using project activities as your objectives, such as "to create an online social network site" or "to offer a training workshop." Rather, the objectives should state the desired outcome of those activities, such as "to increase knowledge" or "to implement the policy in 10 counties." Under each objective, you would then determine what types of activities will best help you achieve those changes.

Sample Goals and Objectives

Some examples of goals and objectives for two different programs might be as follows:

Program 1 Goal: To decrease by 10% the number of traffic deaths of drivers from 16 to 24 years of age by the end of a two-year period.

- Objective 1: To increase by 15% the number of drivers from 16 to 24 years of age who report using seat belts every time they drive by the end of two years.

- Objective 2: To increase by 30% the number of drivers from 16 to 24 years of age who believe that seat belts are safe and effective in preventing traffic injuries by the end of two years.

- Objective 3: To increase by 40% the number of environmental design features, such as road humps, traffic circles, and raised medians that have been proven effective in reducing traffic speed, throughout the County by the end of two years.

Program 2 Goal: To reduce the total amount of electricity consumed by Community Y by 5% by the end of the year.

- Objective 1: To increase the number of residents who report always keeping the thermostat at 68 degrees Fahrenheit or lower during the winter months by 25% by the end of the year.

- Objective 2: To increase the number of residents who believe they can reduce their energy bill by taking small easy steps to change their habits by 40% by the end of the year.

- Objective 3: To pass a city policy requiring apartment owners to install energy-efficient appliances in each building/unit upon entry of a new tenant by six months of commencement of the project.

Effective objectives clearly state who will do or change what by when and by how much. When writing your objectives, keep in mind the SMART format[1] to ensure they will be useful in guiding your program and evaluating your success. The acronym stands for:

Specific—What observable change will occur?

Measurable—What metrics will you use to track the extent of the change?

Achievable—Given your available resources, what type and amount of change is reasonable to expect?

Relevant—Is the objective laser focused to move you closer to your overall goal?

Time framed—What amount of time is reasonable to allocate to accomplish this objective?

Objectives are critical for both planning and evaluation. They must be measurable, for how else will you know if you have accomplished what you set out to do? Consider how much change you can realistically expect to achieve as compared to the baseline data. There is nothing worse for morale than to come up short against unrealistic objectives, particularly when you do achieve a relatively high degree of change. Check the research literature or ask others about their experience for indications of how much change you can reasonably expect. If you cannot find that type of information, you also can decide to measure your success by comparing baseline data to the evaluation data to detect statistically significant differences related to your objectives rather than designating an arbitrary percentage.

PRELIMINARY SOCIAL MARKETING MIX

As discussed in Chapter 3, the social marketing mix helps you to think through a comprehensive strategy for your program. Brainstorming about each element of the marketing mix based

---

[1]Doran, G. T. (1981). There's a S.M.A.R.T. way to write management's goals and objectives. *Management Review, 70*(11), 35–36.

on what you found in your research will prepare you for the next stage of the social marketing process—program and communication design.

Consider each "P" of the social marketing mix in relation to your target audience segments (if you are targeting more than one segment, then you may have a different mix for each). Remember that the marketing mix may change as you have additional brilliant flashes of insight or learn through pretesting that the target audience is less than enthusiastic about your initial approach. Think of the resulting strategy as a living document that provides guidance but can be changed in response to new information:

- Product

  - What is the behavior you are asking the target audience to do?

  - What are the benefits it would receive from adopting the behavior?

  - What is the "competition," and why would the target audience prefer it to the behavior you are "selling"?

- Price

  - What are the costs the target audience associates with the product?

  - What are other barriers that prevent the target audience from adopting the product?

  - How can you minimize the costs or remove the barriers?

- Place

  - What are the places where the target audience makes decisions about engaging in the desired behavior?

  - How can you redesign these places to facilitate behavior change?

What Amount of Change Is Reasonable?

In a meta-analysis of more than 400 health communication programs[2] (not all social marketing based), Leslie Snyder found that the average media campaign affects the intervention community by about 5 percentage points (i.e., if 60% of people were engaging in the behavior before, 65% were doing so after the campaign). Of course, the effectiveness of a particular program depends on many factors, such as characteristics of the audience, as well as the behavior and the quality of the campaign itself. For example, campaigns promoting the adoption of a new behavior or replacing an old behavior with a new one have a greater success rate than those trying to stop an unhealthy behavior people are already doing or prevent the adoption of one.

The meta-analysis looked at effect sizes across many different categories of health campaigns and found a range of success rates:

- Seatbelt campaigns (15%)
- Dental care (13%)
- Adult alcohol reduction (11%)
- Family planning (6%)
- Youth smoking prevention (6%)
- Heart disease prevention, including diet/physical activity (5%)
- Sexual risk taking (4%)
- Mammography screening (4%)
- Adult smoking prevention (4%)
- Youth alcohol prevention and cessation (4%–7%)
- Youth tobacco prevention campaigns (4%)
- Youth drug and marijuana campaigns (1%–2%)

You can use these average results to help estimate what a reasonable amount of change would be for your own program (which of course will be better than average, right?).

---

[2]Snyder, L. B. (2007). Health communication campaigns and their impact on behavior. *Journal of Nutrition Education and Behavior, 39*(Suppl. 1), S32–S40.

- Where do target audience members spend much of their time?
- To which social, recreational, or professional groups do target audience members belong?
- What distribution systems will be most efficient for reaching target audience members?

■ Promotion

- How can you best package the message to reach the most target audience members effectively and efficiently in the places listed above?
- Which communication channels do target audience members pay the most attention to and trust the most?
- Who is the most credible and engaging spokesperson on this issue for the target audience?

■ Publics

- Who are the people outside your organization you need to address to be successful?
- Who are the people inside your organization whose support you need to be successful?

■ Partnership

- Are there other organizations addressing a similar problem or target audience that you could team up with?
- Are there other organizations that could bring needed resources or skills to the project as partners?
- Are there any organizations that would be politically advantageous for you to ally yourself with?

■ Policy

- Are there any policies that would create an environment more conducive to the desired behavior?
- Is there any pending legislation that would affect your program's goals, either positively or negatively?
- Are policymakers knowledgeable about or interested in the problem you are addressing?

■ Purse strings

- Is the funding that you currently have for this project enough to tackle all of your objectives?
- Are there additional sources that you can apply to for funding, if necessary?
- Are there potential corporate partners that might participate in the project in exchange for positive publicity?

CASE STUDY

Strategy Case Study: Eat Smart, Move More North Carolina

Eat Smart, Move More North Carolina (ESMM) is a statewide social marketing program focused on promoting increased opportunities for healthy eating and physical activity in the places where people "live, learn, earn, play and pray."[3] The program focused on moms ages 25 to 54, who are the primary health care decision makers for their families, and their children. The program used two tools to help them segment the audience according to attitudes, behaviors and geography.

The Centers for Disease Control and Prevention (CDC) has created an energy balance audience segmentation framework, which segments people into five groups according to their attitudes and behaviors about nutrition, physical activity, and weight control:[4]

- Actively Balanced—healthy weight, healthy attitudes and behaviors

- Passively Balanced—healthy weight, unhealthy attitudes or behaviors

- Balance Seekers—moderate weight, healthy attitudes or behaviors

- Seeking but Struggling—unhealthy weight, moderate attitudes or behaviors

- Out of Balance—unhealthy weight, unhealthy attitudes or behaviors

ESMM used the CDC questions that determine these segmentation criteria and matched them up with the questions on the Nielsen PRIZM Audience Profile Tool. PRIZM combines U.S. Census demographic data with marketing lifestyle data, media usage data, and GIS mapping capability. This allowed the program to determine how the CDC segments were distributed throughout North Carolina counties. They decided to focus on the "Seeking but Struggling" segment, who would likely be receptive to messages, and the "Out of Balance" segment, which was at highest risk for problems. They mapped out which counties had a higher concentration of each segment, as well as which had a large proportion of both segments, and designed approaches for each segment that were implemented by county.

As an example, the "Seeking but Struggling" segment has the following characteristics:

- Dissatisfied with their weight and recognize the health threat

- Tend to overeat when stressed or upset

- Don't like to exercise but are pleased when they do

- Have low self-efficacy for eating healthy

- Key benefits they value include feeling good about themselves, feeling better physically, and managing weight

- Look for health info on the web

- Belong to a health club

- Joined Weight Watchers

(Continued)

[3]Vodicka, S. (2009, August). *Using technology and science to segment audiences.* Paper presented at the National Conference on Health Communication, Marketing and Media, Atlanta, GA.

[4]Department of Health and Human Services, Centers for Disease Control and Prevention, Division of Nutrition, Physical Activity, and Obesity. (2007). *Segmenting audiences to promote energy balance: Resource guide for public health professionals.* Atlanta, GA: Author.

> (Continued)
>
> The approaches that ESMM took to address the "Seeking but Struggling" segment in the appropriate counties included workshops, a tailored website and online tools, and messages in ads about the following:
>
> - Portion control
>
> - Moving more every day, depicting people walking because that is what this group is more likely to do for exercise
>
> - Preparing more food at home, as they like to cook and to try new foods and recipes
>
> - Avoiding foods and drinks high in sugar, fat, and calories
>
> - Watching less television and moving more (they watch 3 hours of TV per day, on average)
>
> This tailored approach seemed to pay off in the demonstration projects, as recognition of the program grew by 5.7% in 6 months, nutrition improved by 5.7%, and physical activity improved by 3.3%.

CREATING A WORK PLAN

By now, you should have a good idea of the task you have before you. The final step in the planning stage is to create a work plan for program development, implementation, and evaluation. If you have not created a work plan already, then read the rest of this book before proceeding so that you know what to include in the work plan.

The work plan should be as detailed as you can make it, including the following for each objective:

- Tasks and subtasks

- Person responsible

- Deadline

- Resources needed

You also can identify the estimated costs for each task, potential roadblocks, and the evaluation criteria for each objective.

The work plan should help to keep the project on schedule by making sure that all staff know their roles and how they relate to the tasks others are performing. Deadlines can provide the motivation to complete each task on time. As with all things in life, however, whatever can go wrong will go wrong, so make sure to budget additional time and funds to accommodate Murphy's law. You might need to be somewhat flexible and readjust the schedule as the situation requires. The work plan also can serve as a way of tracking progress as you move through the program development process.

WORKSHEET 6:
PRELIMINARY SOCIAL MARKETING STRATEGY WORKSHEET

Target Audience

1. What are the primary target audience segments you have chosen?

   _____

   _____

   _____

   _____

2. What are the secondary target audience segments you have chosen (if applicable)?

   _____

   _____

Goals and Objectives

3. What is the overall goal of your program?

   _____

   _____

4. What are the key objectives of your program? Add as many as necessary on a separate sheet of paper.

   a. _____

                     Who?

   will _____

                     What?

   by _____ by _____

                     When?   How much?

   b. _____

                     Who?

   will _____

                     What?

   by _____ by _____

                     When?   How much?

   (Continued)

(Continued)

c. _____

             Who?

will _____

             What?

by _____ by _____

             When?   How much?

Social Marketing Mix

5. Product

  a. What is the product or behavior you are asking the target audience to adopt?

    _____

    _____

    _____

  b. What are the key benefits the target audience would receive from adopting the product?

    _____

    _____

    _____

  c. What is the competition for your product in the target audience's eyes?

    _____

    _____

    _____

  d. How is your product different from and better than the competition?

    _____

    _____

    _____

6. Price

  a. What are the costs or other barriers that the target audience associates with the product?

    _____

    _____

    _____

  b. How can you minimize the costs or remove the barriers?

    _____

    _____

    _____

7. Place

   a. What are the places in which the target audience makes decisions about engaging in the desired behavior?

   _____

   _____

   _____

   b. Where do target audience members spend much of their time (e.g., physically, socially, professionally)?

   _____

   _____

   _____

   c. What distribution systems will be most efficient for reaching target audience members?

   _____

   _____

   _____

   d. Are there structural/environmental changes that could help enable the behavior?

   _____

   _____

   _____

8. Promotion

   a. Which communication channels do target audience members pay the most attention to and trust the most?

   _____

   _____

   _____

   b. What promotional techniques are the best for conveying your message?

   _____

   _____

   _____

   c. Who are the most credible spokespeople to address your target audience?

   _____

   _____

   _____

(Continued)

(Continued)

9. Publics

   a. Who are the people or groups (in addition to your primary and secondary target audiences) outside your organization that you need to address for your program to be successful?

   _____

   _____

   _____

   b. Who are the people or groups inside your organization whose support you need for your program to be successful?

   _____

   _____

   _____

10. Partnership: Which are the most promising organizations to join forces with for the social marketing program?

   _____

   _____

   _____

11. Policy: What types of policies (organizational or governmental) should you address in your social marketing program?

   _____

   _____

   _____

12. Purse strings: From which organizations will you seek further funding if necessary?

   _____

   _____

   _____

13. Now go back through each element of the social marketing mix and put an asterisk by the most promising ideas to use for developing your program.

Work Plan

Objective	Tasks	Person Responsible	Deadline	Resources Needed	Evaluation Criteria
1.	1.				
	2.				
	3.				
	4.				
2.	1.				
	2.				
	3.				
	4.				
3.	1.				
	2.				
	3.				
	4.				
4.	1.				
	2.				
	3.				
	4.				
5.	1.				
	2.				
	3.				
	4.				
6.	1.				
	2.				
	3.				
	4.				
7.	1.				
	2.				
	3.				
	4.				
8.	1.				
	2.				
	3.				
	4.				

Section IV

Step 3

*Program and
Communication Design*

In Steps 1 and 2, you put in a lot of hard work doing research and building a preliminary strategy. Now comes the fun part. Step 3 focuses on designing your program's approach and developing communications to convey your messages. You will combine the results of your previous research with some creativity to design a campaign that motivates your target audience to adopt your product. This section leads you through the process of pinpointing ways to change behavior through environmental and product design, developing effective messages, identifying appropriate channels, and transforming those messages into communication products.

The section consists of the following chapters:

- Chapter 10: Influencing Behavior by Design
- Chapter 11: Developing Effective Messages
- Chapter 12: Identifying Appropriate Channels
- Chapter 13: Producing Creative Communications

Influencing Behavior by Design

You may not be aware of it as you walk through a grocery store, but every aspect of the experience has been carefully designed to maximize the amount of money you will spend by the time you walk out. This includes elements like placing staples such as milk and eggs on the farthest wall from the entrance so you have to walk through other aisles to get there, putting foods with kid appeal on lower shelves so they can see and lobby for it, and putting impulse items by the cash registers to grab while you wait in line. Even the smell wafting from the bakery has been calculated to increase the number of items in your shopping cart. Though we'd like to think we are buying only needed products, we're not immune to subconscious cues.

That supermarket gauntlet does not even take into account the effects of communication about the products in the form of packaging, point-of-purchase advertising, pricing, or other pieces of information about the products themselves. What if social marketers could similarly affect people's behavior through how their environment or the product itself is designed, without even needing to resort to communicating messages to convince people to change? For example, passing a regulation requiring all residential pools to have childproof fences might be far more effective at preventing drownings than changing the daily behavior of parents and children. Altering the physical or social environment can either make it easier for someone to perform a desired behavior (e.g., vehicles with built-in child safety seats) or make it more difficult to perform an undesirable behavior (e.g., prohibiting smoking in restaurants and workplaces). If you can identify ways to create structural change, you may not need to focus on changing behavior one person at a time—usually a more difficult proposition.

Futurist and designer R. Buckminster Fuller recognized this when he said, "I made up my mind . . . that I would never try to reform man—that's much too difficult. What I would do was to try to modify the environment in such a way as to get man moving in preferred directions."[1] When we design for behavior change, we may be much more successful than if we rely on persuasion.

BEHAVIORAL ECONOMICS GIVES A NUDGE

In recent years, a slew of books—*Nudge, Predictably Irrational, Switch, Sway, Freakonomics,* and others—have popularized the field of behavioral economics as a source of ideas for understanding and changing human behavior. The foundation behind this field is that people do not

---

[1]Tomkins, C. (1966, January 8). In the outlaw area. *The New Yorker,* p. 35.

always rationally weigh out the costs and benefits of a particular choice as classic economics would have us believe. Rather, people are often irrational (though they may not realize it) in choosing behaviors that may not be in their own best interest, but they do so in a predictable way. Their rational mind does not always win out over their more emotional, spontaneous nature; in the book *Nudge,* authors Richard Thaler and Cass Sunstein liken the contrast to Star Trek's logical Mr. Spock doing battle with the impulsive Homer Simpson in our heads.[2]

People have predictable mental biases that affect how they perceive situations and make decisions. If social marketers can take those inclinations into account and stack the deck in favor of the more advantageous choice, we may be able to overcome people's impulses to do things that are not necessarily in their best self-interest. According to Thaler and Sunstein, people are more likely to make an irrational choice if:

- They experience the benefits of the decision now but don't have to pay the costs until later. People who forgo saving for retirement in favor of spending the money now will have painful regrets as they approach their sunset years.

- The decision is one they make infrequently, so they do not have experience thinking through the issues. Your employer may offer an array of health plan options, but because you only have the opportunity to consider the options once a year, you may not be as familiar with the optimal features.

- They do not receive immediate feedback on the consequences of their decision. It's easy to let the air conditioner run all day when the consequences are not clear until the electricity bill arrives at the end of the month.

- They have a hard time imagining the possible outcomes of the decision and are not sure what it means in terms relevant to their lives. Telling people they used 2,000 kilowatt-hours last month may be meaningless; tell them it costs $10 a day in energy costs to keep their air conditioner running, and they will jump to raise the thermostat.

WHERE DESIGN COMES IN

When you think about how to design your approach to take into account this human struggle between choosing behaviors that make rational sense and doing what comes naturally, there are several points at which you can intervene. Many of these biases can simply be addressed through the way you craft and present your messages; Chapters 11 and 13 provide some ideas for how to design and communicate effective messages. Besides communications, the design approach, as described in this chapter, can help you determine how to shape your behavioral product and how to structure the physical or social environment.

Designing Behaviors

As discussed earlier in the context of problem analysis (Chapter 6), your issue may have several different angles from which to choose an approach. The behavior (or tangible item) you choose to promote as your main product will depend on what your audience finds acceptable

---

[2]Thaler, R. H., & Sunstein, C. R. (2009). *Nudge: Improving decisions about health, wealth, and happiness.* New York: Penguin.

and doable, and if they believe it will be efficacious in preventing or reducing the problem. You will have to determine how much is too much to ask them to do. Should the behavior be broken up into small steps, taken on one at a time? Or do they need to go full bore and take on the whole thing at once to have any effect?

Think about different scenarios in which the target audience might perform the desired behavior. Identify the points along the way at which individuals could choose the competition instead. If, for example, you are promoting the reduction of household solid waste, then the action you advocate will be different based on the stage in the purchase and disposal process you target. One possibility would be to urge the consumer to buy products that come in recyclable containers (vs. nonrecyclable containers). Another approach would be to focus on the repurchase point and promote buying refills for old containers that use minimal packaging materials (vs. a new container every time). Or, looking at the point of disposal, the action could be either recycling appropriate nonorganic refuse or composting organic materials (vs. sending it to the landfill).

Another method of pinpointing what behaviors will be the most effective in tackling the problem is to identify the positive deviants—those who have positive health or social outcomes despite having similar

Types of Mental Biases

Some of the cognitive biases people are susceptible to include the following:

- *Anchoring*—The estimate of the size or value of something depends on what you start out comparing it with, such as different price points for similar products.

- *Availability*—People tend to overestimate the likelihood of events that are easily remembered, such as a plane crash, versus less familiar but more likely events such as an asthma attack.

- *Representativeness*—People often impose patterns where none actually exist, such as in coin tosses or in stereotypes based on a few members of a group.

- *Unrealistic optimism*—Most people estimate that they will do better than average on a task than they actually will and that problems happen to someone else.

- *Loss aversion*—The level of unhappiness that people feel about something being taken away from them is much higher than the happiness they feel when they first receive it; once something is theirs, they value it more.

- *Status quo bias*—Most people have a hard time overcoming inertia and will keep going on autopilot rather than making a change.

- *Framing*—People will respond differently to the same information presented in either a positive or negative way (e.g., 10 out of 100 will die vs. 90 out of 100 will survive).

- *Priming*—Simply asking someone what they intend to do in a given situation can affect his or her subsequent behavior.

characteristics to those who are most at risk for the problem—and figure out what they're doing differently to get the good results. Chip and Dan Heath, in their book *Switch,* call this "finding the bright spots" so you can clone them, rather than only focusing on what's broken and how to fix it.[3]

An example from the book illustrates how the design approach led to uncovering the "bright spot" behavior to promote. Save the Children came to Vietnam to address child malnutrition with virtually no budget and a short timeframe in which they needed to make a difference. Rather than jumping to the standard but not very effective solutions of trying to fix

[3]Heath, C., & Heath, D. (2010). *Switch: How to change things when change is hard.* New York: Random House.

poverty, education, and sanitation systems, they first went to a local village and spent time with a group of mothers to identify a potential approach. They decided to weigh and measure every child in the village; when analyzing the data, they found that some of the children were actually well nourished, despite their impoverished families.

Save the Children staff spent time understanding how most families fed their children, then investigated what these families of well-nourished children were doing differently. It turned out that those families did several things that put their children in a better nutritional situation: (a) They fed the children four smaller meals a day, rather than two large ones that their stomachs could not process as well; (b) the parents actively fed the kids, rather than letting them decide how much they wanted to eat; and (c) the mothers collected tiny shrimp and crabs from the local rice paddies to mix in with the rice, along with sweet potato greens, despite these foods being considered either inappropriate for children or low class. Once the program staff discovered the critical differences that together boosted the children's nutritional status, they then designed a program where groups of families of malnourished children would prepare food together, including collecting the shrimp, crabs, and sweet potato greens. Six months later, 65% of the children were better nourished and stayed that way, as a result of having looked for and finding a native solution that came from the villagers themselves.

Sometimes the product is an actual tangible item that needs to be physically designed to be used in a particular context. The city of Kirkland, Washington, with the assistance of Social Marketing Services, Inc., created a program called PedFlag to increase pedestrian safety.[4] Using bright yellow flags placed in holders at crosswalks around the city that do not have a traffic signal, pedestrians make themselves more visible as they cross the street. Research to identify ways to make the PedFlag program more user-friendly changed the color of the flags from their original fluorescent orange, which was confused with construction equipment, to yellow. They added to the flag the same picture of a person crossing the street holding a flag that appeared on the street sign to make it clear what they were for. The buckets holding the flags on either side of the street are sponsored by local businesses, with the slogan "Take It to Make It" emblazoned on them to emphasize the seriousness of the problem. The name of the city was included on the flagpoles to discourage people from stealing them, which had happened when people wanted to use them for waterskiing. Eighteen flags were placed at each of 63 crosswalks to make sure there were enough on both sides of the street. Within 6 months of the new program, 11.2% of people crossing used the flags, with 24.8% of groups crossing with a flag, a substantial increase from before the redesign.[5]

Designing Environments

Besides the product, the environment surrounding an individual affects his or her decisions as well. This can be the physical environment, such as offering safe and clean playgrounds where kids can get physically active, or the social environment, which can be affected by policies such as not allowing smoking in bars and restaurants. Creating a situation that both encourages and supports individual behavior changes increases the likelihood that those positive choices will be sustainable for the long term.

---

[4]City of Kirkland. (n.d.). *PedFlag frequently asked questions.* http://www.ci.kirkland.wa.us/depart/Public_Works/Transportation___Streets/Pedestrian_Flags_-_FAQs.htm

[5]Social Marketing Services, Inc. (2008). *PedFlag usage tracking study.* http://www.pedflags.com/kirklandstudy.html

The Active Living by Design program, at the North Carolina Institute for Public Health, is built on these concepts to help communities design environments that increase opportunities for physical activity and healthful eating. The model includes cross-discipline partnerships that look at the community's needs from a socioecological perspective. The program strategy has a communication and promotion component, but the crux of it involves offering programs with activities and incentives to get people involved; advocacy to create health-supportive policies; and physical projects to impact built environments, remove barriers to physical activity, and enhance safety. See the sidebar for examples of tactics the program uses to carry out these strategies.

Just as policies and structures that facilitate people choosing the most beneficial behavior work well for health issues, they can be used for many other types of choices as well. If you want to encourage people to save money and be fiscally responsible, employer-based savings plans can automatically invest a certain percentage of the paycheck each month, including putting away the new "windfall" each time they earn a raise. Participating in the company's 401K program can be made opt-out, instead of opt-in, so that the default option increases the likelihood that employees will save for retirement.

"Environmental" changes to help the environment also abound. Simply having a recycling bin next to regular garbage cans will increase people's willingness to toss their empty water bottle in the correct container. Replacing homeowners' waste containers for nonrecyclable garbage with ones that are slightly smaller can encourage them to be more thoughtful about what they recycle or compost versus throwing away. Another example for energy conservation is

Healthy Living by Design Tactics

The Healthy Living by Design program has a five-pronged strategy, which is supported by a range of different tactics.[6] Some examples are as follows:

■ Preparation
  □ Develop and maintain partnerships/coalitions.
  □ Conduct neighborhood assessments to identify opportunities for and barriers to active living.
  □ Create interest groups to promote active living environments, such as parks, trails, greenways, and higher density mixed-use developments.

■ Promotion
  □ Develop active living messages and an awareness campaign based on targeted community research (focus groups, surveys, and testing).
  □ Install point-of-decision prompts and cues to action in and around public and private places to promote physical activity.
  □ Educate editorial boards and media outlets about ways of encouraging active living.
  □ Conduct and participate in community events that can educate the public and media about active living.

■ Programs
  □ Organize walking, running, biking, or other clubs to promote social support for physical activity.
  □ Start Safe Routes to School programs to encourage children to bicycle or walk to school.
  □ Create commuter choice or other workplace incentive programs that promote the use of public transit, ridesharing, and active forms of travel.
  □ Establish regular programs to attract people to a walkable town center.
  □ Start neighborhood watch and safety walks to create safe communities.

(Continued)

[6]Healthy Living by Design. (n.d.). *5P strategies & tactics.* http://www.activelivingbydesign.org/our-approach/5p-strategies-tactics

(Continued)

- Policy
  - ☐ Update zoning ordinances, building codes, and approval processes to encourage compact community design and a tighter mixture of activities that make it possible to work, play, shop, and go to school within walking and bicycling distance of people's homes.
  - ☐ Improve funding for pedestrian and cycling-oriented capital improvements and public transit.
  - ☐ Participate in local and regional decisions that improve funding and planning for parks, trails, and greenways.
  - ☐ Enhance local school district requirements to ensure that students in Grades K–12 participate in daily physical education classes.
  - ☐ Establish worksite policies that encourage employees to be physically active.
- Physical projects
  - ☐ Build physical infrastructure such as sidewalks, bike lanes, and trails that encourage walking and bicycling.
  - ☐ Use traffic-calming measures to make walking and bicycling safer and more comfortable.
  - ☐ Increase the availability of high-quality transit service within walking distance of residential, work, and shopping areas.
  - ☐ Install signage to highlight active transportation routes and places that support active living.
  - ☐ Design parks, trails, and greenways to deter crime and enhance safety.

that many European hotels require the plastic room key to be placed into a slot by the door for the lights and air conditioning to turn on. When the guest leaves the room and takes the key out, the energy-guzzling appliances turn off. When policy and structural elements are in place, persuasion is less necessary.

DESIGN PATTERNS

Many of these design approaches follow common patterns that can be applied to different types of issues. All of them have the effect of making either the desired behavior easier to do or the undesirable action more difficult. In all cases, however, the choice of which way to go must be voluntary. Otherwise, it is no longer a choice but a mandate. Our goal should be to make the choice that is the most beneficial to the target audience the one that is easiest or feels the most natural.

Designer Dan Lockton, with David Harrison and Neville Stanton, created a useful toolkit that lays out the various lenses through which you can view a problem as a design challenge, cutting across the fields of designing interactions, products, and architecture.[7] Lockton categorizes the patterns based on how they act on behavior:

- *Enabling*—enable the desired behavior by making it easier than the alternatives
- *Motivating*—motivate the behavior using education, incentives, and attitude change
- *Constraining*—make alternatives to the desired behavior more difficult or impossible

The most common design patterns fall into six categories, which are described below with examples of each.

[7]Lockton, D., Harrison, D., & Stanton, N. A. (2009). *Design With Intent Toolkit v.0.9*. Uxbridge, UK: Brunel University Press. www.designwith intent.co.uk (Version 1.0 is now available as an expanded card deck).

Architectural

Architectural designs draw on qualities of the built environment for inspiration, using the structure of systems to influence behavior. This includes using positioning and layout to affect how people interact with the system, or the sequence in which they do things. The layout of supermarkets, as discussed earlier, falls under this category, as well as things such as the positions of buttons on websites or making stairwells more prominent than elevators to encourage physical activity. A small Dutch city called Drachten used this principle to remove all of its traffic lights, transform intersections into roundabouts, and eliminate road markings. The result has been more careful drivers and a major reduction in serious traffic accidents.

Properties of materials used to create the environment or product can also subtly guide people's behaviors. For example, rumble strips at the sides of the road give tactile feedback when someone strays across the line. Bus benches may be just comfortable enough to sit on while waiting 10 minutes but very uncomfortable to spend the night. Walkways and railings that might have been a tempting playground for skateboarders often have bumpy brickwork or metal plates bolted into the concrete to foil anyone trying to ride their board there.

Errorproofing

Effective design can help to prevent deviations from the target behavior by making it either easier to avoid errors or impossible to make an error at all. Choosing default settings that favor the desired behavior—whether in a computer program or as a policy—will likely find the majority of people not interested in changing the status quo. When determining whether a person will be registered as an organ donor, the default choice makes a huge difference. In most countries, people must explicitly opt in to register, often at the same time as applying for or renewing a driver's license. However, in some countries, people are presumed to be donors unless they make the effort to opt out. We can compare two similar countries that have opposite defaults. In Germany, where people must opt in to the program, only 12% give their consent; in Austria, which has an opt-out policy, 99% are donors.[8]

Errors can also be prevented by using interlocks—systems that only work if the desirable behavior has taken place. People who have been convicted of drinking and driving may have an ignition interlock installed on their car that only allows the car to start after they blow into the breathalyzer to prove they have not had alcohol. ATM machines do not dispense cash until you have taken your card back to ensure you do not leave it behind. Microwave ovens will not function unless the door is fully closed. Once presurgical checklists became mandatory, patient mortality rates were cut nearly in half, and complications fell by more than a third.[9]

Persuasive

The persuasive lens uses contextual information, advice, and guidance to offer feedback and cues, often through technology. Self-monitoring methods let people know their progress

[8]Thaler, R. H. (2009, September 26). Opting in vs. opting out. *New York Times.* http://www.nytimes.com/2009/09/27/business/economy/27view.html

[9]Haynes, A. B., Weiser, T. G., Berry, W. R., Lipsitz, S. R., Breizat, A. H., Dellinger, E. P., et al. (2009). A surgical safety checklist to reduce morbidity and mortality in a global population. *New England Journal of Medicine, 360,* 491–499.

toward a goal, often in real time, or show the effect of their actions immediately. Home energy use monitors that translate the number of kilowatt-hours being used into real dollar costs let people know the effect of turning off a light or keeping the house toasty warm. Biofeedback machines give an immediate aural indication of how tense the body is and can help train users to reach a relaxed state quickly. Similarly, a diabetes monitor lets someone know how that bowl of spaghetti for dinner affected his or her blood sugar afterward.

Persuasive design tactics can also provide cues to action at just the right time, increasing the likelihood that a beneficial behavior will happen. Medicine bottles that sound tones on a timer or scheduled text messages can offer a reminder that it's time to take the next pill. In addition, many pharmacies offer automatic refills of monthly prescriptions and give people a call when it's time to pick them up to ensure that they don't forget the new supply. Automatic speed detectors that let passing cars know how fast they are going give people the opportunity to use the feedback to adjust their speed and slow down. Even the low-tech check reorder form attached to the last set of checks in the box is timed to appear at just the right time for you to order more before you run out.

Visual

The visual lens relates to how meanings and motivation are derived from patterns you see—both literally and figuratively. Making elements prominent or visible can affect whether people act on them. This can be big orange signs urging people to slow down in the construction zone, making recycling containers prominently available next to the regular garbage cans, or placing a large "donate now" button on a nonprofit's home page. Visual feedback can also come from making things transparent, such as the vacuum cleaner that lets you see exactly when it needs to be emptied or transparent "lungs" that demonstrate the effect of smoking. Often, seeing is believing, and one study found that just showing people with high cholesterol levels a scan of their own arteries so they could see the plaque buildup for themselves was enough to make them stay on their medication.[10]

Using metaphors is another design technique that can help people understand how something works by comparing it to another more familiar concept or system. The computer desktop as conceived by Apple with files, folders, and a trashcan gives you a good idea of how each element works. The PITSTOP program in the United Kingdom used the metaphor of the MOT (the Ministry of Transport test of auto safety and emissions required for cars every 3 years) to help men understand the importance of a regular health checkup. At the health checks, information was given in parking ticket, driver's license, and Auto Association card-style formats. They also created a maintenance manual in partnership with the Men's Health Forum (MHF) and Haynes publishers (famous for car maintenance manuals).

Cognitive

Design patterns in the cognitive lens draw on behavioral economics concepts to find ways to affect how people think about the issue and therefore what they decide to do. Use social proof to help people think that others like themselves are doing the behavior. When something is perceived as being popular, people are more likely to do it. Amazon.com recommendations,

---

[10]Bakalar, N. (2006, May 16). Motivation: For patients, there's beauty in the ugly truth. *New York Times*. http://www.nytimes.com/2006/05/16/health/16moti.html

website subscriber "chicklets," and Facebook apps that show how many other friends are using them all work on this principle. Social psychologist Robert Cialdini tested the effect of social proof using the cards that hotels display in their rooms requesting that people reuse their towels at least once during their stay to help the environment. The guests whose cards had a generic message about the environment or helping the hotel reused their towels at a much lower rate than those whose message was that most guests at the hotel reused them, and all of them were lower than the people who received the message that most guests in that room had reused their towels (a 33% increase in response over the generic message).[11]

Framing is another cognitive approach that focuses on message design to affect people's attitudes toward the issue. The way choices are presented can make some sound more appealing than others. This is why the drink sizes at Starbucks start with "tall" and move up from there—small sounds so, well, small. When energy conservation is framed as "saving money" versus "saving the environment," people become much more interested because they can see what's in it for them. Another reframing that has occurred in recent years is that the fast food industry is no longer perceived as selling unhealthy food just because people like it, but it has become the equivalent of the tobacco industry, with its evil persona, trying to kill its customers through obesity.

Security

Finally, the security lens provides a way to look at how to use countermeasures to deter unwanted behaviors. "Surveillance" design techniques make people feel like they are being watched—whether through an open layout floor plan or active monitoring—and thereby avoid negative behaviors. Transparency of political contributions allows others to see who supports whom and to watch for effects of corruption. Surveillance methods can also be used to help elderly people who have fallen in their homes and have a security service that can monitor them and send help.

Atmospherics offer another way to design an environment to elicit or prevent particular behaviors. This uses ambient sensory effects to affect what people see, hear, smell, taste, or feel in either a pleasant or irritating manner. A high-pitched "mosquito tone" that only people who are teenagers or younger can hear has been used to keep young people from congregating in certain areas. (Although teens have turned it around for their own purposes to use as a ringtone so only they know when their cell phone is ringing.) Blue light is used in some public restrooms because it makes it difficult for IV drug users to see their veins and inject themselves. On a more pleasant note, scents such as baking bread or fresh-baked chocolate chip cookies are often used in stores or at real estate open houses to put people in a happy, buying mood.

THE DESIGN PROCESS

When designers approach a new problem, they have a well-defined process they follow to understand the audience and issue in order to design an effective solution. One of the leaders in designing social innovations, IDEO, lays out its Human-Centered Design (HCD) approach as the intersection of desirability, feasibility, and viability—all elements that must be present in a

---

[11]Goldstein, N. J., Cialdini, R. B., & Griskevicius, V. (2008). A room with a viewpoint: Using social norms to motivate environmental conservation in hotels. *Journal of Consumer Research, 35*, 472–482.

Interviewing Techniques for Design Understanding

The IDEO toolkit offers some ideas for how to interview people to get the type of data that will be most helpful in understanding what, how, and why they do things. These include the following:

- *Show Me*—Have the interviewees show you their environment and the things they interact with. Ask them to walk you through the process. Take pictures and notes.

- *Draw It*—Ask participants to visually draw or diagram their experience to get an idea of how they conceptually understand and order their activities.

- *5 Whys*—Ask five "why" questions in a row in response to their answers to help people uncover and express their reasons for doing things.

- *Think Aloud*—Have participants describe out loud what they are thinking as they perform a task. This can give you insight into their motivations, concerns, perceptions, and reasoning.

product for it to work for a particular audience.[12] The HCD process also stands for the steps involved: hear, create, deliver. Stanford University's Design School (or "the d.school") offers a process that overlaps with IDEO's but breaks the steps out further:[13]

1. *Empathize:* Observe users in the context of their entire lives and engage them through qualitative research to determine what they need. Research might include individual or group interviews, ethnographic immersion, asking participants to document aspects of their lives using supplied photo or video cameras, or other ways of involving your target audience members in helping you understand their situation. Look at the problem with a "beginner's mind" and try not to make assumptions. Spend time observing before you start to interpret; move from "what" to "how" to "why."

2. *Define:* Determine an actionable problem statement to guide your efforts through a process of focusing on the issue through what you learned in the first phase. Share stories, and identify patterns and themes that emerged to build a framework that ties together what you observed. Start asking, "How might we. . . ?" questions to frame the issues.

3. *Ideate:* Expand your understanding through idea generation, flaring out to see the problem from as broad a lens as possible. Brainstorm possible solutions moving from the "How might we. . . ?" questions. (Brainstorming tips can be found in Chapter 13.) You can also "bodystorm," setting up a physical experience like a mock shop or doctor's office, to think through the elements of the situation you might not otherwise consider from the chair in your meeting room.

4. *Prototype:* Make your ideas real. Create something that users can start to play with that represents a possible solution to the problem. Try many different possibilities to see what might work. Change a single variable at a time to identify what elements are more successful.

5. *Test:* Put the prototypes into the users' lives to see how they work and refine them based on feedback gathered from the participants. Sort the results by (a) things they liked or found notable, (b) constructive criticism, (c) questions that the experience raised, and (d) ideas that the experience spurred. Figure out how to improve the prototype and move forward with production once you are satisfied with the users' response.

---

[12]IDEO. (2009). *Human centered design toolkit* (2nd ed.). http://www.ideo.com/work/item/human-centered-design-toolkit/

[13]Hasso Plattner Institute of Design at Stanford University. (2009). *d.school bootcamp bootleg.* http://dschool.typepad.com/files/bootcampbootleg2009.pdf

WORKSHEET 7: APPLYING THE DESIGN APPROACH FOR BEHAVIOR CHANGE

1. What is the specific behavior you would like to influence?

   _____

   _____

   _____

2. Who exactly should be doing the behavior (be as specific as possible)?

   _____

   _____

   _____

3. Architectural design:

   a. How can you use positioning or layout elements to either encourage or constrain the behavior?

   _____

   _____

   _____

   b. How can you make it more comfortable for people to do the behavior?

   _____

   _____

   _____

4. Errorproofing design:

   a. How can you make the desired behavior be the default?

   _____

   _____

   _____

   b. How can you force the behavior as a necessary step in another desirable process?

   _____

   _____

   _____

5. Persuasive design:

   a. How can you show the actual effect of the behavior on the overall system for self-monitoring?

   _____

   _____

   _____

(Continued)

(Continued)

    b. How can you provide a cue to action at the appropriate time?

_____

_____

_____

6. Visual design:

    a. How can you make the "right choice" or the cue to action more visible?

_____

_____

_____

    b. How can you use a metaphor of something your users are already familiar with to help them understand how or when to perform the desired behavior?

_____

_____

_____

7. Cognitive design:

    a. How can you demonstrate social proof that others are successfully engaging in the behavior?

_____

_____

_____

    b. How can you frame the behavior or the benefits of the behavior in a way that helps people see it in a more positive light?

_____

_____

_____

8. Security design:

    a. How can you encourage people to do the desired behavior because they think people are watching?

_____

_____

_____

    b. How can you use sensory effects (e.g., sound, smell, light, taste) to encourage the desired behavior?

_____

_____

_____

CHAPTER 11

Developing Effective Messages

Social marketing messages are not just clever slogans but rather well-thought-out communications based on theory and research. To effectively change health and social behaviors, you will need to combine an understanding of behavior change with interpretation of your research results.

THEORIES OF BEHAVIOR CHANGE

To create messages that produce lasting positive effects on your target audience, you should first understand theories of how behavior change occurs. Although some programs use theory as window dressing to show that they were developed "scientifically," a well-designed program uses theory as the support beam on which everything else is hung. A solid theory gives shape to the messages, and without it the program might fall flat.

On the surface, behavior change appears to be a single-step occurrence; either someone engages in a behavior or not. But a major change in a person's lifestyle, such as quitting smoking or starting a compost heap, involves a complex thought process. So much so, in fact, that researchers have proposed many different models to explain the transition from nonadoption to adoption and, more important, to elucidate how to affect that process. These theories also are useful for thinking about changing complex social behaviors as well as those that affect an individual's health.

This section briefly touches on six current theories of behavior change to highlight key issues to consider when developing messages. You may decide to follow a single theory, or you can refer to the synthesis at the end of the section to determine the theoretical elements appropriate to your program. The implications of each theory for message development are illustrated using examples.

The most common theories used to explain health and social behavior are the following:

- Health Belief Model

- Theory of planned behavior

- Social cognitive learning theory

- Transtheoretical Model (stages of change theory)

■ Diffusion of Innovations Model

■ Extended Parallel Process Model (fear appeals)

Health Belief Model

The Health Belief Model[1] attempts to explain the conditions that are necessary for behavior change to occur. The model states that an individual will take action to prevent, screen for, or control a disease or condition based on the following factors:

1. *Perceived susceptibility:* The individual must believe that he or she is susceptible to the condition.

2. *Perceived severity:* The individual must believe that getting the disease or condition leads to severe consequences.

3. *Perceived benefits:* The individual must believe that engaging in the preventive behavior will reduce the threat or provide other positive consequences.

4. *Perceived barriers:* The individual must believe that the tangible or psychological costs of performing the behavior are of less magnitude than the benefits.

5. *Cues to action:* The individual must encounter something that triggers readiness to perform the behavior.

6. *Self-efficacy:* The individual must believe he or she can take action.

As an example, let us get into the head of Julia, a 21-year-old woman in the target audience of a skin cancer prevention campaign. She is blond with pale skin and loves to lie in the sun at the beach. When she remembers to do so, she puts on a sunscreen of SPF 8 so that she does not burn too badly (she says higher SPFs are too "goopy") but longs for a deep tan like that of her friend, Eileen. In fact, most of her friends go without sunscreen and even use baby oil to try to enhance their tans. She certainly has heard of skin cancer but thinks that it only happens to older people and can be removed without any major problems.

Using the Health Belief Model, behavior change messages would include several elements. The campaign would need to convince Julia that she is at high risk for developing skin cancer because of her skin type and sun-related behaviors. She must realize that some types of skin cancer, particularly melanoma, often are deadly and can develop at a young age. Once she is aware of the risk and its severity, a cue to action should take place such as an advertisement urging her to visit a website for more information or reminding her to wear sunscreen effectively. Julia already knows that sunscreen prevents sunburns but does not appreciate its efficacy for preventing skin cancer or know about other behaviors that can reduce her risk such as wearing a hat and avoiding the sun during peak ultraviolet hours. She needs more reasons to use a sunscreen of SPF 15 all the time (benefits could include avoiding wrinkles and preventing her skin from aging) that will outweigh her desire for a tan and her perception of the discomfort of more protective sunscreen.

---

[1]Strecher, V., & Rosenstock, I. (1997). The Health Belief Model. In K. Glanz, F. M. Lewis, & B. Rimer (Eds.), *Health behavior and health education: Theory, research, and practice* (2nd ed., pp. 41–59). San Francisco: Jossey-Bass.

Theory of Planned Behavior

According to the theory of planned behavior,[2] behavioral intention is the most important determinant of behavior. If someone plans to perform a behavior when in a particular situation, then the behavior is much more likely to occur. Intention is influenced by three main factors:

1. *Attitude toward the behavior:* the individual's beliefs about the likely positive and negative consequences of the behavior and the relative weight of importance of each

2. *Subjective norms associated with the behavior:* the individual's beliefs regarding what significant people in his or her life think about the behavior and how strongly that individual is motivated to meet their expectations

3. *Perceived behavioral control:* the individual's perception of the strength of external factors that make it easier or more difficult to carry out the behavior

If the skin cancer prevention campaign is to reach Julia using the theory of planned behavior, then it will need to build her intention to take preventive action. To change her attitude toward protective sunscreen, messages should emphasize the positive consequences of regular use (e.g., younger looking skin, cancer prevention) and downplay the negative consequences (e.g., feelings of discomfort, pale skin). In addition, by finding out whose opinions Julia values most, the program can work with key opinion leaders to change subjective norms about sunscreen use. She might be more easily persuaded to wear sunscreen if she feels that her female peers think it is a good idea or if a doctor recommends it. So long as Julia believes that the norm among her friends is to work hard for a deep, dark tan, she is unlikely to change her behavior. Methods to facilitate the prevention behaviors, such as free samples of sunscreen, skin check reminders for the bathroom mirror, and the presence of beach umbrellas, might help to overcome the factors working against taking action.

Social Cognitive Learning Theory

Social cognitive learning theory[3] states that behavior change is influenced by factors within the individual and the environment. As in the theory of planned behavior, the individual will be motivated to act if he or she believes that the expected positive outcomes of a behavior outweigh the expected negative outcomes. If someone has not previously performed the behavior, then these beliefs generally derive from observation of what happens when others do so. When people similar to the individual perform the behavior and are rewarded for doing so, the individual will be more inclined to follow the role models' examples. The individual can learn how to do the behavior by watching someone else model the process. He or she also will be more likely to adopt a behavior if the individual has a sense of self-efficacy—the belief that one has the skills and abilities to perform the behavior.

Because Julia respects the opinions of her peers most about things such as fashion and skin care, she might be receptive to a peer role model who displays sun-protective behaviors. The role model could be a beautiful woman with light, untanned skin who wears a fashionable, wide-brimmed hat

[2]Ajzen, I. (1991). The theory of planned behavior. *Organizational Behavior and Human Decision Processes, 50,* 179–211.

[3]Bandura, A. (1986). *Social foundations of thought and action: A social cognitive theory.* Englewood Cliffs, NJ: Prentice Hall.

to the beach, makes sure to wear sunscreen, and receives compliments on her skin. Although the actual behavior of putting on sunscreen is not difficult, Julia's self-efficacy will be heightened if she knows exactly when she needs to wear it, what type (SPF) to use, how much to apply, and how often to reapply it. She also may improve her self-efficacy regarding skin cancer prevention by learning what a potentially cancerous skin lesion or mole might look like.

Transtheoretical Model (Stages of Change Theory)

Rather than noting the necessary elements for behavior change, the Transtheoretical Model (also known as the stages of change theory)[4] describes the stages that an individual passes through on the way to adopting a behavior. This model has been used in many social marketing programs for topics ranging from tobacco use to safer sex.

The five stages are as follows:

1. *Precontemplation:* An individual is not aware of the potential problem and does not consider himself or herself at risk. At this stage, messages about behavior change will not receive much attention, and the main goal should be to raise awareness about the problem.

2. *Contemplation:* The individual realizes that he or she might be at risk and begins to consider whether to do something about it. At this stage, emphasizing the benefits of the behavior is likely to move the person to the next stage. Increasing the perceived social pressure for behavior change also will help.

3. *Preparation:* The individual has decided that he or she should take action and learns more about what is involved. If the person encounters many barriers to changing his or her behavior, then the process might stop at this point. Therefore, messages to move the person into action should minimize the perceived barriers where possible and also convey necessary skills.

4. *Action:* The individual performs the behavior once and determines for himself or herself whether it was worthwhile. Positive reinforcement at this stage would make the person more likely to do it again.

5. *Maintenance:* The individual continues to perform the behavior in the appropriate situations. Messages should provide reinforcement and tips on maintaining the commitment such as help with goal setting and overcoming potential barriers.

With any given behavior, an individual might stop at a particular stage in the process or even revert to a previous stage. Someone might move back and forth between preparation and action many times over the course of his or her life, particularly for behaviors requiring long-term lifestyle changes such as weight loss and smoking cessation. Using the stage model, you can segment your target audience by stages and address the segment(s) that most of the target audience falls into or target each segment sequentially over different phases of the campaign.

Julia still is in the precontemplation stage. She does not consider skin cancer as something that could happen to her or believe that she is at risk. Although she uses some sunscreen, the type she uses will not protect her enough from the sun. According to the stages of change

---

theory, intervention efforts should focus on raising Julia's awareness that she is at risk for skin cancer because of her light complexion and sun exposure. She also needs more information about skin cancer and how it could affect her personally. Not until she realizes that she is at risk and can do something about it will she move on to the contemplation stage.

Diffusion of Innovations

Whereas the Transtheoretical Model follows an individual moving through time, the Diffusion of Innovations Model[5] describes a particular innovation moving through a population over time. With any new product or practice, some people will be the first to adopt it, others will wait until most of their peer group has already accepted it, and others never will change their ways. For a particular innovation, individuals will fall into one of the following groups based on when they accept the new idea or practice: innovators, early adopters, early majority adopters, late majority adopters, and laggards (see Figure 11.1). Social marketing programs often end up targeting the late majority adopters and laggards—the hardest people to reach and convince to change their behavior—because the people in the earlier groups have already made the change.

According to this model, the most effective communication channels for disseminating information about a new idea or practice are opinion leaders and peer-to-peer social networks. An individual's decision to accept or reject an innovation encompasses the following issues:

■ Is the innovation better than what the individual currently is using or doing?

■ Is the innovation easy to use or understand?

■ Are other people in the peer group using the innovation? If so, what has been their experience with it?

■ Does the innovation fit in with the person's value system and self-image?

■ Is it possible to try the innovation first before committing to it?

■ How much of a commitment is necessary to use the innovation?

■ How much risk (monetary or emotional) is involved with adopting the innovation?

FIGURE 11.1   Audience Segments in the Diffusion of Innovations Model

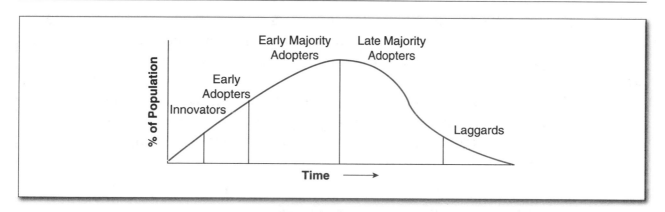

[5]Rogers, E. (1983). *Diffusion of innovations* (3rd ed.). New York: Free Press.

In her peer group, Julia would be among the early adopters of using sunscreen because most of her friends do not use it. Being the first in a group of friends to do something can be scary, and it can be hard to convince someone to lead. In this group, however, Julia is well respected and considered very smart. If the social marketing campaign can get her to start taking protective action, then she might be able to start the diffusion process in her own social circle. By answering some of the questions she might be asking herself about the new behaviors, the campaign will be more successful.

Extended Parallel Process Model (Fear Appeals)

Because fear appeals are so often used in social marketing, it is important to understand when they can be effective and when they may backfire to produce the opposite of the intended effect. The Extended Parallel Process Model[6] states that when people are confronted with messages that arouse fear in them, they will do whatever it takes to dispel those unpleasant feelings. They will either take preventive action to deal with the threat and eliminate it, or control the fearful feelings through denial or avoidance of the issue.

Which of those two directions people take depends on how effective they think the suggested course of action will be in addressing the threat (if one has been proposed) and whether they believe that they can actually carry out the preventive behavior. This model integrates several of the elements of previously discussed theories and specifies how they must be put together to be most effective.

If we were to use a fear-based appeal to try to convince Julia to wear sunscreen, as in the Health Belief Model, we would need to first make sure she believes that she is at risk for skin cancer and that the consequences of not taking action—including possible death—are severe. Offer specific actions that she believes will be effective in reducing the skin cancer threat and that she can do easily. Address the barriers that keep her from taking action—suggest types of sunscreen that don't feel "goopy" or provide evidence that hats block a large percentage of the cancer-causing rays from reaching her face. If she doesn't believe that wearing sunscreen and a hat will make a difference in reducing her risk, then scaring her about skin cancer will only backfire.

Synthesis: Relief From Theory Overload

If the dizzying array of different theories intimidates you, this synthesis provides the essential ideas you need to know. Based on the preceding models and other theoretical composites of behavior change theory,[7] the following list distills the key elements necessary to effect behavior change.

If you do not choose to follow one of the preceding theories strictly, then ensure that the following elements are addressed in your program's messages and interventions if they are not already present in the target audience. To achieve behavior change, the target audience must possess the following traits:

---

[6]Witte, K., & Allen, M. (2000). A meta-analysis of fear appeals: Implications for effective public health campaigns. *Health Education & Behavior, 27,* 591–615.

[7]National Commission on AIDS. (1983). *Behavioral and social sciences and the HIV/AIDS epidemic.* Washington, DC: Author.

- Believe that it is at risk for the problem and that the consequences are severe

- Believe that the proposed behavior will lower its risk or prevent the problem

- Believe that the advantages of performing the behavior (benefits) outweigh the disadvantages (costs)

- Possess the skills to perform the behavior

- Believe that it can perform the behavior (self-efficacy)

- Believe that the performance of the behavior is consistent with its self-image

- Perceive greater social pressure to perform the behavior than not to perform it (social norms)

Keep in mind that theory is there to make your job easier—it should not make your program so complicated that it's undoable. As Yogi Berra said, "In theory, there is no difference between theory and practice. In practice, there is."

MESSAGE CONCEPTS

Before you jump right into writing a script or designing a billboard, spend some time thinking about the basic elements of your message based on the theoretical constructs you chose. The concept development stage determines what you will say in your communications rather than how you will say it (the execution). What will be the main selling point for your product? What are the ideas the target audience needs to come away with? How can you present the information in a way that will make people want to pay attention?

One of the best guides to designing memorable and compelling messages is the book *Made to Stick* by brothers Chip and Dan Heath.[8] After analyzing a panoply of communications to find common elements among the most effective messages, they developed a template of six elements that can be applied to any idea to help make it "sticky"—interesting enough for people to want to share with others and packaged in a way that makes it easy to understand and remember. Each of these elements, by themselves or in combination, offers a way to identify promising approaches for communicating about your issue. We'll go through each of the key concepts here to help you think through how to design the central idea of your message to be most effective.

Simple

You are the expert in your topic and probably know just about everything that's important to know about it. Unfortunately, that can be a disadvantage in being able to explain your message clearly and simply to someone who knows nothing about the topic—what the Heath brothers call the "Curse of Knowledge." We often want to cram as much information as we can into our communications to take advantage of our audience's brief moments of attention. But do people

---

[8]Heath, C., & Heath, D. (1997). *Made to stick: Why some ideas survive and others die.* New York: Random House.

with diabetes really need to understand that physical activity improves glucose uptake and insulin sensitivity, or would it be more clear to say that exercise can help keep people with diabetes healthy?

Simplify your message as much as you can; think about how you can trim it down to its core, with nothing extra. If your audience remembers nothing else from your communications, what is the one key message you want them to retain? Proverbs are a great example of messages that have been pared down to their essence yet hold a great deal of information in a few words: A bird in the hand is worth two in the bush, haste makes waste, strike while the iron is hot. . . . Metaphors can also be useful in conveying complex information. Try to whittle your message down to eight words or less while conveying your key fact, benefit, or action step you want the audience to take.

The U.S. National Institute of Child Health and Development, along with an alliance of other organizations, created a parent-focused campaign to prevent sudden infant death syndrome (SIDS). The campaign's core message, "Back to Sleep," distilled the desired action—placing the baby on his or her back in the crib, rather than on the stomach or side, to reduce the likelihood of SIDS—as well as promoting a key benefit that all new parents yearn for. The campaign partnered with Pampers to place the Back to Sleep logo and message on its newborn diapers and packaging as a simple reminder to parents before baby's bedtime.

Unexpected

Our lives are made up of a series of situations that follow the same script, more or less. We know that when we go to the doctor's office, the usual scenario is that we sit in the waiting room for a while, get called into the exam room, endure pokes and prods from the nurse, wait some more, then finally secure our turn with the doctor as he or she breezes in, asks some questions, and sends us on our way with a plan of action. But what if it were the doctors sitting in the waiting room, waiting nervously, while the nurse calls one at a time into the exam room for you to ask all your questions? A campaign showing this turnabout would drive home the point that patients should come prepared with questions to ask their doctors about their symptoms and treatment.

Demonstrate something about your issue that is counterintuitive or surprising. Many probably feel they've heard everything there is to hear about the issue of obesity and are up to their ears in advice to eat healthy foods and exercise more; if you say the same message in the same way over and over, people will tune you out. To grab people's attention on the topic, the New York City Health Department vividly illustrated the link between sugary sodas and gaining weight. Starting with a subway ad showing a bottle pouring soda that turns to gobs of fat in a glass with the headline "Are you pouring on the pounds?" the campaign also grabbed attention with an online video that showed someone drinking that glassful of fat. More than half a million people watched it on YouTube, as people forwarded it to their friends because of the novelty of the image.

Another way to use the unexpected is to create a "curiosity gap" in your audience. Raise an interesting question to which people likely don't know the answer and it will be like an itch that needs to be scratched. Just like we'll watch a bad movie through to see how it ends or wait up late to see election results, you can present your message in a way to create that curiosity so that people will keep paying attention to get the answer.

Mark Horvath of InvisiblePeople.tv creates that curiosity gap by promising to tell the stories of people who are homeless. Most of us see people on the streets every day and have probably wondered how they got there but are too afraid or uncomfortable to talk with them. The Invisible People project posts video interviews that Mark does with homeless people he encounters across the United States, in which they talk about how they became homeless and what their lives are like. In a little more than a year, the InvisiblePeople.tv website has had over 100,000 visitors, all with a tiny budget.

Concrete

Many of the issues social marketers address are somewhat intangible concepts—health, environmental protection, discrimination, poverty. Our challenge comes in presenting these ideas in a relevant and meaningful way to our audience. Making the issue concrete is the trick, using sensory information to help people imagine what it looks like, feels like, or sounds like. This goes back to the discussion of what we need to do when setting objectives—what observable behavior is connected with making the problem better? Don't just tell people to save the planet; give them a simple, discrete action they can take and show them what it looks like to save energy in their home. Flicking the off switch on a light is much more concrete than "reduce your energy use."

The book *Made to Stick* recounts the story of James Grant, the former director of UNICEF, who met with leaders of developing countries to convince them to take action on providing life-saving oral rehydration therapy (ORT) to save the 1.5 million children who die each year from diarrhea. Rather than go into an explanation of dehydration and its effects or how ORT works, he would show them a small packet with one teaspoon of salt and eight teaspoons of sugar (the ingredients of ORT when mixed with a liter of water). When he explained that this simple mixture cost less than a cup of tea and could save hundreds of thousands of children's lives in their country, the issue was suddenly very concrete and solvable.

Credible

Credibility comes in many forms and provides your audience a reason to believe your message. The organization or person who delivers your message can confer credibility, whether it's the U.S. Centers for Disease Control and Prevention or a real member of your target audience. Credibility is in the eye of the beholder, though, so a government agency may have instant acceptance by one group and may be totally distrusted by another.

Besides authority figures—experts, celebrities, or other aspirational individuals—credibility can be established by "anti-authority" figures as well. These are the people who have "been there, done that" and can tell you why they are lucky to have made it out alive; they provide an example of the negative consequences that can happen if your audience does not listen to your message. Debi Austin, who developed cancer and emphysema after smoking for 30 years, is an anti-authority who appeared in ads for the California Department of Health Services. The most memorable moment in her television ad shows her inhaling a cigarette through the stoma in her throat after asking how the tobacco industry could say smoking is not addictive.

Credibility can also be established through facts. Statistics may back up the message, but you need to use them sparingly and contextualized. The quote attributed to Joseph

Stalin— "One death is a tragedy. One million is a statistic."—sums up the potential problem with talking about the size of a problem. Better to let your audience members see the concept in their own lives to verify the credibility for themselves. Friends of the Earth put up a billboard in Hong Kong that was blank except for a clear sticky coating over the graphic and headline. Over a period of weeks, the particulate matter in the dirty air stuck to the billboard to slowly reveal a picture of lungs and the words "Polluted air pollutes." The process itself of the message appearing conferred credibility, as passersby could clearly see the evidence that it was true.

Emotions

When you can bring people's emotions into play with your messages, your audience is much more likely to pay attention and remember what you told them. Strong emotions help to burn memories into the brain; if you are American, you likely have vivid memories of what you were doing on September 11, 2001. Emotions can be evoked in many different ways in association with your messages.

People are hardwired to care about other people. Tell the story of one person who is affected by a problem or has overcome challenges to change his or her behavior successfully. *Made to Stick* details research that shows that focusing on one person is much more effective than talking about a group—even of two people. In addition, when you're trying to generate an emotional reaction, leave the statistics out. Numbers activate the analytical mind, which diminishes the effect of the potential emotional response. Images enhance the emotional response.

Appealing to people's core values can be very effective in evoking an emotional response. Motherhood and apple pie (or whatever your audience most cares about) touch people deeply, and they may not even be aware of their own automatic reaction. If you can figure out how to tie your message to things that your audience already feels strongly about, you can get a similar response for your campaign. Did you realize that "Don't Mess with Texas" is not actually a state motto but the slogan from a long-running and effective anti-litter campaign? By aligning the ads with the already very strong sense of identity and pride felt by many Texans, the feelings transferred to the campaign as well.

As mentioned in our discussion of product in the social marketing mix, the benefits of the product you articulate and promote should go beyond just the features to the emotional benefits that people will receive by adopting the project. The Sussex Safer Roads Partnership created a video ad for its "Embrace Life" campaign that took a different tack from the standard blood-and-guts car crash approach that other seatbelt promotion campaigns have done. Using slow-motion photography, music, no words, and a set that did not even include a car, the ad shows a man miming driving a car in his living room while his wife and daughter watch. Suddenly, the expression on his face indicates that he is losing control of the car, and his daughter and wife run to him and latch their arms around him like a seatbelt. He is safe and secure in their arms. The simple text reads "Embrace life. Always wear your seat belt." This ad, despite its simplicity, hit over two million views on YouTube within a month, with many noting that the ad had brought them to tears and convinced them to wear their seatbelts.

Stories

Stories tend to include many of the "sticky" elements already listed: providing a simplified version of the message, showing an unexpected twist, making an intangible issue concrete, offering credibility through source and details, and evoking emotions. People remember stories, and the good ones are repeated over and over again, passed from person to person. Stories can convey information and help people build their mental catalogs of likely scenarios and how to respond. Vicarious learning can also happen; while listening to a story, people's brains actually mentally rehearse the actions as if they were carrying them out. The next time they are confronted with that situation, they have already thought through one way of dealing with it and seen if it was successful for others. Stories can also serve as inspiration to get people to take action.

Entertainment education takes advantage of the power of stories to draw people in and bring in the emotional angle with the characters they care about. A radio drama called *BodyLove,* a joint project between Media for Health and the University of Alabama, Birmingham, uses this model to reach a primarily African American audience across Alabama and Florida with health information in a soap opera format. Set in the fictional BodyLove hair salon, listeners followed along "with Vanessa Love and her best friend Rosalyn as they struggle to deal with their stressful lives. Can Vanessa keep her cool and her blood pressure down while dealing with her kids and their troubled father, Sonny? Is Rosalyn going to take care of herself in time? Will Sonny defeat his alcohol addiction? And just what is Fadelia's secret?" The program evaluation showed that frequent listeners were more likely than others to talk about diabetes, get screened for diabetes and blood pressure, start or increase physical activity, and start eating healthier.[9]

When you take the first letter of each of the *Made to Stick* elements, you get the acronym SUCCES(s)! When you can combine one or more of these concepts into your messages, you will be much more likely to end up with a message that sticks. In the next chapter, you will figure out which channels to use to disseminate your chosen message.

[9]Chen, N., Kohler, C., Schoenberger, Y., Suzuki-Crumly, J., Davis, K., & Powell, J. (2009). BodyLove: The impact of targeted radio educational entertainment on health knowledge, attitudes and behavior among African-Americans. *Cases in Public Health Communication & Marketing. 3,* 92–113. Available from: www.casesjournal.org/volume3

WORKSHEET 8: APPLYING BEHAVIOR CHANGE THEORIES

This worksheet will help you to identify information you might need to gather and give you a starting point from which to build your messages around a theoretical framework. Select one theory, or take appropriate elements from more than one.

1. Health Belief Model

   a. What is the level of perceived susceptibility among your target audience to the problem you are addressing?

   ❑ High   ❑ Medium   ❑ Low

   b. How severe does the target audience think the consequences of the problem are?

   ❑ Very severe   ❑ Somewhat severe   ❑ Not severe

   c. Does the target audience believe that engaging in the preventive behavior will lower its risk of the problem?

   ❑ Yes   ❑ Uncertain   ❑ No

   d. What are the benefits and barriers of engaging in the behavior, as perceived by the target audience?

   Benefits:

   _____

   _____

   _____

   _____

   Barriers:

   _____

   _____

   _____

   _____

   e. How can you help the target audience believe it can perform the behavior correctly (self-efficacy)?

   _____

   _____

   f. What "cue to action" will you use?

   _____

   _____

   g. How can you address the above elements to motivate behavior change?

   _____

   _____

2. Theory of Planned Behavior

   a. What are the positive consequences target audience members expect from the behavior, and how important is each to them?

   Consequence   *Importance (high, medium, or low)*

   _____   _____

   _____   _____

   _____   _____

   b. What are the negative consequences target audience members expect from the behavior, and how important is each to them?

   Consequence   *Importance (high, medium, or low)*

   _____   _____

   _____   _____

   _____   _____

   c. Who are the most socially influential people in the target audience members' lives, and how does the target audience think they perceive the behavior?

   Person/Type of Person   *Perception of Behavior (positive, negative, or neutral)*

   _____   _____

   _____   _____

   _____   _____

   d. What external factors make it easier or more difficult to carry out the behavior?

   Factor   *Perception of Factor (easier or more difficult)*

   _____   _____

   _____   _____

   _____   _____

   e. Based on your answers to the above, how can you increase the target audience's intention to perform the behavior?

   _____

   _____

   _____

   (Continued)

(Continued)

3. Social Cognitive Learning Theory

   a. Based on the above lists of expected positive and negative consequences of performing the behavior (Items 2a and 2b), which outweighs the other?

   ❑ Positives   ❑ Negatives   ❑ About equal

   b. Does the target audience possess the skills needed to perform the behavior?

   ❑ Yes   ❑ Uncertain   ❑ No

   c. Does the target audience believe that it has the skills and ability to perform the behavior?

   ❑ Yes   ❑ Uncertain   ❑ No

   d. How can you teach the skills or have someone model the behavior for your target audience?

   _____

   _____

   _____

4. Transtheoretical Model (Stages of Change Theory)

   a. If the target audience is in the precontemplation stage, how can you raise its awareness of the problem?

   _____

   _____

   _____

   b. If the target audience is in the contemplation stage, which benefits should you emphasize, and how can you increase the perceived social pressure regarding the behavior?

   Benefits:

   _____

   _____

   _____

   Increase social pressure by the following:

   _____

   _____

   _____

c. If the target audience is in the preparation stage, how can you remove the perceived barriers and teach the necessary skills to perform the behavior?

Remove barriers by the following:

_____

_____

_____

Teach skills by the following:

_____

_____

_____

d. If the target audience is in the action stage, how can you reinforce the behavior to make it likely that it will be repeated?

_____

_____

_____

e. If target audience members are in the maintenance stage, how can you help them to continue their commitment?

_____

_____

_____

5. Diffusion of Innovations

a. Who are the main opinion leaders for your target audience, and what peer-to-peer networks can you use to spread your message?

_____

_____

_____

b. How is the desired behavior better than what the target audience is already doing?

_____

_____

_____

c. Is the behavior easy to perform or understand?

❑ Yes   ❑ Somewhat   ❑ No

(Continued)

(Continued)

d. What experiences have others in the peer group had with performing the behavior?

_____

_____

_____

e. How can you make the behavior fit in with the target audience's value system and self-image?

_____

_____

_____

f. How can you reduce the monetary or emotional risk or level of commitment required for the target audience to adopt the behavior?

_____

_____

_____

6. Extended Parallel Process Model (Fear Appeals)

a. Does your message evoke fear due to the problem or its negative consequences?

❑ Yes, strongly   ❑ Yes, somewhat   ❑ No

b. What is the level of perceived susceptibility among your target audience to the problem you are addressing?

❑ High   ❑ Medium   ❑ Low

c. How severe does the target audience think the consequences of the problem are?

❑ Very severe   ❑ Somewhat severe   ❑ Not severe

d. Does the target audience believe that engaging in the preventive behavior will lower its risk of the problem?

❑ Yes   ❑ Uncertain   ❑ No

e. How will you demonstrate that the solution you propose is effective?

_____

_____

_____

WORKSHEET 9: DESIGNING MESSAGE ELEMENTS

This worksheet will help you to design your campaign messages using the *Made to Stick* elements. You may focus on one element or use a combination to be even more effective.

1. Simple

   a. How can you distill your message down to its essence? Try to convey the main idea in no more than eight words.

   _____

   _____

   _____

   _____

   b. Is there anything you can use as a metaphor the audience already understands to explain the concept?

   _____

   _____

   _____

   _____

2. Unexpected

   a. What does your audience likely already expect to see in messages related to your issue?

   _____

   _____

   _____

   _____

   b. How can you turn that expected scenario around to make it counterintuitive or surprising?

   _____

   _____

   _____

   c. How can you create a "curiosity gap" in your audience? What don't they already know that they might find interesting?

   _____

   _____

   _____

   _____

(Continued)

(Continued)

3. Concrete

   a. How can you use sensory information to help people imagine what your issue looks like, feels like, sounds like, etc.?

   _____

   _____

   _____

   _____

   b. What is the concrete action you want people to take?

   _____

   _____

   _____

   _____

4. Credible

   a. Who would be a credible authority or anti-authority figure to convey the message to your audience?

   _____

   _____

   _____

   _____

   b. Are there statistics that lend credibility to your message?

   _____

   _____

   _____

   _____

   c. How can you help the audience verify the credibility of the message in their own lives?

   _____

   _____

   _____

   _____

5. Emotions

    a. How can you use one person in your message to evoke an emotional response?

    _____

    _____

    _____

    _____

    b. What images are likely to bring out an emotional reaction?

    _____

    _____

    _____

    _____

    c. What values does your audience hold to which you can tie your messages?

    _____

    _____

    _____

    _____

    d. What emotional benefits does your audience see to adopting the behavior?

    _____

    _____

    _____

    _____

6. Stories

    a. How can you use a story to help people vicariously experience a relevant situation?

    _____

    _____

    _____

    _____

    b. Who has an inspiring story that might get people to take action?

    _____

    _____

    _____

CHAPTER 12

Identifying Appropriate Channels

Channel in social marketing does not mean the television station on which you air your commercials. The term refers to the medium that delivers your program's messages. This involves the marketing mix ideas of "place" and "promotion." Which methods will you use to get the message out or distribute the product to the target audience? Before thinking more specifically about which radio stations to use or what to name your Twitter account, consider whether those are really the most appropriate methods for your audience and message. For example, a website is a great way in which to disseminate information to a computer-savvy audience but not for people without access to the Internet.

CHANNEL CRITERIA

There are a nearly unlimited number of channels that you can use. The key is to carefully select the most effective and efficient methods of reaching each target audience segment. Effective means that the way in which you convey the message attracts attention and inspires behavior change. Efficient means that you reach the most target audience members per dollar expended. If you are trying to reach a very small audience segment such as parents of fifth graders in a particular school district, then using television might be overkill; the message will reach many people, but the efficiency of the medium is low relative to the number of target audience members. A more efficient channel might be sending information home through the students themselves, having teachers or school administrators contact parents directly by e-mail.

To identify the best channels to use, find out where target audience members spend their time and get their information. They will not go out of their way to find your message; you must go to them. Through the research you conduct with the target audience, you will learn which channels it pays attention to and trusts. Among different segments, you might find that certain channels are more popular or credible. Remember that there is no one right answer, but there will be better and worse choices based on your target audience and program budget.

Some channels that are commonly used in social marketing include the following:

- Mass media (e.g., television, radio, newspapers, magazines)

- Social media (e.g., blogs, social network sites, online video)

- Websites (e.g., project site, search engine marketing, online games)

- E-mail

- Outdoor advertising (e.g., billboards, transit ads)

- Brochures, posters, and newsletters

- Mobile phones (e.g., text messaging, mobile ads)

- Comic books or fotonovellas (i.e., comic books using photos instead of drawings)

- Direct mail

- Interpersonal communications (e.g., doctors, telephone hotlines, promotoras)

- Word of mouth (e.g., peer-to-peer communications, street teams)

- Entertainment education (e.g., issue placement in television programs, street theater, music)

- Community events

- Workplace competitions

- Point-of-purchase materials

Each type of channel may serve a different role in the campaign (see Table 12.1). For example, a billboard or radio ad is a good way in which to raise awareness about an issue, and a website can provide more in-depth information, but it might take a conversation with a clinician to finally motivate someone to act. Combining a number of approaches also helps you appeal to people who absorb information in different ways by seeing it, hearing it, experiencing it, or discussing it with others. Each channel has its own strengths and weaknesses, and the trick is to use several methods that complement each other. The more times someone is exposed to a message in different ways, the more likely it will stick.

TABLE 12.1 Comparing Channels

Channel	Pros	Cons
Television	<ul><li>Can reach many people at the same time</li><li>Can have ads aired free as public service announcements (PSAs)</li><li>Repetition of messages</li><li>Can provide follow-up through toll-free number/URL</li><li>Visual medium provides more impact and the ability to demonstrate a behavior</li><li>Can reach specialized audience through cable stations or particular programs</li></ul>	<ul><li>Expensive to produce and buy time</li><li>If a PSA, cannot control when it is run</li><li>Short format does not allow for more than awareness</li><li>Message can be obscured by commercial clutter</li><li>Target audience might not be watching when commercial is aired or might skip over commercials</li></ul>
Radio (most of the pros and cons listed under television apply to radio as well)	<ul><li>Can narrowly target specific audiences</li><li>Often playing while people are engaging in other activities</li><li>Less expensive to produce and buy time than television</li></ul>	<ul><li>Smaller audiences reached than with television</li><li>Does not work as well as television to demonstrate an activity</li></ul>

Print media (e.g., newspapers, magazines)	■ Can provide more detailed information than broadcast but still limited ■ Can tailor messages for specific audiences for different publications ■ Goes beyond building awareness by providing detailed information ■ Good for reaching more educated or older audiences ■ Audience can clip, reread, and think about the material ■ Might provide more credibility	■ PSAs often not accepted ■ Not good for less literate audiences ■ Small ads might get lost ■ Readership is dwindling for many print publications
Social media (e.g., blogs, social network sites, online video)	■ Message/campaign shared by trusted network will be more accepted ■ People can engage with issue on a deeper level ■ Information easily spread from person to person ■ Low cost—time is the primary factor ■ Instantaneous dissemination and response possible	■ Requires Internet access ■ If message is not compelling, it will not spread ■ Information overload can be a factor ■ Less control over message as it spreads ■ Can be time-intensive
Websites	■ Internet is often people's first source of information ■ Can optimize website, use search engine marketing to bring in traffic ■ Information can be customized via online tools ■ Easy to share all campaign materials ■ Provides central location for campaign	■ Requires Internet access ■ Online interface may not have enough of a human touch ■ Requires some technical expertise to create and maintain ■ May not be able to find an appropriate domain name
Print materials (e.g., brochures, fact sheets, newsletters)	■ Can convey in-depth information, especially about complex issues ■ Often low cost (with unit prices decreasing with quantity) ■ Good to use as follow-up to requests for more information (resulting from other promotions) ■ Not competing with ads for audience attention ■ Good for how-to information, answering frequently asked questions	■ Audience must have the interest and will to pick it up and read it ■ Not good for less literate audiences
Posters and flyers	■ Good for generating awareness ■ Can be placed in high-visibility/high-traffic areas ■ Can be put in places where decisions whether or not to perform the behavior are made ■ If attractive and eye-catching, people will want to put them up in their homes or offices	■ Posters can be expensive to produce (relative to other print media) ■ Cannot provide detailed information ■ May need to be reposted often
Direct mail	■ Can get mailing lists of very specific types of people ■ Allows you to contact target audience directly, personalize the message ■ Relatively low cost in high quantities ■ Can easily test how effective your promotion was ■ Can send promotional items with your message that people will keep and continue to use (e.g., calendar, key chain)	■ If mailing list is old or inappropriate, then it might not be successful ■ Envelope must stand out and say "open me," otherwise will be tossed

(Continued)

TABLE 12.1 (Continued)

Channel	Pros	Cons
Outdoor media (e.g., billboards, transit ads)	■ Great for reaching commuters ■ Very noticeable, not competing with other ads ■ Repetition ■ Relatively inexpensive way in which to reach many people	■ Cannot provide very much information ■ Message must be understood within seconds
Interpersonal communications/word of mouth	■ One-on-one communication can be very effective, especially if the person is seen as credible to the target audience member ■ Questions can be answered immediately ■ Message can be personalized to address particular benefits and barriers important to that person ■ People who are already fans can be recruited as ambassadors/evangelists	■ Not very efficient for mass audiences ■ Person might be mistrustful, wonder what the communicator has to gain from this if they don't already know him or her ■ People with the most potential influence might not have time or interest to be involved
Professional or organizational channels	■ Trade associations are a good way in which to reach professionals with a credible message (e.g., mailings, ads in their magazines, conferences) ■ Affiliation provides a connection that makes target audience more likely to pay attention to message ■ Conference sessions can persuade and provide information in a memorable way ■ Materials can be distributed efficiently ■ Receiving endorsements from heads of key organizations can do a lot to advance the message	■ There is not always an appropriate organization to work with, or one might not be willing to participate ■ Not all members of target audience may be affiliated with an organization
E-mail	■ Beyond initial investment, very inexpensive to send e-mail messages ■ Instantaneous method of delivery, good for time-sensitive issues ■ Messages may be sent and forwarded many times from person to person ■ Can send messages through listservs to reach many people with similar interest or profession at once	■ Not everyone is Internet accessible ■ Might be difficult to compile an e-mail list of target audience members ■ People may automatically delete messages from addresses they do not recognize or messages may go into spam folder
Point-of-purchase materials (signs, displays, "take one" materials, or live demonstrations where the product is being promoted or sold)	■ Catch people with your message when they are thinking about the product or a related topic ■ Convenient for target audience ■ Presence of your materials provides tacit endorsement of your message by the store	■ Might be difficult to convince businesses to participate ■ Must regularly refill or restock materials
Mobile phones	■ Reach people wherever they are ■ Most people have a phone with them all the time ■ Web content can be accessed by phone ■ Younger audiences are especially heavy users	■ Audience members may have to pay to receive text messages ■ Little space for message ■ People must opt in to receive your SMS campaign or must download mobile app
Entertainment education	■ Audience is more likely to pay attention to content ■ Provide role models, depict consequences, engage emotions ■ May have more credibility with certain audiences	■ Can be difficult to get "issue placement" in television programming ■ May require some level of talent ■ Entertainment must come before education

OUTLETS

Once you have identified the channels that are most appropriate for the target audience, the next step is to think about the particular outlets you might use. Outlets are the specific television or radio stations, magazines, social networks, websites, and other alternatives within each channel that will promote your message.

Although at this point you do not yet need to specify which media outlets you will use, you can start gathering information for when you reach the implementation phase. The most efficient method is to ask members of your target audience which radio stations they listen to and when, which websites they spend time on, or which streets are best for billboards. You can ask these questions in your initial research or during pretesting in Step 4.

In addition to the target audience input, you can get information directly from the media outlets themselves. Your local public or university library's reference desk should have books listing media outlets of every type in your community or nationally (see Chapter 17 for a list of media resources). Contact the outlets that look like good candidates for your target audience and have them send you media kits or download them from their websites.

A media kit usually will include information about the station or publication, audience demographics, a rate card, and information on special issues or advertising opportunities that are coming up. If you tell them who your target audience is, they often can provide specific ratings or subscriber demographics information that will help you to decide whether they are appropriate. If the outlet can send you Arbitron (for radio) or Nielsen (for television) ratings that show its market rank compared to other stations, look on that list for the other stations that reach your target audience to narrow down your search. Websites that accept advertising usually can provide verified information on their traffic statistics as part of their media kits.

Local advertising agencies, public relations firms, advertising clubs, and even local libraries might have additional sources of information you can use to assess audience media habits. They might have the latest Arbitron or Nielsen surveys, market reports on audience demographics, product use and media habits, or information on media rates and circulation. Some of this information can now be found on the Internet as well. In Step 5, you will learn how to choose appropriate outlets and place your advertisements or public service announcements.

FORMATS

The format is the way in which the message is delivered via a media outlet as an advertisement, a news story, an opinion piece, and so forth. Or, if you are using a nonmedia channel, then the format could refer to the size of the poster, the form the word of mouth will take, or creating a comic book versus a fotonovela. The format you choose will help shape the message and will affect your budget.

If, for example, radio is popular among your audience, then you can use several different communication formats through that media channel. You could produce radio advertisements for airing as public service announcements or paid commercials, you might appear on a station's talk show as a guest, you can pitch a news story to the station about your topic, or you could even create a popular song containing your message to be played in the station's regular rotation. Find out which formats appeal most to your target audience and use those.

Your communications can take many different forms, which are limited only by your imagination (and budget). Some ideas include the following:

- Daily and weekly newspapers (e.g., paid advertisements, public service advertisements, news stories, feature articles, inserts)

- Radio and television stations (e.g., paid advertisements, public service advertisements, guest on a talk show, news stories, entertainment programming, reality shows, public access cable)

- Billboards and transit ads (e.g., outside and inside buses, taxis, subways)

- Movie theater slide ads before the show

- Text message campaign

- Smartphone app

- Bathroom stall posters

- Parade float

- Sponsorship of the local high school sports team

- Advertisements in a professional sports game program or announcements on the giant scoreboard screen

- Hand out flyers at a large event (e.g., concert, sports competition)

- Sponsor a contest on Facebook

- Create videos to distribute online

- Design and publicize a website on your topic

MESSENGERS

A key part of channel selection involves considering who will deliver the message. The chosen messenger can have a great impact on whether the message is perceived as credible, important, and relevant to the target audience. Messengers such as physicians, health educators, hairdressers, and peers could speak to individuals or groups personally, although their effectiveness might depend on the relationship the individuals already have established with the persons delivering the message. If target audience members tend to trust their physicians or talk to their hairdressers about personal issues, then they might respond favorably to an interpersonal approach.

More often, the messenger will be someone the target audience does not know personally. The person might be a recognizable celebrity or public figure, or he or she might portray a generic figure such as a doctor or peer role model. The messenger might not even be a person at all but rather an animated character or an organizational endorsement. Depending on the purpose or style of the message, certain messengers will be more appropriate than others.

To determine who should deliver the message, consider the following criteria:

- Does your research from Step 1 provide any clues about who influences the target audience's behavior on this issue?

- Who does the target audience admire or seek to emulate?

- Who does the target audience trust to give it accurate information?

- To whom does the target audience usually ask questions about the topic?

- Will the target audience respond better to an authority figure? Peer? Celebrity? Animated character?

- Will the target audience immediately recognize who a potential messenger is or who he or she is supposed to represent?

- Is there a celebrity or public figure that is already associated with your issue?

- If a potential messenger is a celebrity or public figure, is he or she a role model on the topic? Might this person have anything in his or her past that could contradict your message (e.g., domestic violence, drug use, arrests)?

- Would you be able to get that person as your spokesperson? If so, is this person worth the money it would require (if his or her service is not volunteered)?

WORKSHEET 10: CHANNEL SELECTION WORKSHEET

1. Which channels are most likely to reach your target audience? (check all that apply)

   ❑ Television

   ❑ Radio

   ❑ Newspapers

   ❑ Magazines

   ❑ Billboards

   ❑ Transit ads

   ❑ Social media

   ❑ Websites

   ❑ Mobile phone

   ❑ Posters/flyers

   ❑ Brochures/fact sheets

   ❑ Newsletters

   ❑ Comic books/fotonovellas

   ❑ Direct mail

   ❑ E-mail

   ❑ Interpersonal communications/word of mouth

   ❑ Community events

   ❑ Workplace events

   ❑ Point-of-purchase materials

   ❑ Professional/ organizational channels

   ❑ Music or dramatic presentations

   ❑ Other: _____

2. For each channel you selected, note how you will find information on available outlets:

   a. Channel: _____

   Source(s) of information: _____

   b. Channel: _____

   Source(s) of information: _____

   c. Channel: _____

   Source(s) of information: _____

   d. Channel: _____

   Source(s) of information: _____

3. For each channel you selected, what formats should you use to deliver your message to the target audience?

   a. Channel: _____

   Formats:

   _____

   _____

   _____

   b. Channel: _____

   Formats:

   _____

   _____

   _____

c. Channel: _____

Formats:

_____

_____

_____

d. Channel: _____

Formats:

_____

_____

_____

4. To what types of messengers would your target audience respond best?

_____

_____

_____

CHAPTER 13

Producing Creative Communications

Using the messages you designed in Chapter 11, you will now develop the elements of your creative strategy into the finished communications that will run on the channels selected in Chapter 12. You will draft them to a point where you can pretest them with members of your target audience, then put the materials into final production before implementation begins. As you develop your materials, consider the capabilities and limitations of the channels and vehicles you have selected to use.

George Bernard Shaw once said, "The single biggest problem in communication is the illusion that it has taken place." Your job in this step is to make sure that the communication is not just happening from your end but that your messages are heard by and resonate with your target audience. You'll do this by taking into account all the research you have done to understand their lives and mind-sets, in order to craft ads and other promotional elements that speak to them and engage them more deeply.

THE CREATIVE BRIEF

To move from Point A (messages and channels) to Point B (finished communications), we use a strategic thought-organizer borrowed from advertising called a "creative brief." This is a short one- to two-page document that lays out the key facts and strategic approach to guide the creative development of your communications; it provides the springboard from which great ideas can grow and acts as a check to make sure the creativity doesn't stray too far from the strategy. If you will be working with an advertising or public relations agency to design and produce the creative communications, the creative brief is an important tool to guide their efforts.

The creative brief consists of the answers to a series of questions that briefly summarize the results of your research and strategic decisions. The resulting strategy document will guide the development of your communications, whether advertisements, websites, workshops, or social media outreach. Getting the "what to say" right at this stage is more important than the "how to say it." See Worksheet 11 for the creative brief format, which includes the following elements:

Target Audience

Be as specific as possible about who the communications will be designed to reach. Lay out the segmentation criteria you selected, along with your formative research, to paint a portrait

Sample Creative Brief for a Fall Prevention Campaign

Target Audience

Seniors ages 75+ who are living independently in their own homes or in senior communities in the state of California. Ambulatory. Active lifestyle filled with activities and friends. Main fear is being dependent on others.

Communication Objectives

As a result of the communications, the audience will

- Believe that they are at risk for a potentially debilitating fall
- Enact at least one preventive modification to their home, such as removing loose rugs from the floor or installing grab rails in the bathroom
- Increase their amount of exercise to at least 20 minutes five times a week

Barriers

- Belief that falls are something that happen to other people who are not as careful as they are
- Stigma attached to using canes, walkers, and home modifications—that's for "old people," not them
- Like their home the way it is and don't want to install modifications that interfere with the way it looks
- Discomfort when exercising
- Their doctor has not recommended they take preventive action.

Key Promise

If I take preventive action to make my home hazard free and strengthen my muscles, I can remain independent and in my own home.

Support Statements

- Falls are among the most debilitating events that can happen to seniors and are the most common type of injury that leads to immobility and premature placement into nursing homes. Two thirds of deaths from unintentional injuries among this population are from falls.

(Continued)

of your target audience members. Construct an identity for them by thinking about who a typical audience member might be—his or her name, information about job and family, current behavior, and feelings about adopting a different behavior. Create as rich a description of this person as you can so that he or she will feel real to you as you develop your campaign. You can even find a picture in a magazine or online that represents what this person looks like.

Communication Objectives

Make clear what outcomes you expect from the target audience being exposed to your communications. These objectives must be very clearly aligned with the overall goal and objectives for your social marketing program and will likely include knowledge, attitude, and behavioral changes. What "action step" are you asking the target audience members to take? Do you want them to visit a website for more information? Make an appointment with a doctor? Eat less fat? The person who is motivated by your message is primed to take action; do not lose that opportunity. Include a way for people to follow up on your message, whether it is by providing a phone number or a URL or by directing them to the appropriate professional.

Barriers

Several types of obstacles may create resistance to adopting the product among the target audience; this is where the price element of the marketing mix comes in. They must be minimized or removed so that the reward clearly outweighs the costs. These barriers may include the following:

■ Physical barriers (e.g., inaccessibility of services, lack of transportation, monetary cost)

■ Emotional or psychological barriers (e.g., fear of social disapproval or rejection, fear of failure, dislike of the product)

■ Social or cultural barriers that may prevent someone from adopting a behavior because it goes contrary to "how things are done" or affects something with symbolic importance (e.g., promoting abstinence from alcohol in a college fraternity, suggesting that Los Angeles residents give up their cars)

If major barriers exist, then you will need to change the target audience members' perceptions by either removing the barrier or minimizing it in their minds. If they do not know how to perform the behavior, then give them the skills. If they think the product is too expensive, then either reduce the price or show why it is worth the money. If they do not think that people like themselves use the product, then show that they do.

Key Promise

If target audience members perform the action you advocate, then what will they get out of it? Show the good things that will happen if they use the product. Consider the competition and what makes your product stand out. They need to see the product as the solution to a problem or issue that affects them; the benefits should be relevant and believable. Your formative research should have helped you identify the key benefits that the target audience values most. State the key promise in a single simple sentence, if possible. For example, "If I drive a hybrid car, I will use less fuel and will save money as a result."

(Continued)

■ About one third of seniors living at home will fall at least once during a year, often leading to hospitalization.

■ Two thirds of falls among the elderly are preventable.

■ Assessing your home for potential tripping hazards and installing unobtrusive modifications is easy.

■ Regular exercise increases strength and improves balance, endurance, and body mechanics among older adults. Muscle conditioning prevents the likelihood of falls and increases the duration of independent living.

Tone/Image

■ Serious, hopeful, and empowering
■ Imagery will depict independent seniors enjoying life.
■ Peer testimonial may be effective.

Media

■ One television commercial (30 seconds)
■ Two radio commercials (60 seconds)
■ Trifold brochure
■ "Prescription" pad listing preventive actions for doctors to hand out
■ Wall calendar with pockets for appointment cards, other notes

Openings

■ Television—evening news broadcast
■ Radio—AM talk radio
■ Doctors' offices
■ Senior centers
■ Seniors' homes

Creative Considerations

■ Television commercial should reflect the diverse population of California.
■ Create radio ads and print materials in English and Spanish.
■ Text on print materials should be in large type.

Showing the negative consequences that might happen as a result of choosing your product's competition can also bring your point home to target audience members. The consequence must, however, be meaningful to them. For example, the threat of death often is not enough to prevent drunk driving by teenagers; they believe that they are immortal. By focusing on more immediate concerns, such as the loss of their driver's licenses and thus their independence, messages may have more impact.

The "consequences" approach requires several caveats. The consequences must be believable; do not exaggerate to make your point or else the audience will dismiss the entire message. Also, using "fear appeals," or trying to scare the audience into doing something, often can backfire. People might become paralyzed by fear and shut out the message. This technique works best when you provide a solution or an action that they can take within the same message. Of course, any fear appeal you use must be something that the target audience can do something about.

Support Statements

You can promise your target audience members everything they desire, but if they do not believe you, then your message is moot. Credibility can come from the scientific facts you use to back up your message, as well as information from the formative research. You also can show the truth of your message through demonstrations or testimonials as to the benefits of adopting the behavior.

Target audience members rely on many different characteristics of the execution to determine the believability of your message. The manner in which you deliver the message, as well as the messenger used, helps to establish credibility. Will you use an authority figure? A celebrity? A target audience member? Will you present a "slice of life" scenario in which actors talk about the product in an everyday setting? Or, will you use animation or a catchy jingle to convey information? Visual and auditory cues, as well as the quality of the execution, provide the target audience with reasons to believe you or discount your message. Be careful not to let the presentation interfere with the content or undermine the believability of your message.

Tone/Image

Every communication conveys its message in a particular style. Whether it is the dry formality of a letter from the Internal Revenue Service or the heart-tugging sentimentality of a phone company commercial, the delivery affects how the recipient perceives and responds to the message. Before you proceed to turning your messages into finished products, you will need to decide the feelings and image you want to evoke with your communications.

Tone refers to how the message is presented. The words and delivery style could be serious, humorous, dramatic, hip, friendly, folksy, stern, understanding, street-smart, frightening, cynical, or any other descriptive adjective. The tone must be appropriate for the subject matter, audience, and format. When the message itself is very serious, a humorous tone might contradict the meaning of the words. On the other hand, humor can be very effective in drawing someone in to your message. The tone you use can help establish a "personality" for your product.

The image that your audience has of the target behavior guides its response to your communications. An established, well-known type of behavior such as exercise might already hold a particular image for your target audience (although it could be different for each segment).

For example, individuals might think of exercise as being for people who already have active lifestyles, who are younger and healthier, or who are obsessed with their looks. If the image of the desired action is negative or neutral, then your communications might seek to change it or, for a previously unfamiliar behavior, to create a new image. The image must be consonant with the target audience's perception of itself and should be appealing and accessible to it.

Every element of your communication executions contributes to the image that an individual forms of your product. This includes the tone, graphics, wording, music, messenger, and even paper stock used. The image should be distinctive and consistent throughout your campaign materials.

Media

Which types of media will you be using to communicate your message? Be as specific as possible about the number and types of communications you will be developing. For example, you may decide that for your campaign, you need one 30-second television ad, four 60-second radio ads, a website, a Facebook page, and a media kit. Or you may not be using traditional or online media at all but creating a word-of-mouth-based campaign that involves "seeding" your product with community influencers, street teams that hand out samples and engage people in conversations about the product, as well as materials that people can use to share the product with their friends and family. Both types of campaigns will need communication materials to be created, and a creative brief can guide the development of each.

Openings

The concepts of place and aperture come into play to determine the openings that will allow your communications to get noticed by your audience. People are more likely to pick up on messages when they are already thinking about the subject or involved in some way. When you were last considering buying a car, how much more attention did you pay to automobile commercials than you would normally? Your target audience might have similar windows of opportunity through which you can pass your message.

To improve your chances of success, try to expose target audience members to the message at a time that they will be most receptive and able to act on it. This might be when they are already thinking about the subject, when they are in a position to take some type of action, or just before they need to make a decision. For example, messages about healthy snacking may be effective at grocery stores, where people are making decisions about the foods that they will have available at home; on afternoon drive-time radio, as people are coming home from work hungry; or perhaps on magnets or stickers that people will see each time they go to the refrigerator or vending machine.

Other Creative Considerations

This last section is where you would note anything else that is important to take into account in developing the communications. Do they need to be made in more than one language? Should the production team leave space for local programs to customize with their own information? What ethnicities or nationalities should be included in graphics? Anything that will affect the words or visuals used should be included.

BRINGING OUT YOUR CREATIVITY

The creative process can be the most difficult part of social marketing for some people. If you have not hired an outside agency to assist you in developing your program, then this is a point at which you can consider bringing one in to help with final message development, production, or graphic design. Of course, if you have the resources within your own organization or through freelancers, then you might be able to coordinate this process yourself. You also might consider adapting materials from other organizations that match your needs; you do not always have to reinvent the wheel.

Although there are no formulas or cookbook solutions, some guidelines can help direct your creative thinking. To be most effective, your communication should have three characteristics:[1]

1. *It must* be relevant and meaningful to the target audience.

2. *It must* be original, stating the message in a new way.

3. *It must* "break through the clutter" and be noticed.

Of course, while meeting these criteria, the material also must fit the goals and objectives originally specified as well as the overall creative strategy. You could have a brilliant idea, but if it does not meet your objectives, then you must set it aside.

Often, the best way in which to get your creative juices flowing is a brainstorming session, either by yourself or with a group of people working on the project. If in a group, you might want to also include people such as your receptionist, interns, and the human resources director—anyone who has a creative spirit or is willing and able to come. Have plenty of butcher paper or flipchart pages available so that you can record all the ideas that emerge during the session.

Pick an idea to concentrate on for a set amount of time (5 to 10 minutes) such as a slogan or campaign name or scenarios for a radio ad. Call out ideas as they come, and do not censor yourselves. Free-associate from other ideas that have already been put on the table. The time limit will provide a sense of urgency and force quick thinking. When the time is up (unless great ideas still are coming), look back over everything that was written and cull the most promising ideas. Spend more time elaborating on those and developing them into whole concepts.

Here are some ideas for getting started on your brainstorming:

- What do people expect to hear about your product? Now, think about what would be unexpected. Are there dramatic visuals you can use? Refutation of "common knowledge"? An unusual way in which to present the facts?

- How can you evoke an emotional response to your message? Which emotions are appropriate? What types of people should be portrayed? What type of situation would make sense?

- Play with the words associated with your product. Can you discover any double meanings that could change the interpretation of a common saying or phrase?

---

[1]Wells, W. (1989). *Planning for ROI: Effective advertising strategy.* Englewood Cliffs, NJ: Prentice Hall.

- If your product were a person, what would its personality be like? What would it look like? What would a cartoon character representing your product look like?

- Ask "what if?" questions that are contrary to how things are. "What if men had babies instead of women?" "What if we had transparent skin and could see our internal organs?" "What if time ran backward instead of forward?" "What if there were 'health police'?" Answer the questions in as many ways as you can.

As you brainstorm and develop your messages, remember this thought from French philosopher Emile Chartier: "Nothing is more dangerous than an idea when it's the only one you have." There is no such thing as one right answer, so keep looking from different angles until you have several right answers from which to choose.

LANGUAGE ISSUES

The language you use in your communications will affect how well the target audience comprehends and processes the ideas. Here are some suggestions for helping the audience pay attention to your message and act on it:

- Personalize the message by addressing the individual directly through the use of the word *you* and the imperative verb tense when appropriate (as in Nike's "Just Do It"). For example, use "Ask your physician about your medications" rather than "Seniors should ask their physicians about their medications."

The 12 Types of Ads

In 1978, Donald Gunn, the creative director at the Leo Burnett advertising agency for many years, spent a year studying the best ads that were out there to identify common patterns that defined them.[2] He found 12 "master formats" into which nearly all of those effective ads fell. This list can give you some inspiration for how to structure your ads—whether television, radio, or print. The categories are as follows:

1. The Demo—Show the product's capabilities.

2. Present the Need or Problem—Position your product as the solution to a problem in your audience's lives.

3. Problem as Symbol, Analogy, or Exaggerated Graphic—Represent the problem in a way that makes the point symbolically, such as the man who turns into a monster when he's sick but returns to human form after taking medicine.

4. Comparison—Show how the product is superior to the competition.

5. The "Exemplary Story"—Depict a situation in which the benefits of the product come to the rescue.

6. The "Benefit Causes Story"—A back-to-front story, where you see the benefits first, then later learn that the product was the source of the benefits.

7. "Tell It"—In this format, someone offers a testimonial, either to the camera or to a fictional friend or neighbor. It could also be a "talking head" presenting information about the product.

8. Ongoing Characters or Celebrities—A recurring character or well-known celebrity touts the product and becomes associated with the brand.

9. Benefit as Symbol, Analogy, or Exaggerated Graphic—Similar to the earlier format that depicts the problem as such, this shows the benefit in a metaphorical way.

10. Associated User Imagery—Show people using the product that the audience aspires to be like—whether celebrities or a certain type of person (e.g., athletic, hip).

11. Unique Personality Property—Highlight something unique about the product, such as its name, origin, or characteristics, which is potentially attractive to the audience.

12. Parody or Borrowed Format—Parody a well-known movie, television show, or even another ad with a new twist.

---

[2]Stevenson, S. (2007, July 23). There are 12 kinds of ads in the world. Resist them all! *Slate Magazine.* http://www.slate.com/id/2170872/

- Give the feeling of immediacy by using the present tense and words that make the subject of the sentence feel closer such as *this* instead of *that* or *here* instead of *there*. For example, use "These wetlands need protection if the legislation passes." rather than "Those wetlands would need protection if the legislation passed."

- Starting off with a question will pull people in if they can answer yes. Examples include "Do you wish you could cook healthier meals but don't know how?" and "Do you have high blood pressure? If so, you should know. . . ." If you have done your research, then you should know what questions will draw in your target audience members. If you are not sure that they will say yes or give the "right" answer to the question, then do not ask.

- Use positive appeals rather than negative messages to effect attitude change about your product. Show why condoms are beneficial rather than just saying "Don't have unprotected sex." Or, highlight the benefits of exercise instead of discussing the problems associated with obesity. This approach works best when the audience has mixed feelings about the behavior.

- Be careful when communicating about risks; it can be easy to misunderstand probabilistic concepts. Refer to risks built up over time rather than single incident probabilities because people often underestimate cumulative risk. For example, the risk of contracting HIV in a single sexual act is fairly low but increases substantially over hundreds of encounters.

- If you want to compare the risks of one activity to another, then choose a comparison risk similar in factors such as whether it is voluntary, the level of dread associated with it, the amount of control someone has over its occurrence, and the level of knowledge about it. It would be more appropriate, for example, to compare the risk of contracting AIDS through sharing intravenous drug needles with the risk of contracting lung cancer from smoking rather than the risk of contracting breast cancer (which is not clearly linked to risky behaviors).

- In print and online materials, write at the reading level of your target audience. All too often, people who are used to writing in a professional style in their jobs forget that the people they are writing for might not have a college degree or even a high school diploma. Define any words that the audience might not know, and minimize the use of technical jargon. Use simple English whenever possible, keeping the number of multisyllabic words down. In Chapter 15, you will learn how to assess the readability level of print materials.

- Keep the materials focused on one or a small number of points, particularly if dealing with a time- or space-limited medium. If you are developing a series of materials, such as radio or newspaper ads, then base each one on a single message and use the same identifier to show they are all part of the same campaign.

- If you are designing a billboard or poster that will be read quickly and from a distance, keep the number of words to a minimum. Eight words is about the most that someone can read as a billboard whizzes by. A poster can have more words if people will have time to look at it. The letters also must be large enough to be legible from a distance.

Writing Television and Radio Scripts

Writing scripts for television or radio ads is not magic. You just need to know the basics and follow them. Do not try to pack too much into your ads. Focus on one or two key points. Limit the number of characters to avoid confusion. Stay away from wild special effects or music that will detract from your message. Your ad also must capture the audience's attention immediately and hold it.

Television spots generally are either 15 or 30 seconds long, whereas radio spots are 30 or 60 seconds long. Although not the case for television, radio time often is sold in 60-second blocks, with the same price for 30- or 60-second spots. If you are submitting a public service announcement (PSA) to be read live on the air, it can be as short as 10 seconds long; you can provide several differently timed versions of the PSA for the station to use as time allows. In writing your scripts, try to use the shortest amount of time to get your message across. Generally, 5 syllables equal 1 second, and a 30-second spot can fit about 75 words.

The scripts for radio and television ads are similar, with one major exception. On the radio, you need to create a picture in your listeners' minds through words, sound effects, and music. Television provides that picture, so you must think visually as you develop the script. In addition to writing the dialogue for each shot, describe how the characters look, the location of each scene, key props (objects) that are included in each scene, and any special camera angles or effects. The dialogue must sound believable; remember that you are writing for the ears of your target audience members, not for readers of your organization's annual report. If you are providing a phone number or URL on television or radio, repeat it verbally or make sure you leave it up on the screen for a long enough time for someone to copy it down.

Here is an example of a 30-second radio script developed for the "Don't Kid Yourself" campaign:

Jason and Miranda

SFX (sound effects): Audio has slightly tinny sound, as through TV speakers	Jason: Miranda. I've waited so long for this. . . .
	Miranda: Oh Jason, me too. . . .
Passionate sounds, soap opera music swells	TV Announcer: *The Greedy and the Gorgeous* will be back after these messages.
Music abruptly cuts out, as with mute button	Viewer 1: Do you believe Miranda is going to bed with Jason? He's been with half the women on the show.
	Viewer 2: And you never see him take out a condom. Lucky Miranda lives in TV-land, or she'd end up with AIDS.
	Viewer 1: Yeah, or a baby spitting up on her beautiful clothes.
	Viewer 2: Wait, they're back.
Music swells	Miranda: Oh, Jason, come to me now, now. . . .
Music ducks under, fades out	Narrator: In real life, sex has real consequences. Don't kid yourself. Call 1-800-230-PLAN.

Creating Effective Online Video

Online videos can be a relatively quick and inexpensive method of communicating your message without incurring big production and distribution costs. You can shoot with a small pocket video camera like a Flip or Kodak zi8 and upload your videos to sites such as YouTube, Blip.tv or Vimeo, or the nonprofit-specific DoGooder.tv. But even though the expectation for online video is that it does not need to be professionally produced, you should be strategic and make yours as well done as possible. Keep in mind that "viral" is not a quality you can check off as you create the video but is an outcome; you can try to create a video that people will want to spread to all their friends, but unless it is compelling enough to strike a chord with your audience, you won't have a "viral video."

Some tips for creating effective online videos include the following:

- Keep it short and sweet—no more than 2 minutes and preferably even less.

- Think about your story visually. How can you convey the message in pictures and sound to make it more than just a video version of a brochure?

- Where will the "viral" factor come from? Will you use humor to make people want to pass it along? An emotional angle? Critical new information their friends need to know?

- If you are including interviews, make sure your camera work is steady (use a tripod if possible) and zoom in close on your subjects' faces.

- Good sound is critical. Even with excellent visuals, if the audio is hard to hear, people will not stick around to watch. Invest in a good external microphone if your camera's built-in mic is not sufficient.

- Use video editing software to bring together your footage with B-roll (generic shots depicting your issue), music, and on-screen graphics. Many computers come with this type of software (e.g., Windows Movie Maker or iMovie) preinstalled.

- Include a call to action. Once you've inspired people with your video, don't forget to give them the next step to move forward with a link to more information.

CREATING DRAFT MATERIALS

Now is the time to put it all together by creating drafts of the materials, including the words you will use and the graphic design or other production formats. These will serve as stand-ins for the finished materials as you pretest them with the target audience. By making these prototype materials look as close to their final forms as possible, you will get a better idea during the pretesting of which elements work and which do not. You might find out that the colors you used have negative connotations or that the audience cannot tell what the person in the picture is doing. By making any needed changes before going into production, you will know that your materials are as good as they can possibly be. These changes will be much less costly than if you had already printed up 10,000 brochures or produced a television ad and then found a problem.

Of course, you should not spend an excessive amount of money on creating prototype materials, particularly if your budget is tight. A television ad does not need to be fully produced for viewers to understand the concept. The people pretesting the materials need to have a good idea of what the finished product will look like, but this can be accomplished using storyboards, without having the final piece on hand.

For print materials, you can easily lay out a brochure, flyer, or rough draft of a poster with your word processing or publishing software. Even if you do not have the artwork yet, you can arrange the text and create "dummy" spaces for the graphics. Work with a graphic artist to come up with sketches of visual concepts to go along with the words you will use. If you want to design the materials yourself with your own graphic software, you can buy high-quality computer clip art or stock photographs that look like they were created just for your project.

For audiovisual materials, you first will need to develop a script. The script should include the lines for each character or the announcer, any actions they will take, sound effects needed, and/or special visual effects. You can create a rough version of a radio spot by drafting amateur actors, co-workers, or friends with some acting ability to record the script. You can do this at a local recording studio or, if necessary, in a quiet room with a digital audio recorder.

Create a rough version of a television spot by making a storyboard that depicts each scene through drawings or photographs, with the appropriate part of the script displayed underneath each panel. From this, you can create a "real-time" version by videotaping each picture in time with a soundtrack of the script; if you use drawings, this is called an "animatic," whereas for photographs, it is called a "photomatic." Another option is to make a video of people (actors or otherwise) acting out the script in a setting as close to the final set as possible.[3]

Digital elements of the campaign, such as websites, social media channels, games, or ads, can be more easily mocked up to be displayed either as screen shots for feedback on graphical elements and layout or as an online demo for pretesters to experience the functionality. Worksheet 12 leads you through the decisions to consider as you create your campaign's online presence.

If you will be placing your message on other types of materials, then you should create a mockup of the piece. For a water bottle, buy a plain water bottle and glue the design onto it. If you are having key chains made, then cut out a piece of cardboard in

Using Mobile in Your Campaign

Mobile phones have become an indispensable tool for people around the world and in many developing countries are the primary way that people access the web. The always-on and always-near nature of mobile technology makes it an attractive way to reach people, if your audience is among those who use their phones for more than just making calls.

Some of the ways you can incorporate mobile technology into your campaign include the following:

- SMS (text messaging) campaigns—People opt in to receive periodic text messages from your campaign. These could be campaign messages, reminders, or coupons.
- Direct response/interaction—When people text a particular word to a "shortcode" of five to six numbers, they receive information back (e.g., when people text their ZIP code to the code "KNOWIT" [566948], they can get a list of nearby HIV testing centers). This can be used for things such as requesting information, voting, or entering a contest.
- Mobile sites—Websites can be optimized for viewing on web-enabled mobile phones so people can access your site from anywhere.
- Mobile apps—Many companies and organizations create applications (or "apps") for smartphones such as the iPhone or Android that make it easy to find certain types of information or perform a function.
- Mobile content—You can create content specifically for viewing/downloading onto mobile devices, such as videos, games, or ringtones.
- Mobile ads—Ads can appear on popular mobile sites, in mobile games and videos, or before downloading content.

The Text4Baby campaign, a public-private partnership among more than 100 organizations, including the Centers for Disease Control and Prevention, Johnson & Johnson, and CTIA—The Wireless Foundation, launched in January 2010 with the goal of improving health behaviors and outcomes for new and expectant mothers.

(Continued)

---

[3]For an excellent step-by-step guide on how to create rough drafts for broadcast materials, see Appendix D in National Cancer Institute. (1992). *Making health communication programs work: A planner's guide.* Washington, DC: U.S. Department of Health and Human Services.

(Continued)

Geared toward low-income women who are more likely to use mobile phones than the Internet, participating mobile operators agreed to send text messages at no charge to the recipients. Women enter their baby's due date when they sign up and then receive regular messages geared specifically to their baby's stage of development or age through the first 12 months of life. Outreach partners such as state and local health departments, federal agencies, health plans, professional associations, corporate and retail partners, and media partners all promote registration via mobile sign-up (text BABY or BEBE to 511411) or the website (www.text4baby.org).

the right shape, paste or draw on the design, and put it on a key ring. You can make a prototype of nearly anything with a little ingenuity or assistance from an artist.

When you pretest your materials, the target audience must be able to visualize them in their final form. With concrete details to comment on (rather than a vague description), the feedback will be much more helpful. After pretesting, you most likely will need to return to the program and communication design stage to refine your product based on the response from members of the target audience. Worksheet 13 at the end of the chapter leads you through the planning steps you will need to complete as you produce draft and final versions of your materials.

CASE STUDY

Program and Communication Design
Case Study: Save the Crabs, Then Eat 'Em

The Academy for Educational Development (AED) faced a messaging dilemma in its project for the six-state public/private Chesapeake Bay Program partnership, which aimed to restore the ecosystem of the bay and protect its water quality into the future.[4] The issue was that area residents had message fatigue from previous campaigns to "Save the Bay," and the behaviors that needed to happen were relatively complex.

The primary problem in the Chesapeake Bay was that nutrients from agricultural waste, sewage treatment plants, lawn fertilizer, and other compounds were being directly deposited or washed into the bay, upsetting the ecological balance by promoting the growth of algae. The campaign was to focus on targeting an untapped source of potential nutrient reductions—the residents of the greater D.C. area who fertilize their lawns to excess. The behavior it would promote was to fertilize lawns in the fall, rather than the spring, to avoid fertilizer runoff, which is damaging to many bay species. This fall fertilization made sense as the target behavior because lawn care is something that individuals have control over, which can have direct impact in the bay, and changing the season of fertilization is not hard to do. Because it is a public behavior, social reinforcement can play a role. Results of a phone survey showed that most people had no strong personal connection to the Chesapeake Bay, and numerous barriers existed because of ingrained beliefs and behaviors, both on the part of homeowners and lawn service professionals.

In considering how to appeal to D.C. homeowners, AED realized that it could use a culinary appeal, rather than an environmental appeal, to get them to care. The Chesapeake Bay was well known for its blue crabs, and area residents were passionate about their seafood, with many seafood restaurants in the greater D.C. area. Rather than a "Save the Bay" approach, they shifted to a "Save the Seafood" message—an unexpected twist on the message. This humorous element emphasized that the benefit of holding off on lawn fertilization would be continuing to have delicious blue crabs and other seafood on their plates when they wanted it. The tagline became "Save the Crabs . . . Then Eat 'Em."

---

[4]Landers, J., Mitchell, P., Smith, B., Lehman, T., & Conner, C. (2006). "Save the crabs, then eat 'em": A culinary approach to saving the Chesapeake Bay. *Social Marketing Quarterly, 12*(1), 15–28.

The campaign became a brand called the Chesapeake Club to emphasize the idea of participation, belonging, and social norms. The campaign partnered with local professional lawn services to offer an eco-friendly option to homeowners who did not make the decisions about fertilizing their lawns themselves. Using television and print ads at the time of year when people would be starting to think about fertilizing their lawns, the campaign directed people to a website with more information. In addition, the campaign had posters in the Washington Metro system, as well as drink coasters distributed to seafood restaurants, and they conducted public relations activities.

The irreverent message got people's attention, even with a relatively small advertising budget. A postcampaign survey found that 72% were able to recall a major theme of the campaign (i.e., brand name, tagline, or what they were asked to do). In addition, 37% were able to remember the Chesapeake Club brand and/or the "Save the Crabs, Then Eat 'Em" tagline without any prompts. While there was not a statistically significant difference between people exposed to the campaign in whether they intended to fertilize in the spring as usual (42% exposed vs. 46% not exposed), more people who were exposed were planning on not fertilizing at all that year (30% exposed vs. 22% not exposed; statistically significant).

WORKSHEET 11: CREATIVE BRIEF

1. Target Audience (Describe each target audience segment as one person. What is his or her life and personality like? What does this person think, feel, and do in relation to your issue?):

_____

_____

_____

2. Communication Objectives (What do you want them to do as a result of the communication?):

a. _____

_____

b. _____

_____

c. _____

_____

3. Barriers (What obstacles keep your audience from taking action?):

_____

_____

_____

4. Key Promise (What will happen if the target audience adopts the product? Make it as concise as possible.):

_____

_____

_____

5. Support Statements (What are the reasons your audience should believe the key promise? How will you establish credibility?):

a. _____

_____

b. _____

_____

c. _____

_____

6. Tone/Image (What feelings should the communications evoke?):
   a. What tone will you use in your communications to elicit the desired response from your target audience? (The list includes common responses, but do not limit yourself to these.)

❏ Serious	❏ Hip	❏ Businesslike
❏ Humorous	❏ Folksy	❏ Emotional
❏ Dramatic	❏ Frightening	❏ Other _____
❏ Friendly	❏ Cynical	❏ Other _____

   b. How else can you convey the desired image in addition to using words (e.g., music, graphic design, characters' appearance)?

   _____

   _____

   _____

7. Media (What types of media or communication methods will you use? Be specific as to quantities, formats, etc.):
   a. _____
   b. _____
   c. _____
   d. _____
   e. _____
   f. _____

8. Openings (When and where should you reach your audience with your communications?):
   a. At what times, places, or situations will the target audience's "aperture" be most open to your message?

   _____

   _____

   b. How can you use your chosen media/communication methods to best reach the target audience at those times, places, or situations?

   _____

   _____

9. Creative Considerations (What other audience or programmatic needs should be taken into account as the communications are developed?):

   _____

   _____

   _____

WORKSHEET 12: DESIGNING AN EFFECTIVE WEBSITE

1. What are your objectives for the website? (Make sure they fit with the overall communication objectives for the campaign.)
   Objectives:

   _____

   _____

   _____

2. What specifically do you want people to do on your website?
   a. _____

   _____

   b _____

   _____

   c. _____

   _____

3. How does the website fit in with the other pieces of your social marketing strategy?

   _____

   _____

   _____

4. What characteristics do you want for your website's look and feel? What adjectives would
   you use to describe it?

   _____

   _____

   _____

5. What are some possible domain names for the website? Are they available?

   _____

   _____

   _____

6. What content will you include on the website?

   _____

   _____

   _____

7. What information should be front and center on the home page?

_____

_____

_____

8. What are the main questions people ask about your campaign/issue? Turn these into a Frequently Asked Questions (FAQ) section.

_____

_____

_____

_____

9. What interactive and/or social elements will you offer on the website?

_____

_____

_____

10. How will you integrate your social media activity from other sites into the website and vice versa?

_____

_____

_____

11. How can you make the content shareable?

_____

_____

_____

12. How will people find your site?

_____

_____

_____

(Continued)

(Continued)

13. Make sure you build in:

   ❏ Search engine optimization (so people can find your site)

   ❏ A descriptive, easy to remember domain name

   ❏ A way for people to contact you online

   ❏ Easy, intuitive navigation

   ❏ Clear, uncluttered site design

   ❏ "About Us" page

   ❏ Appropriate reading level

   ❏ Look and feel consistent with rest of campaign

   ❏ Privacy policy

WORKSHEET 13: MATERIALS PRODUCTION WORKSHEET

1. Audiovisual Materials

   a. Type of materials to be produced:

Medium	Length	Number of Spots
❑ Television	_____	_____
❑ Radio	_____	_____
❑ Online video	_____	_____
❑ Podcast	_____	_____
❑ Other _____	_____	_____

   b. Production assistance needed:

   ❑ Producer

   ❑ Director

   ❑ Actors/voiceover talent

   ❑ Camera operator (for television/video)

   ❑ Studio technician (for radio)

   ❑ Video/audio editor

   ❑ Music composer

   ❑ Additional production crew members

   ❑ Other _____

   ❑ Other _____

   c. Audiovisual production tasks:

Task	Person Responsible	Deadline
Writing script	_____	_____
Creating draft materials for pretesting	_____	_____
Selecting producer and crew	_____	_____
Securing production facilities	_____	_____
Hiring actors/voiceover	_____	_____
Scouting locations	_____	_____
Coordinating props and wardrobe	_____	_____

   (Continued)

(Continued)

Task	Person Responsible	Deadline
Creating or choosing music	_____	_____
Copying the script for all involved	_____	_____
Coordinating rehearsals	_____	_____
Directing production	_____	_____
Editing video or audio	_____	_____
Duplication/posting of final product	_____	_____

d. Audiovisual production budget:

Item Description	Unit Price (per day, copy)	Quantity	Total Cost
Production facility	_____	_____	_____
Producer	_____	_____	_____
Director	_____	_____	_____
Production crew:	_____	_____	_____
_____	_____	_____	_____
_____	_____	_____	_____
_____	_____	_____	_____
Actors/voiceover talent	_____	_____	_____
Music	_____	_____	_____
Materials/props/wardrobe	_____	_____	_____
Draft materials for pretesting	_____	_____	_____
Distribution	_____	_____	_____
Miscellaneous expenses	_____	_____	_____
Other expenses:	_____	_____	_____
Total audiovisual production expenses	$ _____		

2. Print/Outdoor/Other Media

a. Type of materials to be produced:

Medium	Size	Number of Versions
❏ Newspaper/magazine ads	_____	_____
❏ Posters	_____	_____

❑ Brochures   _____   _____

❑ Billboards   _____   _____

❑ Transit ads   _____   _____

❑ Other _____   _____   _____

b. Production assistance needed:

❑ Artist

❑ Graphic designer

❑ Photographer

❑ Copywriter

❑ Publication writer/editor

❑ Printer/production facility

❑ Other _____

❑ Other _____

c. Media production tasks:

Task	Person Responsible	Deadline
Selecting production team	_____	_____
Developing visual concepts	_____	_____
Creating artwork	_____	_____
Copywriting ads	_____	_____
Writing/editing publications	_____	_____
Creating overall graphic design	_____	_____
Creating draft materials for pretesting	_____	_____
Determining specs and quantities	_____	_____
Soliciting bids from printers	_____	_____
Selecting printer	_____	_____
Coordinating printing process	_____	_____
Spot-checking printed materials	_____	_____
Distributing materials	_____	_____

(Continued)

(Continued)

d. Media production budget:

Item Description	Unit Price (per hour/day, copy)	Quantity	Total Cost
Artist	_____	_____	_____
Graphic designer	_____	_____	_____
Photographer	_____	_____	_____
Copywriter	_____	_____	_____
Publication writer/editor	_____	_____	_____
Draft materials for pretesting	_____	_____	_____
Printing of each piece:	_____	_____	_____
_____	_____	_____	_____
_____	_____	_____	_____
_____	_____	_____	_____
Miscellaneous expenses	_____	_____	_____
Other expenses:	_____	_____	_____
_____	_____	_____	_____
_____	_____	_____	_____
_____	_____	_____	_____

Total print/other media production expenses $ _____

3. Digital Media

a. Type of medium to be produced:

Medium	Size	Number of Versions
❑ Website	_____	_____
❑ Social media site	_____	_____
❑ Software/application	_____	_____
❑ Mobile site	_____	_____
❑ SMS (text messaging) campaign	_____	_____
❑ Other _____	_____	_____

b. Production assistance needed:

☐ Web designer

☐ Software programmer

☐ Copywriter

☐ Mobile marketing provider

☐ Other _____

☐ Other _____

c. Digital production tasks:

Task	Person Responsible	Deadline
Selecting production team	_____	_____
Developing site design/function	_____	_____
Creating content	_____	_____
Programming site/application	_____	_____
Writing terms of service	_____	_____
Selecting domain name/web host	_____	_____
Selecting mobile provider/shortcode	_____	_____
Securing approval for mobile campaign on carriers' networks		
Creating draft site for pretesting	_____	_____
Finalizing site/app/mobile	_____	_____
Distributing/promoting site/app	_____	_____

(Continued)

(Continued)

d. Digital production budget:

Item Description	Unit Price (per hour/day, deliverable)	Quantity	Total Cost
Web designer			
Software programmer			
Copywriter			
Mobile marketing provider			
Domain name/web host costs			
Mobile shortcode			
Test messaging costs			
Miscellaneous expenses			
Other expenses:			

Total digital media production expenses $ _____

Section V

Step 4
Pretesting

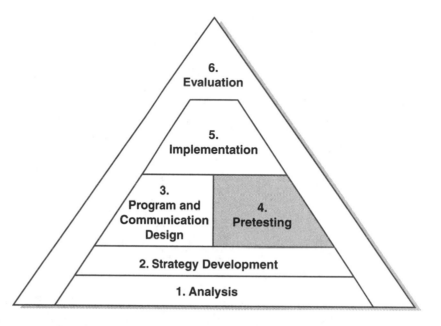

SECTION OVERVIEW

If a tree falls in the forest but nobody is there to hear, did it make a sound? Likewise, if you conduct a campaign but the target audience members do not understand or notice, does it make a sound? Of course, you hear it because you are there with your chainsaw, yelling "Timber!" and watching one tree fall after another. But is it possible that you are living in a different forest from the target audience?

An essential part of developing a social marketing program is pretesting your communications with the target audience. That way, you will know how to get its attention and ensure its comprehension of the messages so that your target audience will hear the trees fall.

The extensiveness of your pretest activities will depend on your situation. If you have very limited resources, do not skip this step; just use some less costly pretesting methods. If you are spending a great deal of time and money on the development of your campaign, then a comprehensive pretest period before implementation will help you to get the most out of your investment. Ideally, you would have two phases of pretesting: the first to test messages and concepts and the second to test materials based on the concepts that were well received.

This section consists of the following chapters:

- Chapter 14: Pretesting Principles
- Chapter 15: Conducting the Pretest
- Chapter 16: Using the Pretesting Results

Pretesting Principles

Pretesting will help you to know whether the materials you have developed will generate the effect you desire. This is an essential part of the social marketing process and is a hallmark of a well-designed program.

WHY PRETEST?

Pretesting might seem like an "extra"—nice to be able to do but not feasible given your time or budgetary constraints. But there are many reasons to pretest your materials or other elements of your social marketing mix with the target audience before finalizing them. By pretesting, you can accomplish the following:

- *Ensure that the target audience comprehends the messages.* Although you understand all the words you used, the target audience might not. Your materials might be at too high a reading level, the announcer might speak too quickly, or a concept might not be explained clearly. You might not notice, but your audience will.

- *Detect other interpretations of your message.* The campaign slogan might seem clever to you, but the words might mean something completely different to the target audience. This might be due to slang words used in that group or ambiguous wording on your part. Chevrolet purportedly found this out the hard way when the automaker introduced the Nova in Latin America (*no va* means "doesn't go" in Spanish).

- *Catch potentially costly mistakes.* By having many people look over your materials, potential problems will more likely be found—anything from minor typos to mistakenly using a picture of someone from a nontargeted ethnic or socioeconomic group (e.g., Japanese instead of Chinese). Having other professionals conduct a review as well will increase the chances of the content being accurate. Pretesting helps you to avoid the cost of completely redoing unusable materials after production.

- *Tune back in to the "real world."* You might develop messages based on points in your research that you think are critical, only to find out in pretesting that the target audience does not respond to your brilliant insights. You might be told that your humorous approach is too "corny." Or, some people might find your messages too graphic or offensive. The target audience will serve to check ideas that seem good in theory but do not work in practice.

■ *Make the materials more appealing.* Depending on the audience, certain visual or other design elements, such as bright colors, a compelling graphic, and a musical style, will make it more likely they will pay attention to your campaign. The pretests will help to identify whether the target audience would pick up your materials or notice your messages in the cluttered media.

■ *Identify details that subvert the message.* In pretesting, you will ensure that each element of the presentation supports and reinforces the message. You might learn that the background music is distracting, that the person in the picture looks too happy, or that the footage includes people wearing unwanted gang symbols.

■ *Select from among several potential approaches.* If you developed more than one version of your messages or materials, then you can determine which approach works best by pretesting each with the target audience.

The benefits of pretesting are well worth the slight delay in implementing your campaign. It is better to have excellent materials later than to provide mediocre materials immediately. If these are materials you will be using for years to come, then a difference of a few weeks in development will not mean much in the long term. Build a pretesting period into your project timeline to ensure that you have plenty of time to get feedback and make changes (if needed).

If you have sufficient resources, then you may wish to divide pretesting into two phases. The first phase would involve pretesting the messages and concepts once you have developed them to identify those that are most effective. The second would pretest the materials developed based on the selected messages and concepts to determine how best to execute the idea. Using this method allows you to concentrate on one element at a time, building up the materials in a sequential manner.

PRETESTING PITFALLS

Although pretesting can do a lot to improve your materials, it is not infallible. The results are only as good as the quality of the research and interpretation. Even when pretesting is performed well, however, there are no guarantees that the program will be successful. Pretesting can give you an indication of the strengths and weaknesses of your materials, but it cannot definitively determine what will work.

Qualitative research methods, such as focus groups, are the most common form of pretesting. These methods help you to learn what the target audience members think about all aspects of your campaign, using their own words. You must be able to interpret the aggregated results to decipher what it all means. When you find many different opinions on the same issue, it might be difficult to know what to do with the information.

Be careful when interpreting qualitative research results, for they are not as straightforward as cold, hard numbers (although the latter can be tricky as well). You cannot necessarily extrapolate your results to the target population as a whole. If 3 out of 10 people in a focus group say the same thing, this does not mean that 30 % of the people in the target audience feel that way.

Picking up on group consensus or key points takes skill and discernment. Having a nonrepresentative sample of focus group participants also can cause skewed results.

Watch out for other types of bias that might be introduced into the research situation. For example, participants might provide the responses that they think you want to hear, or they might indicate agreement with the more outspoken members of a group even though they really feel differently. Testing might occur in an unnatural setting, different from the way in which people normally experience the particular campaign element you are testing. Or, the draft materials you use in your pretesting research might be so dissimilar from the final version that the feedback you received no longer is valid.

You also can run into problems when using the results of pretesting to revise your materials. Although you might think that you understand what the participants were saying, it is possible to misinterpret their comments, leading to changes that do not address the real issue. In another scenario, you might clearly understand the point made in pretesting but execute the change poorly from the target audience's point of view.

By now, it should be ingrained that the program development revolves around the target audience members. Do not, however, let them dictate every change that is to be made in your materials. Their word is important, but it is not gospel. Some of the suggestions you receive might be good but do not fit your campaign strategy, some might be unfeasible given your budget, and some might be just plain bad advice.

Avoiding these pretesting pitfalls might not be easy, but being aware of them will help. One way in which to minimize problems of unclear directives from the target audience is to pretest your materials with as many people as possible. After a while, a clear consensus might emerge. Using multiple pretesting methods, you may elicit different types of information, which can help you to better understand the responses you receive. With data from several sources, you can compensate for the weaknesses of each method.

You might want to convene a group of people working on the project to assist with interpreting the results rather than one person being solely responsible. This can check any biases a single researcher brings into his or her interpretation and also can bring in more heads to help decipher unclear points. To be extra careful, you can pretest the materials again once you believe that they are in their final form. This is especially important if you tested materials in a format that is substantially different from the way in which the target audience will experience them in the real world such as using storyboards for a television ad or black-and-white sketches of a poster.

PRETESTING CRITERIA

What criteria will you use to assess whether your materials meet your objectives? How will you define *effectiveness?* The following list suggests some of the measures you can use to determine whether you need to make changes in your overall campaign, in particular elements, or in minor details:

- *Comprehension.* Do target audience members understand the main points and secondary information? Do they understand every word being used? Are there any difficult concepts that need clearer explanations?

■ *Relevance.* Do target audience members feel that the materials were made for people like them? Can they use the information in their own lives?

■ *Noticeability.* Do the materials attract attention and jump out at the target audience? Will they break through the clutter?

■ *Memorability.* Do target audience members remember the messages and materials after they have been exposed once? Several times?

■ *Credibility.* Do target audience members think that the messages are credible? Do they recognize and trust the spokesperson or perceived source of the materials?

■ *Acceptability.* Are the materials and messages acceptable to the target audience? Do they fit within the target audience's values and culture? Are controversial or uncomfortable topics dealt with in a sensitive manner?

■ *Attractiveness.* Do target audience members think that the materials are attractive? Would they pick up the brochure, stop to read the poster, or watch the television commercial?

■ *Knowledge, attitude, and/or belief change.* After being exposed to the materials, did the target audience increase its knowledge about the subject or change its attitudes or beliefs? Did they intend to adopt the behavior change?

■ *Strong and weak points.* According to target audience members, what are the best things about your materials? If they had to change something, what would it be?

CHAPTER 15

Conducting the Pretest

Some planning is essential before starting any pretest activities. First, decide which pretesting methods you will use. Then, prepare for the pretests by developing the appropriate type of questionnaire and recruiting the participants. Interviewers or focus group moderators also will need to be trained or brought on board for the project.

Pretesting ideally should include both qualitative and quantitative research methods. The strengths of one method can help to compensate for weaknesses of another. Common pretesting methods include the following:

- Focus groups
- Intercept interviews
- Self-administered questionnaires
- Theater or natural exposure testing
- Readability testing
- Usability testing
- Expert and gatekeeper review

The following subsections provide guidance on using these methods to pretest your materials.

FOCUS GROUPS

Chapter 7 discussed the mechanics of conducting focus groups. In addition to exploratory research, focus groups are an effective format for soliciting reactions and feedback about the effectiveness of your strategy and communications. The basic structure of the groups is similar, but keep these additional considerations in mind when using focus groups for pretesting:

- Be sure that everyone can see or hear the materials or media. Make copies for all participants if they need to be able to read the text, or read the words aloud for them. Pass around illustrations or sample prototypes of your materials.

■ Rotate the order in which you present different versions of the materials in each focus group. This will reduce any bias that might arise based on comments made about the versions that were seen first.

■ Ask for general reactions first before you focus on specific design or text elements of the materials.

■ If you are trying to decide between several different graphics, show the pictures by themselves without the text to the group and ask what message they think the graphics convey. This can help you ensure that all elements of your communications match the message you want the audience to take away.

■ Encourage negative reactions if only positive ones are emerging. Participants might be hesitant to criticize the materials, especially if they think you were involved in their development. Ask a question such as, "If you had to change one thing about this, what would it be?"

■ After showing all versions, you can ask the participants to rank them in order of preference. This can be done as a group or written down and turned in individually.

INTERCEPT INTERVIEWS

Intercept interviews (sometimes called "central site" or "central location" interviews) are an efficient way in which to collect quantitative data, particularly for pretesting. Trained interviewers are stationed at a location commonly visited by the target audience such as a shopping mall, street corner, or supermarket. The interviewer then approaches people who appear to fit the target audience definition and asks them whether they would take a few minutes to answer some questions. If so, the interviewer first asks the respondent several questions (called a "screener") to determine whether he or she is a member of the target audience or specific segment you are researching. If all of the criteria are met, then the interviewer takes the respondent to a separate room or a quiet place to sit during the interview.

The interview generally lasts no longer than 15 to 20 minutes. You will get a higher participation rate if you offer an incentive such as money, a gift certificate, or food. Read the message concepts or show the draft materials to the respondent, and then ask for his or her reactions.

The questions should be in primarily multiple-choice (e.g., "Do you think the situation in the ad was very believable, somewhat believable, or not at all believable?") or short-answer format (e.g., "Where would you go for information about your health?"), with a minimal number of open-ended questions (e.g., "How would you describe the message of the ad?" or "What do you like and dislike about this poster?"). Open-ended questions, which allow the interviewee to answer a question at length, take more time and thought to answer and can be more difficult to transcribe. When pretesting several different versions of message concepts or materials, rotate the order in which you present each piece. This helps to avoid any systematic bias based on whether the materials are seen first or last.

Intercept interviews are a way of reaching a large number of people quickly and relatively inexpensively. But because the respondents are not selected randomly from the population, this method is not necessarily statistically representative or projectable to the entire target audience. You can get a good idea of which elements work and what needs to be changed as well as preferences among different versions of an ad. You should do as many interviews as necessary to begin to see patterns emerge; if most people agree on the same points, then 50 interviews with each segment might suffice, but if there are major disagreements, then you might need to conduct about 100 interviews with each segment.

If you will be conducting your intercept interviews on privately owned property such as a shopping mall or fast-food restaurant, obtain the consent of the management from the outset. Some market research companies have offices in shopping malls and specialize in intercept interviews and focus group recruitment. If you do not have a small army of volunteers or staff who can be trained as interviewers, then consider whether contracting with one of these companies is a more efficient use of your time and money.

SELF-ADMINISTERED QUESTIONNAIRES

Self-administered questionnaires are a pretesting method that gathers responses from many people simultaneously without requiring a large investment in staff time. These questionnaires can be administered to a group of people to fill out and return on the spot, to individuals in intercept interviews via an online survey, or to a large sample through the mail. If you use this method to pretest, then either show the respondents the materials in person or include them along with the questionnaire. This method might not be feasible for testing certain types of materials by mail (e.g., television and radio ads), because of the costs of duplication and mailing, but sending video or audio links via e-mail is very easy.

Consider using this method when you do not have the staff to conduct individual interviews or when you cannot meet with people in person because of time or distance. Self-administered questionnaires also allow for anonymity, which might be necessary in the case of highly sensitive topics.

Pilot test the questionnaire with 5 to 10 members of the target audience before using it to ensure that the questions and answers are clear and understandable. If you will administer the questionnaires via an online survey or by mail, then you must provide very explicit instructions because there will be no one to answer questions that might arise. Respondents will be more disposed toward filling out a short questionnaire with primarily multiple-choice questions than a 10-page survey with many spaces for long answers. Also, keep in mind the reading level of your respondents as you design the questionnaire.

The main disadvantage of using self-administered questionnaires online or by mail is the probability of a low response rate. There are several ways in which to increase the number of responses:

- Contact the potential respondents before sending out the questionnaires to request their participation. If they are not familiar with your organization, consider partnering with one that can credibly endorse the importance of your research.

- Follow up with the respondents by e-mail and/or telephone after they have received the packets and encourage them to return the questionnaires.

- Make it easy for respondents to participate by providing an active link in an e-mail that they can click and go right to the survey. If using mail, be sure to include a stamped, self-addressed envelope for them to return the questionnaire.

- Overrecruit a higher number of respondents than is statistically necessary so that if many do not return their questionnaires, you still will have the numbers you need for analysis.

- Provide an incentive for the individuals to respond such as a dollar bill enclosed with the survey or a chance to win a prize in a drawing of all respondents.

As with any survey, there is a possibility that the people who did not respond are different in some way from those who did; this is called nonresponse bias. You can reduce this bias by following up with interviews of a small sample of the nonrespondents and analyzing their answers. If there is no difference from the main sample, then nonresponse bias probably is not a problem. But if there is a difference, then you can extrapolate from that sample to the larger group of nonrespondents and add those responses back into the analysis.

Usually when using quantitative methods for pretesting, you are most interested in the numbers and percentages of people who think or respond in a particular way. If you do not have statistical expertise or statistical software, then you can tally up the responses to each multiple-choice question manually. Online surveys will automatically provide you with basic statistics for each question, without requiring additional data entry. If you have more statistical resources, then you also can compare whether people in a particular category differ from those in other categories (e.g., males vs. females, different ages, different segments). For open-ended questions, look at all of the responses together and create categories of similar answers. You can tally the categories and perform a more detailed qualitative analysis.

THEATER OR NATURAL EXPOSURE TESTING

The drawback of many pretesting methods is that the target audience does not experience the materials in the same setting as it would during the actual campaign. Theater testing and natural exposure testing are more sophisticated means of assessing the effectiveness of campaign materials such as television, radio, and magazine ads. Websites and online ads can also be tested in this way. These methods present the campaign's advertisement in the midst of other ads without telling the audience what they are evaluating. These techniques might not be practical if you have a small budget or lack the technical expertise to execute them well.

Theater (or "forced exposure") testing involves the recruitment of target audience members to a central location to ostensibly preview and evaluate a new television program (for radio, the process is essentially the same). During the session, respondents see a television program interspersed with advertisements for various products and services, either once or a number of times. The ad being pretested is inserted in the middle of the other commercials. At the end of the program, participants are given a questionnaire and asked some standard questions about their opinions of the program to continue the ruse. Then, they are requested to recall and write down the ads that they saw and the main message of each ad. At the end, the facilitator shows the test ad again and asks questions specifically about that item.

"Natural exposure" testing occurs when respondents view or hear the ad in a normal setting such as on their own television or radio at home. Day-after recall tests are one such method in which respondents are asked about the ad after it has run. On the day after it airs, a sample of approximately 200 people who saw it are interviewed, after having been told that they will be reviewing the program in which it was embedded. The questionnaire determines how many people who saw the program remembered seeing a particular commercial and whether they can remember any of the specific messages. In a variation of this approach, respondents might be prerecruited on the day the program will be aired and asked to watch. They are contacted the following day to answer the questionnaire. Cable systems in some communities will allow you to air television advertisements in specific blocks of households, so you can limit your follow-up to those that you know received the ad in their homes.

READABILITY TESTING

In printed materials, the readability of the text is critical, particularly for audiences that are likely to have lower reading levels than the general population. You can assess the readability of printed text either by hand (using a standard formula called the SMOG Readability Formula) or through a computer program (some grammar checkers and word processors provide a basic version of this feature). This will tell you the approximate level of education needed to understand the material.

Readability testing is a quick and easy method that does not require involvement of the target audience. However, it should be used as an adjunct to, rather than a replacement for, pretesting with the intended users. The results do not guarantee that an audience of a certain reading level will understand the material, but it can give you an indication of whether it is appropriate. Readability testing generally is recommended for materials that have a lot of text such as websites, print ads, and brochures.

Readability tests analyze the number of polysyllabic words and/or sentence length in a particular document. Longer sentences and more syllables mean that a higher reading level is needed by the intended audience to fully understand the material. Keep in mind that if the text includes many medical words, even if they are defined and understandable to the target audience, the score will be higher.

These tests look only at the basic structure of the text, that is, the technical details. However, making text more readable also involves the logic of each sentence; how the sentences flow into each other; the use of headings, subheadings, and bullet points; and the use of active verbs. For less literate audiences, pictures illustrating the text also might increase comprehension of the text. There is no substitute for pretesting with the target audience to assess all the different factors contributing to readability. See Appendix E for the SMOG Readability Formula.

TABLE 15.1 Comparing Pretesting Methods

Pretesting Method	Pros	Cons
Focus groups	■ Group interaction might encourage more discussion and responses ■ Excellent technique for obtaining qualitative information from many respondents at once ■ Can gather information relatively quickly	■ Should not be used when you need quantitative data ■ Participants might feel inhibited about expressing opinions if different from others ■ Participants might not be representative of target audience as a whole ■ Can be expensive
Intercept interviews	■ Quick and relatively inexpensive method ■ If location is chosen well, can interview many target audience members ■ Interviewer can clarify responses if necessary	■ Not true random sample ■ Can be difficult to tell who is target audience member ■ Interviews must be short ■ Might need permission to do interviews on private property
Self-administered questionnaires	■ Inexpensive and easy to gather many responses if done online ■ No need for interviewers ■ Can distribute by mail or in person for hard-to-reach audiences ■ Respondents can remain anonymous	■ May be difficult for low-literacy populations to read and fill out ■ Low response rate probable ■ Cannot clarify meaning of responses ■ Cannot control how participants are exposed to materials
Theater or natural exposure testing	■ Exposure to materials similar to actual campaign	■ Can be expensive ■ May require special screening facility or service
Readability testing	■ Cost free and easy to use ■ Does not require involvement of target audience	■ Only checks text ■ Cannot be used by itself
Usability testing	■ Best way to assess effectiveness of noncommunications elements ■ Observes how people would use a website/product in the real world	■ May be more difficult to code the interactions for analysis
Expert and gatekeeper review	■ Helps ensure factual accuracy and effectiveness ■ Might increase chances of public service announcements being run by an outlet or of participation by partners	■ Professionals might be too busy to assist ■ Does not substitute for target audience feedback

USABILITY TESTING

When your social marketing program includes elements that go beyond communications and require people to interact with their design, it's a good idea to conduct usability testing. This applies to websites—especially if they include functionality that goes beyond standard navigation and text—as well as other types of tools, products, or environmental design components. In this type of testing, you will observe how people interact with your products or designs. You can either let them use the product as they think it is supposed to be used without direction from you or provide them a task to complete and watch how they go about it. After you observe many people, you will see what works, as well as what is confusing and needs to be fixed, and learn the most frequently asked questions. If you are testing an environmental design change, such as redesigning a building lobby to make it easier to choose the stairs rather than the elevator, you can study the building traffic patterns to determine how people move through the lobby.

EXPERT AND GATEKEEPER REVIEW

In addition to testing the materials with the target audience, it often is helpful to include professionals in the field and representatives of intermediary organizations in the review process. The "experts" might include people with extensive knowledge of the subject matter or audience to ensure that the information provided is technically accurate and appropriate or professionals with health communication and social marketing expertise to assess the effectiveness of the product design. They can help identify any potential trouble spots that might not be brought to light with other forms of pretesting.

"Gatekeepers" are those you must work with to reach the target audience. They might be the staff of a partner organization that will be distributing the materials to their clients or members. They might be the physicians who have agreed to urge their patients to quit smoking. Or, they might be the public affairs directors at the television stations on which you plan to air your public service announcements. Without the cooperation and support of these people, you could have a difficult time distributing your materials and getting your message out to your audience. The nurse who is supposed to give patients your campaign materials probably will not do so if he or she thinks they have major problems. This goes back to the idea of who your internal and external publics are. You might need to get the "buy-in" of several different groups, each of which might want to review the materials.

Provide the draft versions of the materials to the experts or gatekeepers you deem most relevant to your project, along with a questionnaire on the aspects on which you want their opinions. You also can gather this information through telephone or in-person interviews and meetings. Have the reviewers evaluate the materials on accuracy, comprehensiveness, appropriateness for the target audience, clarity, and design.

WORKSHEET 14: PRETESTING PLANNING WORKSHEET

1. Which of the following methods will you use to pretest your messages and materials? (check all that apply)

   ❑ Focus groups

   ❑ Intercept interviews

   ❑ Self-administered questionnaires

   ❑ Theater or natural exposure testing

   ❑ Readability testing

   ❑ Usability testing

   ❑ Expert and gatekeeper review

   ❑ Other _____

2. Focus group planning

   a. Who will moderate the focus groups?

   _____

   _____

   _____

   b. Who will serve as assistant moderators?

   _____

   _____

   _____

   c. Where will the focus groups take place?

   _____

   _____

   _____

   d. With which segments will you do separate focus groups?

   Segment 1: _____

   Segment 2: _____

   Segment 3: _____

e. When will each focus group take place?

Segment 1:

Date: _____ Time: _____ to _____ a.m./p.m.

Date: _____ Time: _____ to _____ a.m./p.m.

Date: _____ Time: _____ to _____ a.m./p.m.

Segment 2:

Date: _____ Time: _____ to _____ a.m./p.m.

Date: _____ Time: _____ to _____ a.m./p.m.

Date: _____ Time: _____ to _____ a.m./p.m.

Segment 3:

Date: _____ Time: _____ to _____ a.m./p.m.

Date: _____ Time: _____ to _____ a.m./p.m.

Date: _____ Time: _____ to _____ a.m./p.m.

f. How will you recruit participants for the focus groups?

_____

_____

g. What will you offer people as an incentive to participate?

_____

_____

h. Work plan:

Activity	Who	Deadline
Develop topic guide	_____	_____
Create mockups for pretesting	_____	_____
Locate facility	_____	_____
Set dates/times of groups	_____	_____
Select/train moderator(s)	_____	_____
Recruit participants	_____	_____
Confirm attendance with participants	_____	_____
Conduct focus groups	_____	_____
Transcribe audio/write up notes	_____	_____
Analyze results	_____	_____
Write report	_____	_____

(Continued)

(Continued)

3. Intercept interview planning

   a. Who will serve as interviewers?

   _____

   _____

   _____

   b. What location(s) will you use to find participants and conduct the interviews?

   _____

   _____

   _____

   c. Between what dates or on which days will you conduct the interviews?

   _____

   _____

   _____

   d. What will you offer people as an incentive to participate?

   _____

   _____

   _____

   e. Number of responses needed: _____

   f. Work plan:

Activity	Who	Deadline
Develop questionnaire	_____	_____
Develop "screener"	_____	_____
Test questionnaire	_____	_____
Select/train interviewers	_____	_____
Select site/get permission	_____	_____
Conduct interviews	_____	_____
Input data	_____	_____
Analyze data	_____	_____
Write report	_____	_____

4. Self-administered questionnaire planning

   a. How will you select potential respondents?

   _____

   _____

   _____

b. How will you distribute the questionnaires to potential respondents?

_____

_____

_____

c. What will you offer people as an incentive to participate?

_____

_____

_____

d. Number of responses needed: _____

e. Work plan:

Activity	Who	Deadline
Develop questionnaire	_____	_____
Test questionnaire	_____	_____
Write introductory letter/e-mail	_____	_____
Send out/distribute questionnaires	_____	_____
Compile questionnaires	_____	_____
Input data	_____	_____
Analyze data	_____	_____
Write report	_____	_____

5. Theater or natural exposure testing planning

a. Which type of testing will you use?

❑ Theater ❑ Natural exposure

b. How will you recruit participants for the tests?

_____

_____

_____

c. What will you offer people as an incentive to participate?

_____

_____

_____

(Continued)

(Continued)

   d. Between what dates or on which days will you conduct the tests?

_____

_____

_____

   e. Number of responses needed: _____

   f. Work plan:

Activity	Who	Deadline
Develop test materials	_____	_____
Develop questionnaire	_____	_____
Test questionnaire	_____	_____
Recruit participants	_____	_____
Set date(s)	_____	_____
Locate theater facility	_____	_____
Select theater test facilitator	_____	_____
Contract with testing service (if using natural exposure test)	_____	_____
Input data	_____	_____
Analyze data	_____	_____
Write report	_____	_____

6. Readability testing planning

   a. What is the approximate reading level of your target audience?

      _____ grade

   b. Using the SMOG Readability Formula, what is the approximate reading level of each of your print materials?

Material	Grade Level
_____	_____
_____	_____
_____	_____

7. Usability testing

   a. What exactly will you be testing?

_____

_____

_____

b. How will you conduct observations of people using your project/design?

_____

_____

_____

8. Expert and gatekeeper review planning

a. Which experts will you ask to review your materials?

_____

_____

_____

b. Which gatekeepers will you ask to review your materials?

_____

_____

_____

c. How will you collect the feedback from the reviewers?
   - ❏ E-mail
   - ❏ Online survey
   - ❏ Mail
   - ❏ Telephone
   - ❏ Individual interviews
   - ❏ Group meetings
   - ❏ Other

d. Work plan:

Activity	Who	Deadline
Develop questionnaire	_____	_____
Identify potential reviewers	_____	_____
Contact potential reviewers	_____	_____
Compile questionnaires/feedback	_____	_____
Analyze data	_____	_____
Write report	_____	_____

Using the Pretesting Results

With all of the feedback about your materials that you have gathered from the target audience and other sources, you might be wondering, "Now what do I do?" The results might conflict with each other, there might be no consensus, or you might simply not be sure where to start. At this stage, you will analyze and interpret your pretest results, make changes to the materials based on the feedback, pretest the new versions (if necessary), and then finalize the materials.

INTERPRETING PRETEST RESULTS

Looking at all the reactions, insights, and advice you collected, sift through and categorize the information into appropriate topics (e.g., text, visual design, message concepts). In each topic, label each idea as "definitely change," "possibly change," or "do not change." Try to look at the items objectively, setting aside your own feelings about which elements you like or dislike. In addition, keep in mind that you do not have to make every change that was mentioned during the pretesting.

In your analysis, the "definitely change" items should include the following:

- Factual errors

- Unclear sentences or words

- Changes noted by a clear majority (so long as the changes are reasonable)

- Easy changes (e.g., wording, colors, layout)

- Elements or versions that definitely do not work

Throughout your pretesting activities, you probably will have noted items for this category without much problem. Many of the necessary changes will be obvious as you look at the results. The "do not change" ideas also will be fairly clear in the responses you receive from your pretesting respondents.

However, many other changes suggested by the target audience and/or professional reviewers may not be as clearly necessary. The "possibly change" items might include the following:

- Elements that some people suggested changing but with no clear consensus

- Elements that confused a few people but were understood by most people

■ Elements that might cost a lot of money to change (e.g., redoing an entire television spot, hiring a different spokesperson, using special effects)

In these cases, you will need to use your judgment as to whether the materials will really be more effective with these revisions. If so, are there ways in which you can use the suggestions without altering the elements that worked? Or, can you figure out a way in which to reduce the amount of money it would cost to implement the suggestion (if that is the concern)? You might need to prioritize the opinions you have received from different groups involved in pretesting such as target audience members, professional reviewers, and campaign partners. If there is substantial disagreement, then the target audience generally should be the ultimate arbiter (except in cases of factual error), but recognize that internal politics within the program might dictate some decisions as well. You might need to concede some points if you encounter resistance from gatekeepers or others who must provide their approval to go forward with the campaign.

WHEN ARE YOU DONE PRETESTING?

The pretesting stage can go on indefinitely, moving back and forth from message and materials development to pretesting until your results show that not a thing should be changed. For those of us in the real world, however, there soon comes a point of diminishing returns. You probably will not have enough time or money to continue the cycle for very long, and more pretesting does not guarantee effectiveness.

If pretesting elicits substantial changes in the look of the materials, messages, or medium, then you might need to go back and pretest the essentially "new" materials. If the materials do not change extensively as a result of pretesting, then you probably can assume that you are done. You will have to draw the line somewhere between the pretesting and redesign stages.

Final Materials Production Issues

Radio and Television Advertisements

■ Contact the stations on which you will be running the ads to find out their format requirements and how they prefer to receive the ads, such as via e-mail or on a DVD.

■ If you are considering using a cable television production facility, then check with your chosen stations whether the quality will be sufficient. The quality of spots taped by public access channel facilities is not necessarily high enough for regular broadcast television.

■ Determine the final number of copies you will need of the ads for duplication purposes. Also, think about whether you want the cases in which the ads will be delivered to provide any information about your campaign beyond your organization's name, spot titles, and times.

Print

■ For printed materials, you will need to work with the printer to determine the process it will use, the ink colors (the price generally increases with the number of different colors), and the quality of paper you need.

■ When the materials require folding, stapling, or other special treatment, it usually is more efficient to have the printer use its machines than for you to do it yourself.

■ If you plan to ship large quantities of the materials to other locations and your printer is not local, then it might be more cost-effective to have the printer send the materials directly to the other sites than to have your organization ship them again.

■ For newspaper or magazine ads, find out the desired format from each publication. This includes the advertisement sizes, file type, and resolution quality (dots per inch) the publication requires.

FINALIZING THE MATERIALS

After you have determined exactly how the materials will look or sound, you will need to finalize the design and produce the materials in sufficient quantities for the campaign. This includes printing posters, brochures, or other written material; duplicating television or radio ads; producing billboards or other outdoor ads; and manufacturing other types of items. Finalize the design and function of the website, and tie it in with the other materials; include the URL of the website on the ads, and offer the ads and other materials for viewing or download from the website. Solicit bids from different printers or production houses to find the most affordable vendor for your needs. You might be able to procure in-kind donations of materials/services or receive discounts if you are a nonprofit organization or can convince the vendor that yours is a worthy cause. Do not be afraid to ask; the worst vendors can do is say no, and they might even say yes.

> **Digital**
>
> - Make sure to test all aspects of your website, game, or mobile application on different operating systems, browsers, and platforms to be sure it works correctly.
>
> - You can recruit a small number of your supporters to act as beta testers, giving them full access to the site to try out and provide feedback about usability and bugs prior to making the site publicly available.
>
> - Consider the differences between the capabilities of older and newer systems your users may have, and build in different levels of functionality based on the detected system.
>
> - If you are creating a site that will feature user-generated content, preseed the sections with some of your own content to give users an idea of what you are looking for and to avoid the site feeling empty before you reach a critical mass of users.

Leave plenty of time for printing and other production work. Deadlines are notorious for being broken, and the people providing various pieces might not finish them on time, so your products might be finalized only shortly before implementation is set to begin. If necessary, you might be able to submit a rush job and pay a premium for the convenience, but advance planning will save you money and headaches.

Review all materials before they go into final production. Check the proofs from the printer to catch any final errors or misalignments of the color plates. Do not decide to make major alterations in the text or graphics at this stage because such changes will be much more expensive to make. Also, listen to or watch the master audio or video file before duplication to ensure that everything is in the proper order and was created exactly as you want it.

All individuals appearing in any of your materials (e.g., photographs, videotape, audiotape, personal stories) should sign a release form. This will allow you the unrestricted use of the materials in which they are involved so that you can use them indefinitely and in whatever fashion you deem appropriate. Professional actors and other talent might have restrictions because of union rules, but try to secure a "buy-out" through a one-time fee that allows you to use the materials indefinitely.

PILOT TESTING

The best way to gauge the potential success of your social marketing program is through pilot testing (also known as "test marketing"). This is the ultimate pretesting method. By bringing together all of the elements of the marketing mix in a real situation, the pilot test provides a "dress rehearsal" before launching the program in all locations. But if the campaign is designed for one city or community, then a pilot test might not make as much sense as it would for a statewide, regionwide, or national program.

Before you spend a substantial sum on a program that might not work in the real world, a pilot test allows you to work out the kinks and to assess the effectiveness of the marketing effort. Commercial marketers often try out a new soft drink or shampoo in a few cities around the country to gauge consumer response before introducing it nationwide; that way, if it bombs, they can quietly withdraw the product and go back to the drawing board, having spent thousands rather than millions of dollars. They also can test different pricing, packaging, and distribution strategies to see which work best.

The key to getting projectable results is in the selection of the test markets. Without pilot sites that are representative of the demographics and geographic area of the campaign, the findings might be skewed and inapplicable to the region as a whole. For example, if one of the cities used as a pilot site has a large college, then the 18- to 24-year-old population might respond differently from how it would in a primarily working-class town.

Select representative communities for the pilot sites using criteria such as the following:

- Demographics (including percentage of the target audience)

- Population size

- Resources (e.g., community organizations, funding availability)

- Prevalence of the disease or problem

- Willingness of community organizations to participate

- Political climate

- Ease of travel by program staff to site

- Media available in community

You might need to use several pilot sites to test the effects of the campaign in different types of environments and population mixes such as in metropolitan cities, smaller cities, rural areas, college towns, and cities with large numbers of retired people. If there are striking cultural differences within the geographic scope of the program such as among the West, Midwest, Northeast, and South of the United States or even between Northern and Southern California, then you should choose pilot sites in each region to detect any salient differences.

The test market can help to diagnose strengths and weaknesses of the program so that each element can be fine-tuned. Pilot testing helps the staff become experienced in operating the program and in measuring real-life costs. The pilot test differs from the full program only in its scale; implementation and evaluation occur in the same way whether it is a test market or the full-scale program (see Sections VI and VII for more information on implementation and evaluation). In fact, you might end up exploring more elements in the pilot test than you ultimately use in the regionwide implementation because you might drop some elements that did not work.

Monitor the process and outcome evaluation activities very closely to catch any potential problems or opportunities that should be addressed prior to the full implementation. Look for anything that could not be foreseen through pretesting such as problems with recruiting campaign partners, distributing the materials, or reading the phone number on the billboards. Qualitative information, such as interviews or focus groups with the target audience, can help you to know what those who have been exposed to the campaign think about it and whether they have any suggestions for improving the visibility and effectiveness of the campaign.

CASE STUDY

Pretesting Case Study: Control Your Diabetes. For Life.

The National Diabetes Education Program (NDEP), sponsored by the National Institute of Diabetes and Digestive and Kidney Diseases of the National Institutes of Health (NIH), and the Centers for Disease Control and Prevention (CDC) created the "Control Your Diabetes. For Life." campaign with the goal of helping people with diabetes engage in healthful behaviors to control blood glucose levels.[1] Development of the campaign involved reviews of the literature, advisory groups of diabetes educators and researchers, and focus groups with the many target audience segments addressed in the campaign. The focus group findings drove the development of the campaign's basic messages for each segment, which were then pretested in additional focus groups. The basic message, which was adapted to the needs of each group, was that they should take care of their diabetes so they could avoid diabetes complications, enjoy a better quality of life, and be around for their family members and loved ones.

NDEP found in its pretesting that people with diabetes were perceived as more effective spokespersons than celebrities. Men tended to respond more to fear-arousing messages, whereas women preferred messages that used testimonials from other patients or that demonstrated social support for people with diabetes. Overall, respondents favored "happy endings" in the messages that provided hope and empowerment, more than fear-arousing portrayals of the consequences of the disease.

In a series of 20 focus groups with members of specific ethnic groups, they were able to refine the messages more. In general, they preferred messages delivered by people of their own racial/ethnic backgrounds that reflected their own culture and values. For example, the importance of intergenerational relationships was a motivating factor for African Americans, and the setting of a family reunion was a familiar backdrop for ads for this group. American Indians saw diabetes as an epidemic that threatened their very survival and preferred ads that emphasized this with the message to control diabetes to ensure that Native American values and traditions would continue to be passed down to future generations. The Hispanic/Latino focus groups pointed out the fatalistic attitudes often associated with diabetes in this population and the need for messages to emphasize that diabetes is something that they can control. Asian Americans and Pacific Islanders were the only group that responded positively to factual messages from physicians who were seen as credible sources of health information. Those who had come from Asian countries with a history of totalitarian regimes also pointed out that the word *control* had negative connotations to them, so the wording was changed to "manage your diabetes" for that group. The final communications that were created for each group ended up having some messages and elements in common, but they were able to be tailored to the needs of each group based on what was found in the pretesting phase.

[1]Gallivan, J., Lising, M., Ammary, N. J., & Greenberg, R. (2007). The National Diabetes Education Program's "Control Your Diabetes. For Life." campaign: Design, implementation, and lessons learned. *Social Marketing Quarterly, 13*(4), 65–82.

Section VI

Step 5
Implementation

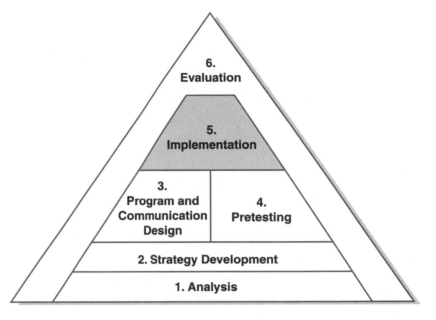

SECTION OVERVIEW

The implementation phase is where all your hard work pays off. Everything that you have developed finally sees the light of day and has a chance to work its magic on the target audience. A well-planned implementation increases the probability of reaching the right people and having the desired effect on changing behavior.

Think about NASA preparing to launch a rocket into space. Long before the craft is revving on the tarmac at Cape Canaveral, Florida, years of research and testing go into its development. Scientists orchestrate every detail of the mission, from takeoff to landing. They anticipate possible problems and plan solutions in advance. Everyone knows his or her role and is ready when the moment comes.

If you could be even a fraction as prepared as NASA in the implementation of your social marketing program, then you would have a high likelihood of success (and you do not even have to be a rocket scientist). For a flawless launch of your program, consider the following analogy:

T minus 3. Develop an implementation plan to guide you.

T minus 2. Plan media buys, social media, and public relations strategies.

T minus 1. Put monitoring systems and program elements in place.

T minus 0. We have liftoff!

This section consists of the following chapters:

- Chapter 17: Developing an Implementation Plan
- Chapter 18: Planning and Buying Traditional Media
- Chapter 19: Engaging in Social Media
- Chapter 20: Generating Publicity
- Chapter 21: Monitoring Implementation

Developing an Implementation Plan

Rather than jumping into implementation as soon as your materials are ready, take some time to plan each necessary step. The implementation plan covers all of the preparatory activities as well as what will happen after the program is introduced. A comprehensive plan includes the following elements:

- Deployment plan
- Public relations plan
- Social media engagement plan
- Internal readiness plan

DEPLOYMENT PLAN

How will you put all the pieces of your program in place prior to implementation? A deployment plan will help you to think through all the steps involved in producing your materials and getting them from Point A to Point B (it is not always a straight line), as well as installing any structural or environmental features of your program prior to launch. The questions to consider in creating the plan include the following:

What are your dissemination channels? Do you need to set up accounts on various social media sites or design a website? Do you have partner organizations that will hand out brochures and put up posters? Do partners need to be brought on board? Do you have radio, television, or other media materials that will be placed with media outlets, either as public service announcements or as paid advertisements?

What noncommunication elements of the strategy need to be put into place before launch? If there are changes to the environment that need to occur, have the necessary measures been taken to make them happen? This may involve physical construction, installation of items for the target audience to use, redesign of forms or processes, or other changes that are part of the strategy.

How many copies of each communication piece do you need? Estimate the potential demand for items that will be requested or picked up by the target audience so that you know the quantities to produce. Add enough extra leeway that you can replace materials if they are used up early in the campaign. For television or radio spots, print advertisements, or other media, create enough copies for all of the outlets you will use. Make extra copies for yourself and your partners to have on hand in case additional opportunities emerge in which you can use them.

How will you keep track of your inventory? If you do not already have one, create an inventory tracking system. This might be as simple as creating a form that you fill out each time materials are sent out. Or, it might be as advanced as a computerized database that automatically deducts the number of materials sent from the total inventory. At the end of each week or month, assess whether you still have sufficient quantities to last through the campaign. You can give your campaign partners a reorder form to make the process as easy as possible when they need more materials.

Does everyone know how to distribute the materials? Whether your own staff or that of other organizations, ensure that all involved know what to do once they have the materials in hand. Provide very clear instructions as to how the materials are to be distributed. Will they be placed in waiting rooms? On countertops of local businesses? Will they be handed out directly to their clients? Spell out clearly what you want done with the materials, or they might end up sitting in the box.

PUBLIC RELATIONS PLAN

The media can be a very effective ally in getting your message out to your target audience. Use public relations strategies to attract coverage by the "free" media such as news outlets and talk shows. The particular methods you can use to generate publicity are covered in Chapter 20, but you can start to think about how to incorporate the media into your implementation.

Use a kickoff event to introduce your campaign to the media and the community. This could be a press conference in which you preview your ads and explain how and why the campaign was developed. Other ideas include the following:

- Walk-a-thon or fun run
- Health fair
- Expert panel discussion
- Online launch across social networks
- Concert
- Disease screening
- Celebrity appearance

The event you offer should meet three criteria. First, it must attract members of your target audience. Second, it must communicate your message. Third, it must be considered newsworthy enough by the media for them to cover it or be interesting enough to generate social media buzz.

Your public relations plan also should specify which media outlets you will target. If your campaign covers a large city, state, or even more territory, then you might have an overwhelming

Media Directories

Bacon's Media Directories
(866) 639-5087
http://www.cision.com

BurrellesLuce Media Contacts
(800) 368-8070
http://www.burrellesluce.com/Media_Contacts

Gebbie's All-in-One Directory
(845) 255-7560
http://www.gebbieinc.com

Vocus
(301) 459-2827
http://www.vocus.com

number of choices of television, radio, newspapers, and magazines to sift through. You can narrow down your choices by consulting a directory of media outlets that identifies the audiences targeted or the type of programming each offers. Some cities also might have media directories specifically for their local areas; check your local library.

Build a media contact list that includes the critical information about each outlet. You should be able to get much of the data from a media directory, but to be safe, contact each station or publication to make sure that you have the most up-to-date information. Staff turnover is high in the media, and to have the best chance of getting your materials to the right person, you need to know who covers your topic. Keep an eye out for which reporters or columnists cover key "beats" (topics), such as health, environment, children and families, metro (local issues), social issues, and government agencies, and who the relevant people are in the newsroom, such as the assignments editor and editorial page editor.

Wire services, such as Associated Press, United Press International, and Reuters, are an efficient way of reaching many news organizations with your story at once. Most newsrooms subscribe to at least one wire service, through which they learn of breaking news as it happens. Some newspapers and news websites use stories they get off the wire word for word, whereas others use them as background for original articles. The wire services usually have bureaus in major cities, state capitals, and some smaller cities. There might even be an independent wire service that gathers and distributes information particularly for your state or region. Some wire services specialize in distributing information for nonprofits, such as AScribe and the Nonprofit Newswire. Many wire services publish "daybooks," which provide details of upcoming events that their subscribing news organizations might want to cover. Your media contact list for the wire services should include most of the same people noted previously as well as the names of the relevant bureau chiefs.

SOCIAL MEDIA ENGAGEMENT PLAN

In addition to having your social media tools set up on time for the program launch (and ideally much earlier than that to be able to start to build a base of followers), you will need to create a plan for how your program will engage with people via social media. Decide who on the project will be responsible for coordinating the overall content used on the different types of social media sites. You may want several people to interact as individuals on their own accounts as representatives of the program or as a team through a single account that funnels everything through one place.

Depending on which tools you are going to use in the campaign—whether it's blogs, social networks, Twitter, online video, or other social sharing sites—create a plan for how much time the responsible staff member(s) will spend on interacting through those venues. You can create an editorial calendar to guide the themes to focus on from week to week or even day to day (e.g., guest blogger every Wednesday, resource round-up every Friday).

A social media policy will be important to guide how those representing your organization or campaign engage online. Some of the factors to include in the policy include the following:

■ Who is authorized to act as an official representative for the project

■ Approval process for online content

■ Level of personal content that is appropriate

■ Criteria to decide who to follow/friend on the official account

■ Disclosure guidelines when commenting on blogs and other sites

■ Information about the project that is and is not appropriate to share online

Set up a social media monitoring system (described in Chapter 19) to start tracking where conversations about your issue and program are happening online. You can create a set of criteria to determine when to respond to blog posts, tweets, or other online comments. For example, depending on the amount of time you have to devote to social media, you may want to prioritize your interactions to people from your own specific community (if you have a local program) or to those who are talking about your specific campaign or organization. The Air Force created a flowchart to help its staff know when and how to respond to comments on blogs (see Figure 17.1), and this model could also be used to determine responses to other types of social media conversations as well.

INTERNAL READINESS PLAN

Because you probably have been the main person thinking about the social marketing program from Step 1 until now, you know the campaign's goals and objectives, target audience, main messages, and planned procedures inside and out. Do not forget, however, that others in your organization might have only a vague notion of what you have been doing. To prepare others in your organization for implementation and to bring them on as part of the social marketing team, educate your staff, volunteers, and partners' staff about what you are trying to do. You can gather people for a short meeting to explain the campaign or conduct an intensive training on social marketing and how the campaign was created.

Depending on how involved others in the organization will be in the implementation phase, you might need to spend time going over each person's role. If, for example, you are publicizing a toll-free number, then be sure that the people answering the phones know what to do, particularly with common questions or requests. Create a telephone protocol that makes it easy for the phone answerers to know what to say or key questions to ask. Or, if nurses are supposed to hand out a "prescription for exercise" from the campaign, talk to them about who the target audience is and how best to incorporate the prescription into the visit. Clinic managers might need

FIGURE 17.1   Air Force Blog Assessment Flowchart

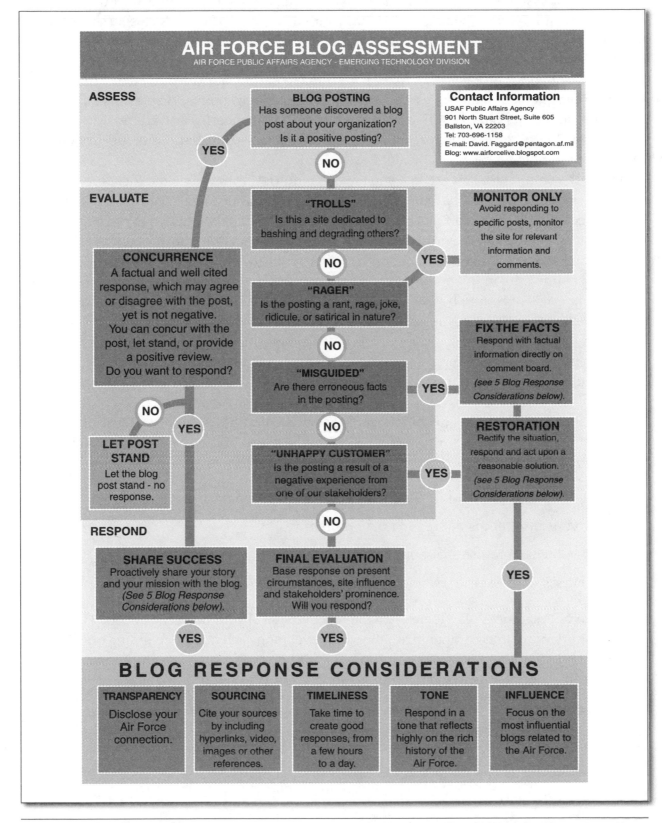

Source: Air Force Public Affairs Agency, Emerging Technology Division, 2008 (first published online at http://www .webinknow.com/2008/12/the-us-air-force-armed-with-social-media.html).

to be explicitly told to put up posters and to set campaign materials on the tables in the waiting rooms. Do not assume that everyone knows what to do, even if it is obvious to you.

Be very clear in your expectations of what your partners will do. Work closely with them to prepare for implementation and ensure that they perform their roles correctly. Set discrete objectives for what you want to accomplish through the partnership, and give the partners tasks that are reasonable. The easier you make it for them to participate, the more likely they will do it right. Give them digital copies of your materials, talking points, display racks for your brochures, and other aids. Listen to their suggestions and concerns, and address them whenever possible. Also, make sure to acknowledge your partners' contributions to the program and thank them publicly when possible.

During the campaign, you are likely to receive inquiries from the media for more information and you may get reactions from the community, both positive and negative. To avoid panic-stricken receptionists and staff, have a plan in place prior to implementation to respond to these types of situations. Anyone who answers the phone or interacts with others outside of the program should know what to do if faced with a persistent reporter or an irate caller.

Designate one person in your organization to serve as the spokesperson for the social marketing program. This could be the project director or someone else who is comfortable with public speaking and knows the project well. You also can designate someone to serve as a backup in case the primary spokesperson is not available. All calls or communications requiring any type of public comment regarding the campaign should be directed to these people. They should be prepared to respond as needed and ideally should have some media relations training.

Create some talking points to help the spokesperson communicate the key ideas of the campaign to the media or others who might call with questions. These points should include the following:

- Facts about the problem including local statistics (if you have them)
- How your program is addressing the problem
- Why you chose to use that approach
- Responses to foreseeable objections to your program

The internal readiness plan focuses on the reactive side of your outreach efforts. This can be just as important to your campaign as other public relations activities, depending on who contacts you and what they do with the information. If your organization is unprepared when a reporter calls, then the headline story in the local news the next day might feature your program's critics along with an inappropriate quote from your receptionist.

WORKSHEET 15: BUILDING A MEDIA CONTACT LIST

Use this worksheet as a model for your media contact list. You can use one page for each entry or create a database that includes each field.

Broadcast Outlets

1. Date entered: _____

2. Station call letters: _____ Frequency or channel number: _____

3. Main phone number: _____

4. Does the station accept press releases by: ❑ Fax? ❑ E-mail? ❑ Website submission?

5. Fax number: _____

6. E-mail address: _____

7. URL: _____

8. Newscasts

Time of Broadcast	Relevant Segments (e.g., health, consumer news)	Deadline/When to Call	News Director	Phone/E-mail
_____	_____	_____	_____	_____
_____	_____	_____	_____	_____
_____	_____	_____	_____	_____
_____	_____	_____	_____	_____

9. Public affairs programs:

Day/Time of Broadcast	Name of Show	Deadline/When to Call	Producer of Show	Phone/E-mail
_____	_____	_____	_____	_____
_____	_____	_____	_____	_____
_____	_____	_____	_____	_____
_____	_____	_____	_____	_____
_____	_____	_____	_____	_____

(Continued)

(Continued)

10. Talk show programs:

Day/Time of Broadcast	Name of Show	Deadline/ When to Call	Producer of Show or Host	Phone/E-mail
_____	_____	_____	_____	_____
_____	_____	_____	_____	_____
_____	_____	_____	_____	_____
_____	_____	_____	_____	_____

11. Notes/other information:

_____

_____

_____

Print Publications

1. Date entered: _____

2. Publication name: _____

3. Main phone number: _____

4. Does the publication accept press releases by: ❑ Fax? ❑ E-mail? ❑ Website submission?

5. Fax number: _____

6. E-mail address: _____

7. URL: _____

8. Publication type:

❑ Newspaper ❑ Magazine ❑ Online Version of Print

❑ Newsletter ❑ Journal ❑ Other _____

9. Publication frequency:

____ Daily ____ Weekly ____ Monthly ____ Other _____

10. Deadlines (e.g., time, day of week, month):

_____

_____

_____

11. Best time to call: _____

12. Editors:

Title	Name	Phone Number/E-mail
Assignments editor	_____	_____
Editorial page editor	_____	_____
Features editor	_____	_____
Metro editor	_____	_____
Political editor	_____	_____
_____	_____	_____
_____	_____	_____

13. Reporters/columnists:

Beat/Column	Name	Phone Number/E-mail
_____	_____	_____
_____	_____	_____
_____	_____	_____
_____	_____	_____

14. Notes/other information:

_____
_____
_____

Online News Sites/Blogs

1. Date entered: _____

2. Website name _____

3. URL: _____

4. Website type:

   ❏ News site   ❏ Blog   ❏ Online Magazine

   ❏ Podcast   ❏ Video   ❏ Other _____

(Continued)

(Continued)

5. E-mail address: _____

6. Relevant topics covered:

_____

_____

_____

7. Update frequency:

____ Daily   ____ Weekly   ____ Sporadically   ____ Other _____

8. Bloggers/editors/writers:

Name	E-mail	Role/Topics
_____	_____	_____
_____	_____	_____
_____	_____	_____

CHAPTER 18

Planning and Buying
Traditional Media

For those who have never done it before, buying ad space or broadcast time on radio, television, print, outdoor, or online advertising can be somewhat intimidating. But you do not have to be an advertising whiz to be able to place your own advertisements in the media. With an introduction to how it all works, you can navigate the world of media buys yourself to save your organization money and have more control over the process. Or, if you have a more complex media buy, you may decide to work with a professional media buyer who knows the ins and outs and can save you time and money.

Traditionally, advertising agencies receive a 15% commission when they place an ad, which is paid by the media outlet. The client pays the full cost (or "gross rate") to the agency, and the agency then pays the station or publication the "net" rate, which is 15% less than the gross rate. The 15% is built into the cost of the ad, so even if you are not working through an agency, you might be able to negotiate that rebate. Alternatively, you can work with an independent media service, which is staffed by experts in media placement and rate negotiation. These firms generally work for a commission of 10% or less or a fixed fee negotiated with you, which can save you money over the traditional commission structure. An hourly or flat rate removes the inherent disincentive for them to negotiate aggressively on your behalf that a commission-based fee fosters.

PAID VERSUS FREE MEDIA

Why pay to place an ad when you can have it run as a public service announcement (PSA) for free? Actually, your campaign will benefit much more as a result of investing money into media buys. Of course, if you do not have enough money to pay for your media placements, then PSAs are an alternative. Distributing your ads directly online through video sites such as YouTube is also a cost-effective way of reaching your audience if you promote them through your other outreach efforts and make them compelling enough that people want to share them.

The chief advantage of buying media time or space is that you can direct exactly when and where the ad runs. If you know that members of your target audience tend to listen to a particular radio station as they drive to work in the morning, then you can ensure that your ad will run at that time. Or, if you want to place your ad in the sports section of the newspaper, then

Determining Reach and Frequency

The two main variables you need to consider as you plan your media buys are reach and frequency. Reach refers to the number or percentage of people who see or hear your ad at least once during a given period of time (usually 4 weeks). Frequency is the number of times the average person or household sees or hears your ad during that period of time. You might not be able to pinpoint your target audience segments beyond basic demographic descriptions unless the outlet providing the ratings information has additional variables available for analysis.

One way of comparing the relative efficiencies of various media vehicles in reaching your audience is by calculating the cost per thousand (CPM) to reach your audience for each station or publication. Just divide the cost for each option by the number of people you will reach through that medium (divide the number of people by 1,000 first). For example, a television ad that reaches 800,000 people at a cost of $10,000 (10,000 divided by 800 yields a CPM of $12.50) is less efficient than a newspaper ad that reaches 50,000 people at a cost of $300 (300 divided by 50 provides a CPM of $6.00).

To decipher the Arbitron and Nielsen charts, you need to know that a rating point equals 1% of the total audience. Gross rating points (GRPs) are the total number of rating points in your overall advertising schedule, or the percentage of people you will reach. This is a function of reach multiplied by frequency; for the same amount of money, you can reach more people less often or fewer people more often.

The charts will show both the ratings for each station (the percentage of the audience who have watched or listened to a particular station at least once during that period of time) and the audience share of each station (out of all the people watching television or listening to the radio at that moment in time, the percentage who were tuned to a particular station). You probably will be more interested in the ratings so that you can determine the percentage of the total audience you are reaching, not just those who happen to be flipping the channels at a given moment. Target rating points (TRPs) refer to ratings based on your specific target audience.

The salespeople at each station can help you calculate when and how many times you need to run the advertisement to reach a certain percentage of the target audience. You can either ask them to suggest a schedule that will maximize the TRP you can achieve within your budget or tell them the percentage of the target audience you would like to reach, as well as how many times on average (in essence, the TRP), and they will provide a figure. Most stations and media services have computer programs that will help them determine the most efficient and effective schedule based on your specifications.

you can guarantee that by purchasing the space. The more flexible you can be, the less the placement will cost, but you lose the benefit of targeting your audience precisely.

When you submit broadcast or print materials as PSAs, you are relying on the good graces of the media outlet to run them at all, let alone in a favorable position. If you have ever watched television at 3 a.m., you probably have seen several PSAs in the commercial breaks. But when was the last time you saw one during prime time? Unless your target audience includes a lot of insomniacs, you cannot count on reaching many people with PSAs. Once in a while, you might encounter a public service director who feels strongly about your message and schedules it in a prominent spot, but that is the exception rather than the rule. Developing long-term relationships with the public service directors at major media outlets and educating them about your issue can help improve the visibility of your PSA. Or, you might be able to obtain in-kind donations of media time from corporate or media partners. Repetition and access to the target audience are the keys to effective media placement, and these are hard to obtain through PSAs.

BROADCAST MEDIA BUYS

If you are not working through a media service, call the radio or television stations that you know or think that your audience watches or listens to. Ask to speak with someone in advertising sales, and talk to an account executive about what you wish to accomplish through your social marketing program. Tell him or her about the target audience you are trying to reach, particularly its demographics. Ask each outlet to send you a media kit (or download it from their website), which includes information about the station, its rate card, and a chart of the latest Arbitron (for radio) or Nielsen (for television) ratings for your target audience. The ratings will give you an idea of where the station ranks compared to others in the same market (geographic area) for your audience's demographics at certain times of the day. Look at the rankings to see whether there are other stations listed near the top that you should consider.

You can purchase radio and television ad spots at particular times of day ("dayparts" in broadcast parlance) or for specific programs. Or, you can select "run of station" (ROS) programming, which means that the station determines when your spot fits into its schedule throughout its on-air time; this usually is the least expensive option and provides coverage throughout the day. Consider your target audience's lifestyle and when it is most apt to be listening to the radio or watching television. High school students are not likely to have access to radios during school hours but might listen while socializing after school or on weekends. Stay-at-home moms might have an opportunity to watch late morning talk shows on television but turn the tube over to the kids when they get home from school. The account executive can help you figure out the best times or programs for your needs.

If your campaign is nationwide, then you should work with the network salespeople who sell space at a national level. This means that you will not have to contact every station across the country but rather will deal with only a few people. More likely, you will want to reach people within a particular state or metropolitan area. In that case, you will buy spot television or spot radio by working directly with the stations in that market. In some cases, the same company might own more than one station in the area you want and could provide less expensive "combo" rates if you purchase ads on two or more of its stations. Do not forget about cable television; it allows you to reach a very specific niche (e.g., ESPN, Telemundo, HGTV, Syfy) and to run commercials within a small geographic area. As of 2009, 86% of U.S. households subscribe to a cable or satellite television provider,[1] but those without it might be the very audience you need to reach. Talk to a cable salesperson to determine the stations and programs that might work for you.

When determining how to structure your advertising schedule, consider whether you want to run your spots in rotation or in flights (see Figure 18.1). Scheduling the ads in rotation means that the station airs them regularly during a specific period of time. The spots can rotate horizontally (scheduled at the same time each day to reach regular drive-time listeners or viewers of a particular program) or vertically (at different times throughout the same day to catch the audience members whenever they might tune in). Scheduling in flights means that the spots run for a set amount of time (whether 4 weeks, 6 weeks, or another period), then are not run for the same amount of time, and then appear again for another flight. This helps stretch your budget by making it seem that the ads have been running during the entire period. Your ads should run a minimum of 10 times per week, although 18 often is used as the norm. Some times of the year are more expensive than others, such as the Christmas holiday season, so you might want to plan your campaign around those periods.

Once you have looked over the stations' rate cards or received price quotes and have narrowed down the most appropriate outlets to reach your audience, it is time to talk to the account executives again. Think of the price on the rate card as the "suggested retail price"; rates almost always are negotiable. Ask whether the station offers a nonprofit rate (if appropriate) or

---

[1]Leichtman Research Group. (n.d.). *Gap in satisfaction between cable and DBS subscribers narrowing.* http://www.leichtmanresearch.com/press/052109release.html

FIGURE 18.1   Sample Flight Plan

Contact information:	Jane Smith
	The Health Council
	123 Main Street
	Springfield, XY 12345
	Phone: (123) 456-7890
	Fax: (123) 456-7891
	E-mail: jsmith@springfieldhealthcouncil.org
Station:	KXYZ-FM 109.9
Spots:	Save a Life 30 seconds
	Go for It 30 seconds
Dates:	February 1 to March 28 and June 1 to July 26

Rotation:

Daypart	Number of Spots/Week	Daypart	Number of Spots/Week
Monday–Friday		*Saturday–Sunday*	
6 a.m–10 a.m.	10	10 a.m.–3 p.m.	5
10 a.m.–3 p.m.	10	7 p.m.–12 midnight	5
3 p.m.–7 p.m.	10		
7 p.m.–12 midnight	10		

Total ads per week:	50
Total weeks:	16
Total ads:	800
Cost per ad:	$100
Total cost:	$80,000

whether it can reduce the price because of the public service nature of the ads. You might be able to get a "buy one, get one free" rate, where for every ad you buy, you receive another ad as a PSA (which the station can place anywhere in the schedule). Or, the station might offer special promotional opportunities such as broadcasting live from your organization's event, including information about your program in its newscast, and naming your organization as a sponsor of one of its regular features (e.g., "This traffic report is brought to you by the Regional Bicycle Coalition. Bike to work tomorrow and leave the traffic behind.").

Once you are ready to make the buy, make a list of all the information you need to know or need to convey to each station so that you can keep it all straight. Talk to the salespeople at each station to find out what is available that meets your specifications and to try to bring the price down or get more value in other ways. Once they have provided a proposed package of spots that is acceptable to you in GRPs and price, reserve the spots verbally. Within a day or so, the station will provide you with a written confirmation or contract detailing your agreement, or your contact might ask you to send a "flight plan" with all your specifications. Find out when the station needs to have the spots (usually at least 48 hours before the schedule begins) and what audio file format it prefers.

After the ads have gone on the air, you will receive an affidavit of performance certifying when your ads were broadcast (generally at the end of each month). This should include any ads run as PSAs as well. Check the affidavit against your original order to make sure that the station delivered as promised. If new ratings have come out since you ordered the spots, you might wish to assess whether your ads achieved the GRPs originally promised. If you notice any problems, talk to the salesperson immediately to see whether he or she can rectify the situation through "make-goods" (running the ad again if it was not run correctly or at all) or credits for future advertising.

PRINT MEDIA BUYS

The process and principles involved in purchasing advertising space in a newspaper or magazine are very similar to those of broadcast media. The concepts of reach and frequency apply in the same way, but the audience reached is measured by the publication's paid circulation rather than by ratings points. Of course, more people might see the publication than are counted in the official circulation figure as a result of "pass-along" readership (others reading the same copy) and copies that are given away.

To identify the publications that will reach your target audience, you have several options. One source of information is the Standard Rate & Data Service (SRDS), which publishes several directories with information for advertisers on newspapers, consumer magazines, and business publications. The SRDS directories offer information on each publication's intended audience, circulation, rates, and production requirements as well as other useful pieces of information. Another helpful source is Mediamark Research, Inc., which regularly publishes data on readership of consumer magazines according to demographics. If, for example, you wanted to know which publications reach a higher than average proportion of men from 18 to 34 years of age who are married with no children and earning more than $50,000 a year, you might find that you should consider magazines such as *Fortune, Wired,* and *Men's Fitness.* Other media directories, such as those listed previously, will let you know what publications are published in a particular geographic area. Many public libraries have these directories available at their reference desks.

When you have an idea of the publications that are most likely to reach your audience, contact each newspaper's or magazine's display advertising department (display ads are provided

Radio and Television Dayparts

Advertising rates generally are determined by the daypart in which the ad runs. (Please note that slight variations in times may occur according to station or region of the country.)

Radio Dayparts

Morning drive-time	6:00 a.m.–10:00 a.m.
Midday	10:00 a.m.–3:00 p.m.
Afternoon drive-time	3:00 p.m.–7:00 p.m.
Night	7:00 p.m.–12:00 a.m.
Overnight	12:00 a.m.–6:00 a.m.

Television Dayparts

Early morning	6:00 a.m.–9:00 a.m.
Daytime	9:00 a.m.–3:30 p.m.
Early fringe	3:30 p.m.–5:30 p.m.
Early news	5:30 p.m.–7:00 p.m.
Prime access	7:00 p.m.–8:00 p.m.
Prime time	8:00 p.m.–11:00 p.m.
Late news	11:00 p.m.–11:30 p.m.
Late fringe	11:30 p.m.–1:00 a.m.
Late night	1:00 a.m.–6:00 a.m.

in a graphical layout, as opposed to classified ads, which generally involve lines of print only). Ask an advertising salesperson to send you a media kit (or download it from the website), including a rate card, readership demographics, production requirements, and a few recent sample issues. When you receive the kit, look everything over and consider whether that publication is likely to appeal to your target audience and whether the editorial content is compatible with your advertisements.

Among the pieces of information in the media kit that are most important for you to note and understand are the following:

- *Publication schedule.* Is the publication daily, weekly, monthly, or quarterly? What day is each issue sent out? Is it different from the date on the cover?

- *Closing dates.* By when do you need to reserve the space verbally? What is the deadline for getting the ad to the publication? What is the space cancellation date (after which you must pay for the ad even if you decide not to run it)?

- *Size of advertising units.* Does the publication sell space by the column-inch (the number of columns wide by the number of inches deep), by another unit, or by preset modular sizes (e.g., one-half page, one-eighth page)? How wide are the columns in the publication? What is the size of the page?

- *Cost.* What is the price per column-inch (or other unit)? Does the publication offer nonprofit rates? Does it offer frequency discounts? If so, do you need to sign a contract to receive the discount? Are there combo deals you can get with ads on the publication's website?

- *Format.* What graphic format does the publication require? Can it lay out an ad for you if you supply the text? Can you supply preprinted inserts to disseminate in copies of the publication?

- *Placement.* Does the publication charge extra to place an ad on the page or in the section you request? What sections are available, and are there any special issues or advertorials coming up?

- *Geographic targeting.* Is it possible to place the ad in publications that will go to only certain parts of the metropolitan area or regions of the country?

Call and speak with a salesperson at each publication to reserve space in the issues in which you would like to place your ad(s). Be prepared to provide the publication date(s), the size of the ad(s), and any special instructions you have regarding placement (see Figure 18.2). Find out the closing date to get the materials to their offices (usually 2 or 3 days before publication for newspapers, 30 to 90 days for magazines), and get a final quote on the rate. Newspapers and magazines usually are not as willing to negotiate on their rates as are broadcast media, but you might be able to get a lower nonprofit rate or a frequency discount if you agree to buy a certain number of ads or amount of space.

Follow the publication's instructions regarding uploading or e-mailing the digital ad files, along with an insertion order, to the production team. The insertion order should consist of a written version of the information you provided when you verbally reserved the space.

FIGURE 18.2   Sample Print Insertion Order

Contact:	Jane Smith			
	The Health Council			
	123 Main Street			
	Springfield, XY 12345			
	Phone: (123) 456-7890			
	Fax: (123) 456-7891			
	E-mail: jsmith@springfieldhealthcouncil.org			
Publication:	The Springfield Gazette			
Ad rate:	$45.60 per column-inch (nonprofit rate)			
Instructions:	Please place the ads in the Sports section			

Issue	*Ad Size*	*Size Provided*	*Description of Ad*	*Price*
March 25	3 columns × 7"	5" × 7"	"Safety First"	$957.60
April 11	2 columns × 4"	4.25" × 4"	"Go for It"	$364.80
April 30	4 columns × 5"	8.5" × 5"	"Save a Life"	$912.00
May 6	2 columns × 4"	4.25" × 4"	"Go for It"	$364.80
			Total:	$2,599.20

After your ads run, you should receive documentation of the fact. You do not need to purchase issues of each publication to check the ads; the publication will send you tear sheets of each page your ad is on. When you receive the tear sheets, check them to be sure that the ads ran as ordered and make sure that the reproduction quality is satisfactory. Any problems should be promptly reported to the salesperson so that he or she can provide a make-good ad or adjust your invoice accordingly.

OUT-OF-HOME MEDIA BUYS

Out-of-home (OOH) media include outdoor advertising such as billboards and painted signs, transit ads, and other types of displays. These media can reach a large proportion of the total population but are more difficult for narrowly targeting demographics below the level of neighborhood. The companies that own the billboards and other OOH media and provide the printed sheets, paint, and construction are called "plants." Different plants may specialize in particular media such as the following:

- Billboard posters and wallscapes
- Painted bulletins (signs)
- Bus and subway signs (inside and outside)
- Subway station and bus shelter displays
- Taxi advertising and mobile billboards

- Airport terminal and shopping mall displays

- Restroom stall posters

- Postcard racks

- Aerial advertising

- Movie theater screens

- "Wild posting" on construction side barricades, building sides, etc.

OOH media buys are sold based on packages called GRP showings, that is, the degree of market coverage you get when you buy a certain number of postings. The quantity you purchase depends on where the displays are located, how many people see them every day, and the percentage of the population you wish to reach. If, for example, you purchase a No. 50 GRP showing, then half the adult population of that market will be exposed to your message every day, and by the end of a month, your advertising will have reached 75% of the audience with a frequency of 15 times each.

Shapes and sizes vary depending on the type of medium. Billboard posters most commonly come in two sizes: 30 sheets (12 feet high by 24 feet wide) and 8 sheets (5 feet high by 11 feet wide). Painted bulletins can range from 10 to 20 feet high by 40 to 80 feet wide. Transit signs depend on the particular system and the location of the signs.

Speak with a salesperson or sales "rep" who sells the type of OOH media in which you are interested. He or she can provide detailed information on rates, where postings will be available, achievable reach and frequency, and demographic coverage. The OOH plant generally provides both the production of materials and ad space. Each plant has a rate card that explains the market and how GRP showings are priced. You also can refer to DOmedia's comprehensive database of OOH vendors of all types (http://www.domedia.com/), which includes information on rates, production specifications, and other key data.

Once you have decided how you would like to proceed, ask the salesperson to take you on a "preride," in which he or she drives you around to view each location you are considering purchasing. This gives you an opportunity to see whether there are any problems (e.g., construction) that might interfere with your target audience seeing the ad.

Most types of OOH media are sold in 30-day increments, although some more permanent signs may be sold in 3-month to 3-year blocks. As with broadcast and print media, you can try to negotiate a better deal than that initially offered. For example, you might be able to get a bonus month or additional posters during the scheduled period. Or, the plant might agree to leave your posters up after your run until someone else purchases that location, which could be several months. You most likely will sign a contract committing to your buy in writing.

Provide the OOH plants with complete posting and painting instructions, along with the produced materials, if you are producing them. Check with the plant for the best format in which to provide your artwork. Find out the deadlines for the posting dates you want and make sure that the plants have the materials in time. Once they are up, you can make a "postride" to ensure that the materials were posted as contracted and that they remain in good condition throughout their scheduled period.

ONLINE MEDIA BUYS

When done in a relevant way, advertising on websites can be effective in reaching your audience. The key is in determining the right type of online marketing and making sure your ads are appearing on the sites frequented by your audience. When you target the people who are looking for information related to your issue or can pinpoint which websites are most popular with the people you are trying to reach, you can be more efficient in reaching them. Unlike the other types of media buys, most online media space is purchased through automated systems and uploaded directly by you.

Search Engine Advertising

Search engine advertising takes advantage of the fact that you can put a link to your campaign in front of people who are at that moment looking for related information. Google AdWords is the most well-known service, and most other search engines offer similar advertising services (e.g., Yahoo! Search Marketing and Microsoft adCenter on Bing). Your ads show up when people search on the keywords and user characteristics you have specified for your campaign. For example, a Montana-based social marketing program to increase animal adoptions from shelters rather than purchases from pet stores might choose to run its ads to people from the state who search for keywords such as

- pet stores
- dog breeders
- (dog or puppy or cat or kitten) adoption
- dog for sale
- animal rescue

Online keyword tools can help you make sure you find all the most likely searches related to your issue. Your ad would be shown in a box by the search results to people who used those keywords. The ad can also run on websites that are part of that service's network (e.g., Google AdSense), when keywords on individual web pages match your criteria, expanding the number of people exposed in a relevant context.

To purchase search engine ads, look for a link from the home page (usually at the bottom) that refers to the advertising program. You will need to create an account, and then the program will lead you through the options. Specify the geographic area, language, keywords to target, the headline and text of the ad, and the URL to which the ad links. You will also need to determine your daily budget—how much you are willing to spend per day—and how much you are willing to pay each time someone clicks on your ads. The more you bid on the cost per click (CPC), relative to the other people who are also bidding on those keywords, the more likely your ad will be shown at or near the top of the list. The service will track how many people click on your ads and what keywords or sites they used; this can help you refine your campaign to focus on what works best.

Social Network Site Ads

Purchasing advertising on social network sites gives you the opportunity to reach your audience in a very targeted way. Because people share so much personal information about themselves and their interests, the sites are able to offer the ability to show your ads to people who have noted specific interests. Beyond standard demographic variables such as geography, sex, age, education level, marital and parental status, networks such as Facebook and MySpace let you dig deeper into interest and occupation categories. For example, on MySpace you can target people who

- Spend time working out
- Are childcare workers
- Count the Bible as their favorite book
- Like to eat junk and fast food
- Go boating in their spare time
- Listen to country music

If you have a community-based boating safety campaign, you can show your ads only to those who list boating as a favorite activity and live in your community. Or if you are reaching out to childcare workers with a campaign to improve the nutritional quality of the food they serve their charges, a customized ad campaign might be welcomed. On Facebook, you can also extend the ads to people who have identified themselves as fans of a particular brand or campaign, as well as to their friends.

To purchase an ad on a social network site on which your audience spends time, first think about what you want the ad to look like. On Facebook, the ad format is standardized, with the only differences being the graphic and text. MySpace runs banner ads, which allows for more customization. Other social networks offer different types of ads as well; for example, hi5 provides the options of taking over the homepage, offering users a branded profile page "skin," sponsoring free branded virtual gifts, adding your video as "preroll" when a user plays a game, or running ads on the hi5 mobile site. Check the advertising section for the social network site in which you are interested to learn about the options and design requirements.

Similarly to search engine ads, advertising on social network sites requires that you set a budget (daily or total campaign lifetime), determine how long you want ads to run, and bid on how much you are willing to pay. You will also need to decide whether you want to pay based on cost per click (CPC) or cost per 1,000 views (CPM). The choice you make will depend on your goals for the ads. Generally, you would select CPC, in which you only pay if someone actually clicks on your ad, when your main goal is to get people to visit your website. CPM advertising is typically chosen when your main goal is to build brand awareness and get your campaign seen by people.

Other Online Advertising

Besides ads on search engines and social network sites, you can purchase various types of advertising on commercial websites of all types—from huge corporate-owned entities to small single-writer blogs. The key is knowing where your target audience spends its time online and placing relevant ads there. For a community-based campaign, you might consider advertising on local news or entertainment sites, community blogs, or local businesses' websites. If your audience has a particular health condition or lifestyle interest, you can contact websites geared toward that group to learn about their advertising options. Services such as Compete, comScore, and QuantCast that measure web traffic can help you identify websites that reach your audience and assist with online media planning.

If you do not want to figure out the specific websites yourself but would rather spread your ads across many different types of websites that reach people with the relevant demographics, contract with an online ad network that distributes ads across the web. Networks such as DoubleClick or Adbrite can schedule your ads on many different websites according to your specifications, shifting more ads to the sites that are better performing. The fee structure is similar to the other types mentioned earlier, with bids based on CPC or CPM. Some like-minded consortia of bloggers have also created their own ad networks, such as BlogHer, which consists of blogs with a primarily female readership, or Pajamas Media, which reaches a mostly conservative-leaning male audience.

The ads that run on these websites generally conform to a standard set of shapes and sizes and range from static banner ads to streaming video. Other types include floating ads that move across the user's screen, pop-ups and pop-unders (new windows that open either in front or in back of the current page), interstitial ads that appear between pages of a site, or ads designed to appear on the mobile version of the website.

To avoid "banner blindness," the widespread ignoring of online ads by website visitors, keep in mind the findings of eye-tracking research that tests what gets people to pay attention to various elements on a web page.[2] In many cases, people simply do not even glance at the ads on a page. The design elements that were found to be most effective in attracting eyeballs were plain text, faces, and cleavage or other "private" body parts (not that I'm suggesting you use those graphics!). In addition, the closer the ad looks to the design of the surrounding page, the more likely people will click on it. Customizing ads for the particular website on which they will run may be more likely to yield results (with the caveat, of course, that you must abide by the publishers' advertising guidelines).

[2]Nielsen, J. (2007, August 20). Banner blindness: Old and new findings. *Alertbox.* http://www.useit.com/alertbox/banner-blindness.html

Engaging in Social Media

When Albert Einstein published his theory of relativity, physicists slowly but surely came to see that this new way of looking at the world made sense, even though it was initially counterintuitive. This didn't mean throwing out traditional Newtonian physics altogether because it still is the best method of describing how objects larger than atoms function. Similarly, social media have emerged as an effective and different way of communicating with people that some organizations have been slow to adopt because it seems counterintuitive: How can we do marketing without controlling every aspect of the message? Once you realize that people talking with and about the brand is a positive thing, the value of social media becomes obvious. But like the contrast between quantum and Newtonian physics, using social media doesn't mean that marketing via traditional forms of media is no longer necessary; each channel is appropriate for different purposes and audiences.

You can think of the relationship between mainstream media and social media as the letter "T"—what blogger Steve Rubel calls "The Magic 'T' of Marketing."[1] Use mass media to do what it does best: to reach the masses. Traditional forms of media such as television, radio, and magazines reach large numbers of people with a relatively shallow message. This is the horizontal bar of the "T." Use social media to then draw the vertical line down, with deeper engagement for a narrower segment of the audience. After the campaign's messages reach a broad swath of the population, the people who want more information or to interact with others around the issue can move to the social media realm to do so. Not every program needs to use both types of media together, but this is a useful conceptual model for how to integrate them.

WHAT ARE SOCIAL MEDIA?

As new online tools have emerged that make it easy for people to connect and interact, a new paradigm in marketing is evolving. In contrast to the traditional website, which is mostly static and centrally managed, social media sites (what some call "Web 2.0") are dynamic, with new content added by the users rather than just the site managers. Traditional websites provide a one-way flow of information, from the site's creator to the user, while social media sites offer opportunities for users to interact with the site's content and other content creators. The older

---

[1]Rubel, S. (2006, May 18). The magic "T" of marketing. *Micro Persuasion Blog.* http://www.micropersuasion.com/2006/05/the_magic_t_of_.html

Building Movements With Social Media

The word-of-mouth marketing company Brains on Fire laid out poetic distinctions for thinking in terms of building movements versus implementing campaigns, which makes particular sense for health and social issues:[a]

Campaigns have a beginning and an end.

Movements go on as long as kindred spirits are involved.

Campaigns are part of the war vocabulary. (target, launch, dominate markets . . .)

Movements are part of the evangelist vocabulary. (evangelize, passion, love . . .)

Campaigns are dry and emotionally detached.

Movements are organic and rooted in passion.

Campaigns rely on traditional mediums.

Movements rely on word of mouth, where the people are the medium.

Campaigns are part of the creationist theory—we're going to create something cool and people will talk about it.

Movements are part of the evolutionist theory—whatever we co-create with the fans they can own and run with it, which will evolve over time.

Campaigns are you talking about yourself.

Movements are others talking about you.

Campaigns are an ON/OFF switch.

Movements are a volume dial—and there's no zero.

Campaigns add to awareness.

Movements add to credibility.

Campaigns are "you vs. us."

Movements are "let's do this together."

a. Brains on Fire. (2009, July 8). *Lessons learned in igniting word of mouth movements.* http://www.changethis.com/60.03.BrainsOnFire

Internet model requires some level of technical knowledge of HTML or other programming languages to design and post web pages. Many social media sites make it simple to build a web page or a whole new online presence with no technical knowledge whatsoever. There is nothing wrong with the traditional model, which plays an important role; sometimes all we want is to read an article with information provided by a trusted organization.

The Cluetrain Manifesto, marketing's equivalent of Martin Luther's 95 Theses nailed to the church door, presaged the emergence of social media marketing in its very first thesis: "Markets are conversations."[2] This shift has driven and changed the expectations of consumers so that they are no longer content to simply receive information passively. They are now "The People Formerly Known as the Audience," in the words of Jay Rosen.[3] They want—and expect—to be able to interact with the information, talk back to the person or organization that created it, and adapt it and share it with their friends. Social media allow people to easily connect with others who have similar interests and to reach thousands of others with one click. They can take something someone else created and turn it into something even better or collaborate with others around the world. Tools such as blogs, social network sites, Twitter, and photo- and video-sharing sites put the capability right at your fingertips.

Social media technology gives "power to the people" to do all these things; they can be a pundit, a publisher, a videographer, a DJ, or a reporter. A middleman such as a news editor or publishing house no longer

[2]Levine, R., Locke, C., Searls, D., & Weinberger, D. (1999). *The cluetrain manifesto.* http://cluetrain.com

[3]Rosen, J. (2006, June 27). The people formerly known as the audience. *PressThink.* http://journalism.nyu.edu/pubzone/weblogs/pressthink/2006/06/27/ppl_frmr.html

serves as a gateway for deciding which information gets to flow to the masses. But remember that social media are not about the technology—they're about people . . . people spreading ideas and messages to each other, just as they have always done. Social media just make it easier for people to talk to each other in large numbers in a short amount of time. It's word of mouth on steroids.

Because the focus is on people talking to people, social media are based on relationships. To be most effective, you need to think in terms of building relationships with the people you're trying to reach, not just sending messages out to them. This happens over time, through ongoing interactions that maintain their interest and are focused more on them than on you. Trust is a key piece of the equation; people usually trust information coming from their

> ## The 10 "Cs" of Social Media
>
> The range of uses for social media can be conveniently summarized by a series of words starting with the letter "C." They include the following:
>
> - Communicate your message
> - Converse with others
> - Connect with people with similar interests
> - Collaborate and Co-create content
> - Collect and Categorize information online
> - Collective wisdom pooled in one place
> - Customize your online work environment
> - Community building
> - Consumer research
> - Customer service
>
> In social marketing, we hope that these activities will eventually lead to the Big C—change.

friends, family, and colleagues (or people perceived as being similar to themselves) more than a company or organization they see as having an agenda to "sell" them something. With social media, think in terms of building a long-term movement through relationships and trust, rather than creating a short-term marketing campaign. Even Kevin Roberts, the worldwide CEO of advertising firm Saatchi & Saatchi, has said, "Marketing is dead. We need to build movements instead."[4]

SOCIAL MEDIA PRINCIPLES

The wide variety of social media tools, with more launching every day, means that no book could explain how to use all of them. There are, however, principles that cut across all the tools that ensure that you will be more effective in your social media interactions. Each tool develops its own set of "netiquette" guidelines over time, but these general rules of the road will help you avoid the biggest missteps on all of the types of sites. And within these broad guidelines, every person or organization puts their own unique spin on how they use social media and interact online and uses it in the way that works best for them.

Be Authentic

In 2009, a plain-looking 48-year-old woman named Susan Boyle grabbed the world's attention after appearing on the television show *Britain's Got Talent* and surprising everyone with

---

[4]Barda, T. (2010, January 27). Profile: Kevin Roberts, Saatchi & Saatchi. *The Marketer.*

her powerful singing voice. Within 9 days of her appearance, her online videos were viewed 100 million times. Her recording debut became 2009's best-selling album in the world after only 6 weeks of sales. There are many other great singers out there; why did people respond so strongly to Susan Boyle? The answer is because they felt she was a real person, like them. She was not a plastic-looking, polished celebrity. Her "realness"—in how she looked, spoke, and acted—was her appeal, and her authenticity laid in the fact that she did not try to be somebody she was not.

People connect with other real people—that's what powers social media. They don't want to have a relationship with a computer or a faceless organization. When people can tell there is a real person behind the words on the screen, they are more likely to respond. So, don't be afraid to let some of your personality come through in your interactions online. That doesn't mean you have to tell everyone details of your personal life or even talk about yourself at all. Just be transparent about your identity and who you are representing, be your wonderful self, and most of all, don't talk like a press release!

Share

Social media are also based on sharing. *Sharing* in this context means two different things: first, sharing information, and, second, sharing control. The people who share the most useful and interesting information are the ones who build a strong following. In social media, the currency is not money but information and helpfulness. Like the Beatles say, "can't buy me love," but you can earn it. You build your social currency online by establishing yourself as a go-to source of information and valuable interactions. The more generous you are with your knowledge, energy, and time, the more online friends and followers you will gain, along with the extent of your influence. This fundamental value of sharing also extends to always providing attribution to where you get your nuggets of wisdom through links back to the originator. Do unto others, and they will do the same to help spread your own original content.

Sharing control is the other aspect of sharing. This is what often scares organizations from engaging in social media; they are used to feeling like they have total control over the presentation of messages about the organization. The fact is that people have always taken messages and information they come across and passed them along with their own spin. The difference is that now we can see what they are saying and respond to it. You never had any power over the actions of other people, but you do have total control over the messages your organization puts out and your reactions to what happens online. Isn't it better to know what people are saying about you, even if it is negative, so you can respond? Once you accept that you can't control what other people do, you can then focus on sharing your message in the most effective way with your audience.

Be Relevant

The biggest sin in social media (or any kind of communications) is being boring. To get people to pay attention to you, you need to offer something of value. That means figuring out what will be most relevant to the lives of the people you are trying to reach. If you are promoting immunizations to parents of younger children, they probably don't care about the latest journal article on cellular immunology. But they'll likely be very interested in knowing where they can get an inexpensive flu shot in their neighborhood or if there are new recommendations for the immunization schedule for their 5-year-olds. To be relevant, you will need to know your audience well and understand what they are most concerned about and need help with. Think about how you can make the information more interesting or useful to them.

Engage in Two-Way Conversation

The biggest difference between social media and traditional media is that these tools allow for two-way conversations. Rather than talking "at" the people we want to reach, we can now talk "with" them. This feature can lead to greater engagement with your issue by giving people the opportunity to ask questions, discuss concerns, and receive social support from you and others. Conversations via your social media activities heighten people's interest and help them get to know you. These interactions with your organization or program can result in the development of a relationship and identification with your cause. You can use social media as just another way of distributing your press releases, but that would be like buying a computer to use as a doorstop. It can certainly work for that purpose, but you would be missing out on the opportunity to build those critical relationships, as well as giving the impression of your organization as being uninterested in talking with its audience.

Be an Enabler

Think about your program as being an "enabler," providing a place for people to gather online to get more information and talk about your issue. Whether you have a blog, Twitter account, Facebook page, or even built your own dedicated social network, you can share links and information, encourage conversations via commenting, and repost others' thoughts. If you can get people talking to each other, providing support and answering each other's questions, you can play a facilitating role, making the focus about them rather than your own organization. Creating an online "home" for your program provides a central meeting place to coordinate activities on- and offline. By facilitating these interactions, you can build a thriving online community that will be receptive to your calls to action.

The most effective way to enable your movement to spread is by finding your fans—the people who are most passionate about the issue or program and are already talking about it—and turning them into evangelists. Give them the tools they need to help spread your messages and bring others into your program. This could be a widget they can post on their blog or website with information linking back to your site, links they can share, and suggested actions individuals can take. Remember that other people spreading your message for you increases its credibility and helps it travel farther. Offering ways to track communal progress on getting people to take action can be very motivating.

BUILDING A SOCIAL MEDIA STRATEGY

Just as you built an overall strategy for your social marketing program and one for the communications within that strategy, you need to think strategically about how you will use social media. Don't jump into writing a blog or starting a Facebook account just because it seems that

Possible Social Media Outcomes

- Listening and learning
- Building relationships
- Building awareness of issue
- Improving reputation of organization
- Motivating content generation by supporters
- Increasing relevant visitor traffic/page rankings
- Increasing perceptions of social norms
- Social support
- Taking action

Source: Adapted from WeAreMedia.org

everyone else has one. You will need to think through what your overall objectives are, who your audience is, and how much time you have to put into social media activities before determining which tools make the most sense.

What Are Your Objectives?

Think through what you hope to accomplish through your social media activities. Which of your program objectives can they best support? If social media do not fit in with your overall goals and objectives, do not use them; this is why you spent time creating those program guidelines in the first place—to keep you on track. If you do see a role for social media, use the SMART format discussed in Chapter 9 to create objectives that will be useful in guiding what tools and tactics you select. Be realistic about what you can expect to achieve through your activities, but don't be afraid to think big.

Who Do You Want to Reach?

You have already defined your target audience as part of your overall strategy. If you do not know their social media habits, now is the time to find out. The best way is to ask them in your formative research. You need to know which sites they spend time on and what types of activities they participate in online. If you find that they do not spend much time online or on social media sites, it does not make sense to try to reach them there. You may find that one segment of your audience is more likely to be online or that different segments are participating in social media in different ways, which may lead to targeted strategies for each group.

What Is Your Capacity?

Using social media is free . . . like a "free puppy" is free. While most social media tools are available at either no charge or very low cost, they still require care and feeding. Staff time to set up and interact on social media accounts is the main expense your organization will incur. However, if you want to customize your sites, you may wish to hire a designer to make them fit with the rest of your campaign or add functionality that does not come with the basic account.

Think about who on your staff makes the most sense to engage with your audience via social media. Many CEOs, executive directors, and government officials have social media accounts that they use to share what they and their organizations are doing. You may decide it makes the most sense for the project director or someone in your communications or public relations department to be the voice of your program online, or there may be several people who engage online from different perspectives. Be careful about using interns to do your social media. They will be the public face of your organization, and you need to be sure they know the issue and program well enough that there will not be negative repercussions from an inexperienced person communicating on your program's behalf. While a blog post is something that is easy to put through an approval process before it goes up, day-to-day interactions are less straightforward to monitor and to check quality control. You may already have a large quantity of content created that can be repurposed for posting on various social media sites in different formats so you do not have to build content from scratch.

How much time does your staff have available to put into social media activities? The amount of benefit you'll see will be proportional to the amount of time spent. Think of the time spent online as an investment in the success of your program. You will need to put more time in at the beginning to get the accounts set up and build your friends/followers base. For those who are new to using these sites as marketing tools, there will be a learning curve that will require more time at the beginning as well. Once you get into a routine, you may be able to keep active enough on your accounts with 5 hours a week or so. Of course, the more time you spend, the more you will get out of it in the end.

> ## What Are Your Audience's Technographics?
>
> Forrester Research's Charlene Li and Josh Bernoff introduced the concept of social technographics, creating profiles of how people participate online, grouped into overlapping categories.[a] By understanding where your audience falls on this "ladder," you can determine where to focus your social media energies in the activities they are most likely to be comfortable with:
>
> - *Creators*—publish a blog or their own web pages; upload videos, audio, or music they created; write articles or stories and post them
>
> - *Conversationalists*—update status on a social network site or Twitter
>
> - *Critics*—post ratings/reviews of products or services; post comments on blogs; contribute to online forums; contribute or edit articles in a wiki
>
> - *Collectors*—use RSS feeds; vote for websites online; add tags to web pages or photos
>
> - *Joiners*—maintain a profile on a social network site; visit social network sites
>
> - *Spectators*—read blogs; listen to podcasts; watch video from other users; read online forums; read customer ratings/reviews; read tweets
>
> - *Inactives*—none of the above
>
> ---
>
> a. Bernoff, J. (2010, March 4). Social technographics: Conversationalists get onto the ladder [Blog post]. http://forrester.typepad.com/groundswell/2010/01/conversationalists-get-onto-the-ladder.html

Which Tools and Tactics Will You Use?

Now that you have thought through your objectives, target audience, and capacity, you can strategically select which social media tools you will use and how you will use them. Keep in mind that you do not need to have a presence on every tool that's out there; selecting one or two that you use regularly and effectively makes more sense than spreading yourself thin. Also, think in terms of how each tool will integrate with the other pieces of your social marketing program. Will your print ads direct people to where they can find you on various social media sites? Will your Facebook page link to your videos on YouTube? Can you use your social media outreach to direct people to where they can get in-person assistance in their local communities?

For each social media tactic—the purpose for which you are using social media—there are numerous options of tools you can select. You may decide to focus on one tactic at a time or engage in several at once, depending on where you are in your learning curve and how much time you have available. The list in Table 19.1 offers some suggestions for the tools you could use for

TABLE 19.1   Tool Options for Social Media Tactics

Tactic	Tools
Listening Tracking when keywords related to your program or issue appear online	■ Google Alerts ■ RSS readers ■ Twitter Search ■ Paid social media monitoring
Conversing Responding to people who are talking about your program or issue	■ Blog comments ■ Twitter ■ Facebook pages
Telling Your Story Sharing information about your program or issue	■ Blogs ■ Twitter ■ Online video (e.g., YouTube) ■ Photo sharing (e.g., Flickr) ■ Podcasts
Helping Supporters Tell Your Story Providing tools they can use to spread the word	■ User-generated content ■ Contests ■ Social network apps ■ Widgets
Generating Buzz Spreading excitement from person to person about your program	■ Social news (e.g., Digg) ■ StumbleUpon ■ Twitter ■ Facebook ■ Blogger outreach
Building Community Bringing people together around a common interest	■ Social networks ■ Twitter ■ Tagging (using a consistent "tag" to mark relevant online content) ■ Gaming/virtual worlds
Collaborating/Collecting Information Identifying useful information and making it easy for others to find	■ Wikis ■ Social bookmarking ■ Tagging

various purposes, but keep in mind that these are only the tools that are most common at the time of the publishing of this book. Some of these tools will be discussed more in depth later in the chapter.

How Will You Measure Success?

As with the rest of your social marketing program, evaluation is an important part of the process to help you adjust your social media approach and improve your effectiveness. The objectives you initially set for what you would like to achieve with social media should guide the types of data you collect to determine your success.

While there are many different social media metrics you can track, those that are most relevant to a social marketing program include the following:

■ Web activity (e.g., pageviews, unique visitors, time on site, where visitors linked from, which links were clicked on most)

- Social actions (e.g., friends/followers/fans, comments, active contributors, ratings, votes, user-created content)

- Mentions and reposted content (e.g., blog links, retweets, social network site posts, social bookmark links)

- Return on engagement (i.e., calculate the cost per social action)

In addition, to be able to tie social media engagement in with other elements of the social marketing program, as well as ultimate outcomes such as knowledge, attitude, and behavior change, you can conduct a survey that assesses links between those.

SOCIAL MEDIA TOOLS

Any guide to the details of using specific social media tools is guaranteed to be outdated almost immediately. Sites come and go, change their features, and sometimes a new category pops up that changes everything in a short amount of time. For that reason, this book will talk about the principles of each broad category of social media tools (i.e., blogs, microblogging [e.g., Twitter], social networks, and social media monitoring) and focus less on the "user manual" details. For every type of site and tool, the Internet is packed with a plethora of articles and blog posts on how to use them. Appendix A points you to some of the best sources online for this information.

Blogs

Blogs offer an effective platform for sharing your story and drawing people in to your issue. A blog is an easy-to-use website that you can update with news, commentary, personal stories, videos, photos, or other types of content. The blog posts can be any length, though in general shorter is better to retain readers' interest (generally 200–400 words). Most blogs allow readers to comment on each post, and this can be a key point of conversation for the program— both between the blogger and readers and among the readers themselves.

Blogs usually offer an RSS ("Really Simple Syndication") feed that sends updates directly to users. Rather than having to bookmark your favorite sites and keep visiting them to see if there is anything new, a browser-based RSS feed reader, such as Google Reader or Bloglines, gathers all the feeds to which you have subscribed and

Types of Blog Posts

- Educational
- Call to action
- Tips
- News
- Commentary
- How-to
- Resources
- Lists
- Interview
- Personal story
- Ask a question, gather responses
- Photo/video blog
- Ongoing feature
- Guest blogger
- Event planning/recap

displays the new content in your account. RSS feeds can also be used to add headlines and/or posts from your blog to your other websites, social network profiles, and e-mail.

Some of the factors you will need to consider as you plan for your blog include the following:

- *Audience*—Who is the blog intended to reach, and what type of content will best meet their needs to meet your objectives?

- *Theme*—What is the blog about? Don't narrowly focus on your product, but make the topic broad enough that you will have plenty to write about.

- *Blogger*—Who will write the blog? Will it be one person or a team? Who is in the best position to contribute interesting content on a regular basis? A consistent, informal "voice" for the blog will be more engaging, especially if the person is enthusiastic about the topic. Make sure you include a bio and picture for the person or people who are contributing to the blog so that readers can better connect with the blogger.

- *Blog design*—What do you want the blog to look like? What functionality should it have? What will you include in the sidebars? The blogging platform you select will influence what you can do with it; the easiest to use is Blogger, while the most customizable is WordPress.

- *Comment policy*—Will you allow readers to post comments on the blog? Will you moderate comments before they appear? What guidelines will you use to determine whether a comment goes through or not (e.g., no obscenities, no ad hominem attacks, etc.)?

- *Schedule*—How often will you post to the blog? Will you create an editorial calendar to guide weekly/monthly themes? Will you post in a particular format on certain days (e.g., news/commentary on Mondays, interviews on Wednesdays, new resources on Fridays)? At a minimum, post weekly, but more often is better.

- *Images*—Will you include images to illustrate the posts? Where will you get the images from (Creative Commons, stock photo sites, your own photo library)?

Tracking Blog Metrics

As you blog, you will want to know how many people you are reaching and track your own outreach activity. There are several ways to collect metrics for your blog:

- *Blog traffic:* Use tools such as Google Analytics or Performancing Metrics to track number of site visitors, number of page views, most popular content, incoming and outgoing links, location and domain URL of visitors, time spent on site, and search terms used to find your site.

- *Blog subscribers:* Using a tool called Feedburner, you can track the number of people subscribing to the RSS feed of your blog on a daily basis.

- *Traffic sent to main website:* Using similar analytic services to the blog, you can track how much of the traffic to your program's main website came from your blog or other social media accounts.

- *Comments:* You can track the number of comments you receive on the blog, as well as the qualitative content. Follow the conversations on other blog posts where you left comments using services such as Backtype or coComment.

- *Ego feeds:* Using a search of your name, your organization or campaign's name, or your URL, you can track every time those words appear online somewhere. Services such as Google Alerts, Technorati, or Twitter Search will notify you whenever someone publishes those words on blogs or other sites.

Once you have created the blog, how do you generate traffic and build community? The best way to grow your blog is to leave it to read and comment on others' posts. Identify other bloggers who write about similar topics or have similar audiences, and add them to your "blog roll"—the list of recommended blogs on your sidebar. Linking to other blogs within your posts will also bring attention from those bloggers to your site and may result in links back from them. Participate in blog "carnivals," which are organized weekly or monthly compilations of blog posts on a specific topic. The more involved you become with commenting and conversing with the existing blog community around your issue, the more people will get to know you and to visit your blog. You can also optimize the text and titles of your blog posts to make them more likely to be found via search engines.

Images can help to liven up your posts and bring an added dimension to the messages delivered by the text. Try to include an image or video in each of your posts and be consistent in the style of image you use to maintain the same general look and feel for the blog. You need to be careful, though, not to use photos or other images that are copyrighted without permission. Most of the images that will turn up in a general search engine query are likely copyrighted and should not be used.

The best way to find images that you can use is to turn to the Creative Commons (http://search.creativecommons.org/). This is an alternate copyright system that has emerged with the new needs of online content creation to make it easy for people to share their work for reuse, remixing, and commercial use. By using graphics that are marked as "Some Rights Reserved" under a Creative Commons license, you do not usually need to request permission and often need only provide attribution to the creator of the photo or graphic. Flickr.com offers a broad range of high-quality photos, many of which are offered for use under a CC license.

You can also use images from stock photo sites for which you may need to pay a small fee. Websites such as iStockphoto.com, stock.xchng, Dreamstime.com, and Fotolia.com offer low-cost stock photos to illustrate just about any concept. The U.S. Centers for Disease Control and Prevention offers a Public Health Image Library of public domain images you can use at no charge (http://phil.cdc.gov/phil/). Similarly, Photoshare.org, which is a service of Knowledge for Health, offers a database of photos that are available for nonprofit educational use upon request.

The Los Angeles Fire Department (LAFD) Blog

Los Angeles Fire Department (LAFD) spokesman Brian Humphrey started the LAFD News & Information Blog (http://lafd.blogspot.com) in 2004 as a way to reach the citizens of Los Angeles "to offer timely and accurate information in an appealing manner that can help people lead safer, healthier and more productive lives."[a] A staff of three public information officers post to the blog, including summaries of incident reports describing recent firefighting or rescue operations in vivid detail, timely safety issues, helpful resources, and upcoming LAFD events. The blog gets more than 500,000 direct visitors each year and as of 2010 has reached about 2.8 million hits.

Anyone who reads local Los Angeles blogs has likely seen comments from Brian on posts related to the LAFD or safety issues, written in his usual friendly and helpful style (and always with his signature sign-off, "Respectfully Yours in Safety and Service, Brian Humphrey"). Even when people are griping or downright nasty on his or other blogs, Brian always responds with good humor, sympathy, and a genuine desire to be of assistance. By commenting on other blogs, he brings new readers to the LAFD blog.

(Continued)

(Continued)

The LAFD blog is only one piece of the overall social media strategy of the department, and it serves as a central point from which to explore LAFD-tagged photos on Flickr, videos on YouTube, Twitter, Facebook, and other social media accounts and participate in polls. Brian, with help from his colleagues, maintains these accounts on his regular shift without any additional budget and has been a trailblazer for public agencies using social media.

When asked how blogging fits in with the agency's overall mission, Brian said, "If you want to be successful in fulfilling your agency mission, you have to communicate. Blogging tools make it among the most affordable and productive mediums for communication." His advice on how to get started: "Lurk for at least six months before you blog, then get your team together, and make it happen. People want access and transparency, and they ultimately come to understand that a blog is a work in progress. They will become both your mentors and your apostles if you let them."

a. Weinreich, N. (2007, February 26). Fireblogger: LAFD blazes the trail for public agencies. *Spare Change.* http://www.social-marketing.com/blog/2007/02/fireblogger-lafd-blazes-trail-for.html

Microblogging

Microblogging (sometimes called "microsharing") refers to providing short updates and links via a service such as Twitter or Google Buzz. As this book is being published, Twitter is the dominant service in this category and so will be the focus of the discussion here. Twitter offers users 140 characters at a time to share their thoughts, indicate what they are doing at the moment, provide useful links or information, or carry on conversations. You can choose whose "tweets" you want to follow and which appear in your timeline as they are published, and others can choose whether to follow you and receive your tweets. You do not have to follow back everyone who follows you, and in fact, the quality of your experience on Twitter will be determined by whom you choose to follow.

When you tweet interesting and useful information, especially when you engage people in conversation, you will be more likely to gain followers. People have many different styles and purposes for using microblogs, and over time you will figure out what works best for you. Some of the ways people use these tools include the following:

- Providing information or commentary
- Conversation—ask and answer questions, build relationships
- "Livetweeting" conference sessions
- Sharing opportunities, such as grants, events, or resources
- Human-powered search engine—to get intelligent answers to a question
- Rally the troops—urge people to take action
- Tell a story
- Inspire others through example
- Bring people together through shared hashtags

- Serve your constituents and provide "customer service" to those using your product

- "Lifestreaming"—share what you are doing at a particular moment

Because you will likely not see the usefulness of Twitter until you are following a critical mass of high-quality people, be selective about who you follow, but start off with a minimum of 30 to 50 people. There are several ways to identify the people who are likely to be of most interest to you. You can find people you know via Twitter's e-mail find function or by searching for them by name. Twitter's list function is a useful tool for finding the people who others have deemed worth following in various categories. You can find people you like and trust and explore their lists (found on the right sidebar of their Twitter profiles) or the lists they are included on (found in the upper right under "listed"). You can also use a tool such as Listorious.com that lets you search for lists by topic. Many people add themselves to Twitter directories by topic, with tools such as WeFollow.com or Twellow.com. You can look at the people who your favorite people are following, conversing with, or retweeting to see if they interest you as well. Another method is to use Twitter Search (http://search.twitter.com) to find people who are talking about a particular topic, which can be limited to a particular community in the Advanced Search function if you have a local program.

The big question is: How do you get people to follow you on Twitter? The number one answer is to make sure that you are providing useful and interesting content that includes interacting with others. If Twitter is like an online cocktail party, you don't want to be the guy who goes on and on about himself, never letting others get a word in edgewise. Don't use Twitter as just a place to post your press releases and send one-way messages about your program. The more you talk to and about other people, the more people will talk about you. Reach out to people you find on Twitter Search who are discussing your issue or program. When you follow people, send them a tweet to let them know why you're interested in them or why they might be interested in what you are doing. Be careful not to mass-follow too many people at one time or send the same message to different people over and over, or you may get tagged as a spammer. Just be yourself, talk to people in the same way you would want to be approached, and let your relationships build organically over time.

Social Networks

Social network sites are the most popular social media category on the Social Technographics ladder, with the largest numbers of people maintaining an account on a site like Facebook or MySpace. A variety of smaller sites have niche audiences focused on areas of interest such as pets or health conditions. Outside of the United States, many other large social network sites are popular, such as hi5, Friendster, Orkut, and Qzone, so before you jump to conclusions about which social network makes the most

Anatomy of a Tweet

The syntactical conventions on Twitter can be somewhat confusing at first, as they are designed to use abbreviations to keep things as short as possible to maximize the amount of space for your message. Some of the key elements of a tweet you need to know are as follows:

- @username—the "@" sign in front of someone's username shows that you are either talking to or about that person. Place the name at the beginning of the tweet to show you are talking to that person.

- RT @username—REtweet—This shows that you are repeating what the person with that username previously tweeted, often with your own commentary before or after.

(Continued)

(Continued)

■ #hashtag—when you see a word with the pound or number sign (#) in front of it, that is a hashtag. Hashtags are used to aggregate tweets from many people on a particular topic, event, or conference. You can use Twitter Search or other services when you want to see what everyone using that hashtag is saying in one place.

■ DM—Direct Message—when you want to send a private message to someone without everyone else seeing it. Will only go through to people who are already following you.

■ URL shorteners—Because of the limited number of characters available, Twitter automatically shrinks long URLs in links to begin with "t.co," followed by a shortened ID.

sense for your audience, do your research to find out. A service called Ning also allows you to create your own dedicated social network around your issue or campaign.

For the most part, social networks are centered on keeping in touch with friends and family. They offer ways to provide status updates or more in-depth blog posts, post pictures and videos, customize user profiles, play games, and converse. Organizations can use these networks to reach their target audiences by creating a profile and reaching out to people to become a friend or fan and encouraging people to enlist their friends and family to the cause as well. You can also post updates or links that your supporters can send to their own networks. In Facebook, you can create a page that serves as the program's central meeting place, where you can have conversations in comments, post events, and send out messages to all fans.

People use different social networks for different purposes and may have accounts on more than one. It's important to understand why and how people use each site, so that the programs' approach can be tailored in a very specific way. See Table 19.2 for a comparison of some of the most popular American social network sites and how you can best reach people on them.

TABLE 19.2   Comparison of Social Network Sites

Network	Audience	Why They Use It	What to Give Them
Twitter	People who want info/networking/stimulation	Meet interesting people, build relationships, get news	Provide value, give interesting things they can share
Facebook	People they know—friends and family	Keep in touch, express brand/cause affiliations, play games	Help them show their family/friends what they care about, give them fun things to do
MySpace	Music/entertainment fans, teens	Express themselves, follow bands	Provide "Bling 4 Good"—badges or graphics that tie into your program
LinkedIn	Professionals—colleagues in same field	Professional networking, information sharing	Help them do their jobs better, answer questions
Ning	People with a shared niche interest	Connect with others who care about topic	Enable connections, build community

Social Media Monitoring

Social media monitoring is a way of listening to the conversations people are having online. This information may be found in blog posts, social networks, Twitter, and other websites of interest. You can find out as soon as something new is posted online related to your issue, organization, or campaign. Use social media monitoring to

- Get an idea of your audience's knowledge, attitudes, and behaviors related to the issue

- Find opportunities to respond to questions, engage in conversations, correct misperceptions, and reach out to assist people interested in your issue

- Direct your strategy and activities in the most effective ways

- Find the people who would be most interested in being part of your online community

- Stay on top of the latest news related to your issue so you will be better able to knowledgeably engage your audience

Many free tools are available online to help you monitor for the keywords of your choice. You can easily set up a social media monitoring system that you can check daily for the latest mentions of the topics and words you are interested in watching. If you have a program for which you would need to track a large number of high-volume keywords, you might consider contracting with a paid monitoring service such as Radian6 or Scout Labs that will catch everything that comes through and provide an analysis of the content of the posts.

First, set up an account on an RSS feed reader such as Google Reader or Bloglines to serve as the central hub of your monitoring efforts. Next, create Google Alerts (http://www.google.com/alerts) for the keywords you selected. Google Alerts are an easy way to receive notification via RSS feed (or you can set them up to come via e-mail) whenever your keywords of interest appear on a blog, in the news, on a webpage, or

---

TuDiabetes Social Network

In late 2006, Manny Hernandez, who has type 1 diabetes, started an online social network using the Ning platform for others with the same condition. He describes the network, TuDiabetes.com, as "an online community where the members help each other out, educate ourselves and share the steps we take every day to stay healthy while living with this very serious condition." Members write blog posts, exchange ideas in discussion forums, share personal photos, and post useful videos. The site has more than 13,000 members, and its sister Spanish-language site, EsTuDiabetes.org, has more than 7,500 members.

For World Diabetes Day, the community participated in "The Big Blue Test," which was an opportunity to see the effect that exercise has on blood sugar levels on a mass scale. At 14:00 local time (2:00 p.m.) on November 14th, 2009, participants tested their blood sugar. They then exercised for 14 minutes, tested their sugar again, and posted the results on Twitter. This shared event reinforced the importance of exercise and made it a social activity.

Selecting Keywords

You will need to determine which keywords you want to track—most likely the name of your program or campaign, the name of your organization, and words that describe the issue your campaign addresses. Make sure you include abbreviations or misspellings. If your program addresses pandemic flu preparedness, you might set up the system to track the following words:

- Pandemic flu
- Pandemic preparedness
- Swine or Avian flu
- H1N1
- Panflu
- flu cityname
- flue prepare

other locations online. If you are receiving the alerts via your RSS feed, you will want them on an "as-it-happens" delivery schedule. If you choose to receive them via e-mail, you can decide, based on the volume, how often you want to receive them. Same-day alerts let you respond in a timely manner if necessary.

You can then set up a Twitter Search feed by going to http://search.twitter.com and doing a search on the selected keywords. When you have the search results, click on the link on the upper right that says "Feed for this query." This will generate an RSS feed that you can subscribe to with your feed reader.

In addition to searches for specific keywords, it is also a good idea to scan relevant blogs or news sources to stay informed and catch items that might have been missed by your keywords. The specific feeds that you select may be a combination of blogs and news sources related to your issue and those about your specific community. Use BlogPulse or Google Blog Search to identify blogs that are relevant to your program and subscribe to them in your RSS feed reader. You can also explore the blogroll in your favorite blogs' sidebar to find other recommended blogs on the topic. In addition to blogs, you can also add news feeds from local or national news sites. Though they may not offer RSS feeds, you can also search message boards (Boardreader.com) and wikis (wiki.com or Qwika.com) manually for your keywords. New search tools are coming out all the time.

After you have the feed reader set up as your social media monitoring system, check it at least once a day, if not several times, to see if you need to respond to anything that comes through. A large number of the items caught in your social media monitoring net will not be of relevance or interest to you and can be ignored. Many of the others can be considered "information only," and once you have seen them, you do not need to take any action on them (or you can share them with your team members).

When you find people talking online about your issue, you will need to decide whether it is a good opportunity to respond. Some reasons to respond to online posts or comments include the following:

- To let people who might be interested know about your program

- To praise or thank people who are getting the word out about your issue

- To answer questions that are asked about your issue

- To correct misperceptions that are stated as facts

- To address criticisms of your program or activities

Ideally, you would respond to each item on the same social media site on which it was posted. So, for a blog post, you would respond in the comments section for that post. On Twitter, you would respond via your Twitter account. Sometimes it will make more sense to respond with an e-mail privately. Some bloggers do not enable their comments and are only reachable via e-mail. They may decide to post your response as an update on their blog themselves. Or you may wish to have a private conversation with a blogger or website manager before making a public response. For news items that come from more traditional journalism sources online, such as newspapers or wire services, you can write a letter to the editor, fill out a feedback form on their websites, or write a blog post with your response.

If you do leave blog comments, reply on Twitter, or send a letter, make sure you follow up to see if the original poster or other readers respond to your comments. Continuing the conversation is important and should not be limited to a one-shot response. Several online services exist that can help you keep track of the comments you leave on blogs or news posts and show when new comments arrive. These include coComment and BackType. On Twitter, you can create an RSS feed for replies to your tweets. Just use Twitter Search to search for "@username" and click the option to create a feed.

Over time, analyze the posts you catch in your social media monitoring system, not just quantitatively but qualitatively as well. What is the general sentiment about your issue or program—positive, negative, or neutral? What other words or ideas come up frequently? Do different segments of the audience have different types of concerns? Extract qualitative insights and use those to refine your messaging and outreach strategies.

WORKSHEET 16: BUILDING A SOCIAL MEDIA STRATEGY[5]

1. Objectives

   a. What do you want to accomplish with social media?

   ❑ Listening and learning

   ❑ Building relationships

   ❑ Building awareness of issue

   ❑ Improving reputation of organization

   ❑ Motivating content generation by supporters

   ❑ Increasing relevant visitor traffic/page rankings

   ❑ Increasing perceptions of social norms

   ❑ Social support

   ❑ Taking action (behavior change)

   ❑ Other: _____

   b. State your objective(s) so they are "SMART"—specific, measurable, attainable, relevant, and time based.

   _____

   _____

   _____

   c. Describe how your social media objectives support or link to objectives in your overall social marketing strategy.

   _____

   _____

   _____

2. Target Audience

   a. Who must you reach with your social media efforts to meet your objectives? Why this target group?

   _____

   _____

   _____

[5]Parts of this worksheet are adapted from the WeAreMedia project http://www.wearemedia.org and NTEN. Project funded by the Surdna Foundation.

b. What social media tools are they currently using? Where do they fall on the Social Technographics ladder?

_____

_____

_____

c. What is your audience currently talking about online related to your issue or program?

_____

_____

_____

3. Capacity

a. Who will implement your organization's social media strategy?

_____

b. How many hours per week can you collectively devote to your strategy?

_____

c. Do you need any outside expertise to help implement your strategy?

_____

d. What sources of content do you have that can be repurposed to post in different formats online?

_____

_____

_____

4. Tools and Tactics

a. What tactics and tools best support your objectives and match your targeted audience?

Tactics	Tool Examples	Implementation Ideas
Listening	Google Alerts, RSS readers, Twitter Search, paid monitoring	
Conversing	Blog comments, Twitter, Facebook	
Telling Your Story	Blogs, Twitter, video/photo sharing, podcasts	
Helping Supporters Tell Your Story	User-generated content, contests, social network apps, widgets	

(Continued)

(Continued)

Tactics	Tool Examples	Implementation Ideas
Generating Buzz	Social news (e.g., Digg), StumbleUpon, Twitter, Facebook, blogger outreach	
Building Community	Social networks, Twitter, tagging, gaming/virtual worlds	
Collaborating/ Collecting Information	Wikis, social bookmarking, tagging	

b. Now, take a second look at what you are planning. What tactics and tools do you have the capacity to implement?

_____

_____

_____

5. Measurement

a. What metrics will you use to track your objectives? How often will you track?

_____

_____

_____

b. What systems and tools will you set up to track those metrics?

_____

_____

_____

c. What qualitative data can you collect to help generate insights?

_____

_____

_____

CHAPTER 20

Generating Publicity

Just as you can get your message out by purchasing advertising time or space, you can promote your program in the spaces between the commercials (what people really want to pay attention to) through public relations. Although getting news and blog coverage often is thought of as free publicity, those press conferences, news releases, and slick media kits are not cheap. The resources and effort your staff members put in make it "earned media" rather than "free." But when you compare the cost of these activities to that of creating a mass media campaign, buying airtime, or advertising space, pitching stories ("selling" your story idea) seems like a bargain. Public relations can be a useful adjunct to your other communications activities if you are able to generate coverage by appropriate traditional and online media outlets. On the other hand, if your target audience does not pay much attention to the news, then these techniques might not be worthwhile for your program.

Using public relations strategies as part of your social marketing program accomplishes the following:

■ Lends credibility to your program and message via news coverage

■ Reaches many people at once

■ Does not require purchase of media time or space

■ Develops mutually beneficial long-term relationships with media

■ Gets your message out quickly and efficiently

Public relations also has some potential disadvantages, including the following:

■ You have less control over how your messages are conveyed.

■ Media coverage is not guaranteed, no matter how good your public relations efforts.

■ You might not reach your target audience members with the media that cover your program.

■ Big news developments might bump your story or take precedence over the press conference you planned for months.

This chapter offers a set of public relations strategy questions to help you consider whether and how to use public relations in your social marketing program. Rather than regarding the media as a fearsome adversary, think of it as a potential ally. Before jumping in, there are certain questions you should ask yourself.

WHY DO YOU WANT MEDIA ATTENTION?

Determine exactly what you want to accomplish through your public relations efforts. Do you want to direct people to your program? Promote a particular attitude or behavior? Advocate for policy change? The answers to these questions will determine who you should try to reach with your message and which media outlets and blogs you should target.

As with every aspect of your social marketing campaign, be strategic in your public relations plan. Set goals consistent with your overall program strategy. You can use public relations methods to accomplish the following:

- Supplement and reinforce your campaign with the target audience

- Reach your secondary audiences

- Increase community awareness of your program

- Put pressure on policymakers to address your issue

Select the target audience for your public relations efforts carefully. This may or may not be the same group you target in your other communications efforts. If you want to reach the same target audience, then refer back to your research on the group's media habits and work through those outlets to get your message to that group. For other audiences, research the media that will best reach them. You probably would not use the same media to reach members of Congress as to reach low-income parents of 2-year-olds. Be as specific in your public relations outreach as you are in the rest of the social marketing program. On the other hand, if your goal in attracting media attention is to publicize your organization and its services throughout the community, then you should contact as many outlets as you can for possible coverage.

Media Advocacy

Media advocacy is a tool that uses the media's power to bring about social change and to influence the public debate on an issue. Of course, political interest groups also engage in media advocacy, but the focus here is on public health or social issues. Practitioners use media coverage to present an issue from a public good point of view and to "frame" the issue in a different way from how people normally think about it. Ultimately, the goal is to put pressure on lawmakers to adopt a particular policy or on corporate entities to change something that they are doing that negatively affects people's health or lives. A social marketing program may incorporate media advocacy techniques into its media strategy if its goals include changing public or corporate policy or countering unhealthful messages in the media.

Media advocates use a variety of skills, such as grassroots organizing, coalition building, lobbying, and media savvy, to create newsworthy events that get their points across. One useful means of getting attention is using what has been called "creative epidemiology" or "social math." This involves reframing statistics into a vivid image that is meaningful to the audience. Instead of saying, for example, that 400,000 Americans die from smoking-related causes each year, you can localize the statistic and give it more impact by stating that 3 people in your city die each hour because they smoked. Or, rather than relaying that college students drink 430 million gallons of alcoholic beverages per year, you can create an image by saying that they consume enough alcohol each year to fill 3,500 Olympic-size swimming pools.

Using symbolism is another effective tool in the media advocacy arsenal, as illustrated by the following example. When tobacco manufacturer Philip Morris Companies, Inc. sponsored a 2-year tour of the Bill of Rights around the country in 1990, tobacco control advocates came together to address what they saw as a usurping of a national symbol to promote smoking and to improve the company's image.[a] At each stop on the tour, local activists garnered media attention by setting up "Nicotina," a figure modeled on the Statue of Liberty that symbolized the problems caused by tobacco. Nicotina held a cigarette in her upheld hand instead of a torch, had the phrase "Give me your poor, your tired, your women, your children yearning to breathe free" at her feet, and stood on a pile of cigarettes purchased by 14-year-old children. On the base of the statue was a running clock showing the number of people who had died of tobacco-related diseases since the beginning of the tour. The advocates also wore and handed out buttons that said "YES Bill of Rights, NO Philip Morris." At nearly every stop, the antitobacco protesters received some media coverage of their health messages and the controversy surrounding Philip Morris's sponsorship of the tour. In early 1991, Philip Morris quietly changed the tour schedule and shortened its length by 2 months.

a. This case study is described in Wallack, L., Dorfman, L., Jernigan, D., & Themba, M. (1993). *Media advocacy and public health: Power for prevention* (pp. 183–188). Newbury Park, CA: Sage.

WHAT IS YOUR "NEWS"?

Often, what we consider newsworthy and exciting in our own programs would make a reporter yawn. Why should people be interested in yet another project addressing AIDS? Or the fact that you just got funded for another year? Or your new online video? The news media have their own criteria for judging what is worth covering, so to get their attention, you will need to frame the issue in an appealing way.

Find an angle that makes your idea stand out and grabs the reporter's interest. The media prefer stories that contain at least one of the following elements:

Timeliness. Look for a news "peg" (an issue that currently is in the news) to tie your information into current events or upcoming holidays. If a well-known celebrity just died of the disease your program addresses, then you can use this window of opportunity to get information on that disease's prevention and treatment to your target audience and others. Or, if there is an annual day, week, or month set aside for your issue, such as Child Abuse Prevention Month, then use that as the peg (although you might need more angles than that to make your issue relevant).

General interest. Make your issue as relevant to people in your own community as possible. Connect the information to a common situation that people encounter or an issue that nearly everyone must address. A stress reduction program might put out a list of "stress-buster" tips for dealing with traffic jams (because very few of us are lucky enough to avoid those). Or, a study showing which fast-food restaurants offer the healthiest selections might attract many people's attention. Those living in colder climates might be eager to see a winter feature on back care tips for shoveling snow.

Local angle. Provide local data or reactions to a national or international news event. People want to know how the big story relates to them. If the results of a national survey on homelessness are released, then provide information on the homeless problem in your community, how it compares to that in the rest of the country, and what people can do about it. If Congress is considering cutting funding for your program, then highlight the plight of some of the people in your community and what it would mean for them.

Conflict. The media love a good conflict, whether it is good versus evil, big tobacco companies versus nonsmoking advocates, or school board members versus each other. Reporters tend to cover all sides of an issue, even when there might not necessarily be a valid second viewpoint. Make their job easy and cast your story, if appropriate, as a struggle of right over wrong. Try not to demonize your opposition, however, because this might make you look like an unreasonable fanatic.

Human interest. Providing a human side to a disease or an issue creates emotional appeal. Telling the story of one person who is affected helps people to connect with the issue and think about it in relation to themselves, particularly if the person is similar to themselves in other ways.

Novelty. When something has not been seen before or is an unusual occurrence, people pay attention. Whether it is a lemonade-powered car or a new advance in contraception, this is literally "news." Do not create a gimmick just to attract media notice, but if you truly have something that is new or different, then use that as your hook.

Celebrity. The whole idea of being a celebrity is that people look at you as you walk down the street. They listen to what you have to say. If you can find a famous person who will serve as your spokesperson or will provide some comments about your issue, people will be more likely to listen than if your public information officer were speaking. The celebrity should be someone who appeals to your target audience and who the media would feel is worth covering.

Superlatives. Do you have something that is the biggest? The best? The fastest? The most effective in clinical trials? The media do not want to know what is second best; they want to run screaming headlines about new breakthroughs or new highs and lows. Use this desire for superlatives to get your story noticed. Is the problem you are working to prevent the leading killer of young children? Does your city have the most low-birth-weight babies in the country? But do not dig too far just to come up with a superlative; the world's biggest gallstone might not be a very big draw.

WHAT TYPE OF MEDIA COVERAGE DO YOU WANT?

The term *media* refers to many different types of entities—radio, television, newspapers and magazines, computer software, and the Internet—that vary extensively within each category.

Each of these channels provides different opportunities to reach particular audiences with a specific type of message.

The standard media formats that you can use to promote your messages include the following:

News. This is factual and timely information about important events or new developments. News stories generally would show up on a television or radio news program, on the front page or metro section of a newspaper, in a newsmagazine or the news section of another type of periodical, or through an Internet news service. Many blogs also specialize in publishing news in a given niche area. A news format provides greater credibility to your information and attaches inherent importance to it. Because a reporter takes your information and rewrites it, you have less control over the content and slant of the story.

Feature. This is a story focusing on the human or emotional side of an issue. Feature stories are more like short stories than news, with an emphasis on helping the reader understand someone else's experiences, thoughts, and feelings. Although a feature story may contain facts and figures and be based on current issues, it generally is not as time sensitive as a news story. Features pop up all the time on television news and radio networks such as National Public Radio. You also can find them scattered throughout newspapers and especially in magazines, which, because of their weekly or monthly publication, prefer stories that are not time dependent. Blogs are a particularly good venue for sharing this type of story, especially when written in the first person voice by the person telling the story.

Editorial. This is a short piece offering the opinion of an individual or organization on a particular topic. Editorials can be in the form of an op-ed (runs opposite the editorial page) by a well-known or well-qualified person, a letter to the editor responding to an article that was published previously, a "community viewpoint" spot on television or radio, or a blog post. In an editorial format, you have more control over how your message is conveyed, although an editor might trim your words to make it fit the space.

Entertainment. This is a program or published item that people watch, hear, or read primarily for fun or diversion. Television or radio talk shows can be a forum in which you can

Writing Op-Eds

Op-eds provide your point of view on a particular issue. Use them to begin a community-wide discussion on a particular topic or to weigh in with your side's arguments in an ongoing debate. To make your op-ed as effective as possible, keep the following in mind:

- Present your opinion clearly and without ambiguity. Every sentence in the op-ed should bolster your case.
- Support your premise with facts and figures. Make statistics relevant to the people reading the article.
- Offer solutions. Do not just write about the fact that a problem exists.
- Keep the op-ed brief. It should be no longer than 800 words.
- Time the submission of the op-ed with a holiday or other event, such as the kickoff of your campaign or recent related news, to make it more newsworthy.
- Have a recognized expert or someone with credentials related to the topic sign his or her name to the op-ed. This will increase the chances that the article will be printed and lends it more credibility.
- Send the op-ed to the op-ed page editor at larger newspapers or to the editorial page editor at smaller publications, as well as posting it on your blog after publication (or instead of publication, if it was not accepted).

Writing Letters to the Editor

A letter to the editor can be used in many ways: to respond to an article or editorial that you disagree with, to agree with a piece and provide supporting facts, or to comment on an issue relevant to your community that has not necessarily been covered by the publication. To increase the likelihood of your letter being published, keep the following in mind:

- Be brief and to the point. A good length for a letter to the editor is approximately 100 words.

- Do not personally attack the author of an article or write in an inflammatory tone. Provide a rational, well-thought-out response to the points with which you disagree.

- Include your name, address, e-mail address, and phone number with the letter. An anonymous letter probably will not be published, and the editor might need to call to confirm that you are indeed the author before printing it.

- Your letter is likely to be edited or shortened to fit the space available, so try to preemptively edit out any unnecessary or redundant sentences before submitting the letter to make it as concise as possible.

- Include the name of your organization in the letter or below your signature if you think it will enhance your credibility.

provide information to a lot of people who might not relate to other formats (although a show with topics such as "My Lover Is an Alien" might not be appropriate). Network-produced programs, whether drama or comedy, provide many opportunities to provide pro-health or social messages if the producers are willing to build those in. Radio call-in shows can reach many active listeners who will pay close attention to what you have to say (whether they agree with you or not). "Dear Abby" has legions of people who hang on her every word. Working your messages into entertainment formats can be effective because the audience is not expecting to learn anything, yet many people form their opinions and attitudes based on what they are exposed to in the entertainment media every day.

Public service. This is information that most types of media provide as a courtesy to the community. Public service programming might include community calendar announcements to publicize upcoming events, a weekly nonprofit spotlight to describe the services of a community organization, public service announcements, or community access cable programming.

WHO WILL YOU CONTACT IN THE MEDIA?

The key to implementing your media strategy is getting your information to the right people at the right places at the right time. Use your media contact list to identify the appropriate person for your purposes at each outlet. If you have an idea for a story on your issue, then contact the reporter who covers that beat or the news director. When you plan an event that you want covered by the media, contact the assignments editor or news director. To be booked as a guest on a television or radio talk show, approach the show's producer or host.

For long-term relationship building, get to know the media gatekeepers at each outlet. These are the people who set the editorial tone of the publication or station and determine what types of stories are covered. At a newspaper or magazine, this is the editor-in-chief or managing editor. At a radio or television station, the key gatekeeper is the station manager, program manager, or public affairs director. Write a letter to the key media gatekeepers in your community introducing yourself and your organization. Explain your issue and why they and their audiences should be interested. Identify exactly what you would like them to do. Increase the number of stories on your topic? Sponsor a public service campaign? Write an editorial on your issue? Follow up with a call to set up a meeting and make your case in person. At the very least, your organization will stand out to them the next time you send a press release or hold a media event.

HOW WILL YOU CONTACT THE MEDIA?

Traditional News Media

In addition to the media gatekeepers, start to establish beneficial working relationships with the reporters and producers at key outlets before you need to pitch them a story. Write to those who cover your issues to give them reactions to their previous stories related to your issue and provide them with an information packet on your organization for future reference. If a reporter or producer knows that you are available as a source, then that person might call you the next time he or she is working on a related story.

When you have news that you want covered by the media, send out a press release to your media list (see sidebar). Individual reporters or outlets might have their own preferences about how they wish to receive releases, so include that information on your media list. Nowadays, most reporters and editors prefer to receive a press release via e-mail; information on where to send it should be available on the outlet's website.

> ## Writing a Press Release
>
> A press release is a succinct summary of the story you are "pitching" to a news organization. To prevent your release from being pitched right into the virtual garbage can, keep the following hints in mind:
>
> - Make the release as short as possible. Ideally, you should keep it to one page, but certainly no more than two pages (400–500 words). If you have more than one page worth of information, then consider turning some of the information into a fact sheet or backgrounder to supplement the press release.
> - Grab the reader's attention with a strong headline (generally eight words or less) and compelling lead sentence.
> - Use recent trends, upcoming holidays, or other "pegs" to establish the newsworthiness and timeliness of your release.
> - Report your information as straight news, without any hype or too many adjectives.
> - Do not forget to include the who, what, why, where, when, and how of the issue. Provide the information in descending order of importance, with the most critical facts at the beginning.
> - Be accurate with your facts, and avoid typos or misspellings of names, to maintain your credibility.
> - Use quotes from key people involved in the news story when appropriate.
> - Provide contact information, including your name, e-mail, and phone number, for a reporter to call with questions about the press release. You might wish to list your cell phone and/or more than one contact in case the reporter needs to reach someone immediately.
> - Use proper press release format, including the date and city in which the news is taking place in the form of a dateline just before the opening paragraph. One paragraph at the end should provide background information about your organization or agency.

The press release text should be in the body of the e-mail, rather than included as an attachment. Never send a press release to more than one person at the same outlet; if two reporters find that they have started writing the same story, then you might ruin your chances of ever getting another story covered. When you have an event, send out a media advisory (see Figure 20.1) with the who, what, why, when, and where of the occasion; this is much briefer than a

FIGURE 20.1 Example of a Media Advisory

MEDIA ADVISORY

LOCAL COALITION IS MAKING SKIN CANCER PREVENTION SOCIAL

The Healthville Cancer Coalition, comprising representatives from 10 local organizations, will introduce its new community-based campaign to prevent skin cancer on May 5, 20XX. The campaign includes billboards that direct people to a website with online videos, a directory of participating local merchants, and an outdoor fun-oriented social network that brings together county residents to stay healthy in the sun. The most recent data on local skin cancer rates also will be announced at the event.

PARTICIPANTS: **Susan McCall**

Chairperson, Healthville Cancer Coalition

Dr. Patricia Smith

Chief of Dermatology, Healthville General Hospital

John Delancey

Executive Director, Healthville Community Foundation

DATE: Tuesday, May 5, 20XX

TIME: 11:00 a.m.

PLACE: Healthville General Hospital Auditorium

123 Main Street, Healthville

CONTACT: **David Solomon**

Healthville Cancer Coalition

(123) 456-7890

---

press release. With every press release or media advisory, make sure you include the URL to a web page where the reporter can find more information. In fact, a social media–based press release submitted through a service such as Pitch Engine or PR Newswire can make it more likely that someone interested in your issue will find you online. By building in social sharing and engagement tools within the press release itself, your message will spread beyond the press to reach even more of the audience directly.

In general, avoid following up the press release with a phone call just to ask if he or she received it. If following up on a media advisory, you can call close to the day of the event to personally invite the press to cover it. Otherwise, an e-mail follow-up is generally sufficient if you have new information to add or have a preexisting relationship with the reporter. Most news organizations work under tight timeframes, so be respectful of the reporter's time when you call. Try to phone in the morning rather than in the afternoon, which is when the deadlines for most outlets fall. Ask whether the person is "on deadline" or if he or she has a few minutes before you go into your pitch. Explain who you are and why your news is important. Be ready to follow up with additional information, and be enthusiastic about the topic as you explain why it is newsworthy. If you are not excited, then why should the reporter be?

Blogger Outreach

As blogs have risen in influence, organizations are reaching out to relevant bloggers to invite them to cover their programs and activities. Many bloggers specialize in writing about a particular niche, and the best are avidly read by others who are interested in that topic. In contrast, some bloggers write about more general content from their day-to-day lives (which may include experiences related to things such as parenting, health and disease, overcoming addiction, disabilities, and other social marketing–related issues). Readers often develop a relationship with bloggers, whether through interacting in the comments section or just in getting to know them through their writing, and this translates to a higher level of trust in the information that they provide.

Many commercial and social marketers have had success in reaching out to a blog's readers by working with the blogger to get the word out (either in a paid or voluntary capacity). Select potential bloggers to work with based on their access to your target audience and the topics that they write about. Though a blogger who your target audience reads might not write specifically about health, social, or environmental issues, he or she may be interested in sharing your information if it is presented in a compelling way. Don't only focus on the bloggers with the biggest audience; many medium-sized blogs reach a smaller but more engaged readership.

A popular blogger named Heather Armstrong, who writes about her daily life on the Dooce blog, learned that she had a basal cell carcinoma on her arm.[1] As she wrote about the process of going from diagnosis to treatment, she generated hundreds of comments on each post by her readers either sharing their own similar experiences or affirming that because of her, they were going to get their own moles checked out by a dermatologist. Though Heather ended up becoming an advocate on her own, this would have been a perfect opportunity for an organization such as the Skin Cancer Foundation to approach her with information she could share with her readers or, at the least, provide links in the comments section. Because her readers spent so much time reading her blog and cared about what happened to her, this experience connected with them more emotionally than if they had simply seen an ad or a news story about the topic.

How do you find bloggers who might be interested in writing about your issue? Search tools such as Google Blog Search, BlogPulse, and Technorati can help identify bloggers who write about relevant topics. Alltop.com is another site that offers human-curated compilations of the best blogs on hundreds of topics. Once you find promising blogs, you can check out the "blogroll" in the sidebar to find links to other blogs recommended by that blogger. Note that you can also reach out to people who communicate via Twitter, podcasts, or video with these techniques as well.

Once you've identified some potential bloggers, spend some time getting to know their blogs to make sure your topic is relevant to what they write about. Read at least three to four recent posts, look at the "About" section to learn more about them, and note whether they provide information about how best to contact them. Some bloggers offer detailed guidelines as to how to send a pitch and what will make them more likely to write about your proposed topic. Because social media are so relationship driven, you will be more successful if the blogger's first introduction to you is through a thoughtful, well-written comment on one of his or her posts than if you start by sending an e-mail asking for something. Look at blogger relations as something that needs to develop over time; start building those relationships now so when the time comes to ask for something, they already know you. Send them useful information that relates to their area of interest, link to their posts in your own blog or social network feeds, start commenting regularly, and provide your perspective on the topics they write about.

---

[1]Armstrong, H. (2006, July 20). Death to Ed. http://www.dooce.com/archives/daily/07_20_2006.html

Many bloggers who are not affiliated with a traditional news organization (which is most of them) are blogging because of a personal or professional passion for the topic. They are not professional journalists and often are blogging in addition to holding a full-time job, so be respectful of their time. Approaching them with a formal press release or a mass-mailed generic appeal is likely to turn them off.

The key to success will be demonstrating how your topic fits in with the focus of the blog and its benefit to the blog's readers. Show that you have actually read their blog beyond the title. Make their write-up easier by providing embedd-able online resources to enhance the story: a linkable URL (a must!), pictures, audio, or video. Provide access to the person in charge of the program or subject matter experts to interview. To reach many people at once, you can offer in-person events for local bloggers, a telephone conference call, or a "bloginar" (a webinar for bloggers). And don't forget, when someone does give you space on his or her blog, say thank you!

WHAT DO YOU HAVE TO OFFER?

Keep in mind that the news media need people like you to help them fill column inches and airtime. You know the topic, you have ideas for interesting stories, and you have access to the people the stories are about. Although you should not contact a reporter every week with a story concept, do not feel intimidated about calling if you truly have a newsworthy idea.

The more you can do to help the reporter do his or her work, the more likely your story will be the one that gets covered that day. Succinct information, such as fact sheets and backgrounders (explaining the events, legislation, or scientific concepts behind your news story), helps the reporter to quickly understand the issue. Photographs or video footage related to the story also heightens your chances of coverage. Provide as many "pieces" of the story as you can of real people affected by the issue, experts willing to be interviewed, and copies of relevant studies. If you want television coverage, then

CDC Blogger Outreach

When an outbreak of salmonella occurred in the United States as a result of contaminated peanut products in early 2009, the U.S. Centers for Disease Control and Prevention (CDC) and the Food and Drug Administration (FDA) needed to get information about the recall of potentially dangerous food items to as many people as quickly as possible. While the issue was all over the news at the time, they also felt they needed to get information and resources out to the public through their already trusted sources. In addition to creating a blog specifically to provide the latest updates about the recall, the CDC used a variety of social media outreach tools to facilitate the spread of information to where people already were spending time online.

CDC staff decided to offer a bloginar (a webinar specifically for bloggers) to quickly get the word out online about the peanut product recall. Rather than focus only on the most obvious type of blogger—those writing on health-related topics— who likely had already covered the salmonella outbreak to some extent, they expanded the invitation list to include less obvious but still relevant blog topics. They reached out to "mommybloggers," whose readers included many parents who might have the affected products in their pantries, as well as bloggers on food, pets (because some pet food was included in the recall), and sports (the bloginar was happening right before the Super Bowl, a big snack food day). Out of approximately 165 invitations, 35 bloggers participated in the bloginar.

The bloginar included presentations from key experts at the CDC and FDA and took questions from the bloggers by phone and Twitter. Some of the questions that these non–health experts asked were things the project team had not yet thought of, which helped them to refine their subsequent messages. The participants were referred to additional online sources of information, as well as badges and widgets they could add to their blogs to offer the latest updates on the recall. Ten of the bloggers who were on the call ended up writing posts, which reached approximately 1,000 people.

make sure that you have visuals to offer such as children playing at a family support center, a counselor speaking with parents, and other compelling action shots.

Conducting a Press Conference

You might wish to hold a press conference to respond to negative publicity about your program, to provide additional information on how a current news event affects your organization or community, or to actively generate attention to an issue your program is addressing. If you do not have major news to announce but wish to inform the media about an issue, then consider conducting a more informal media briefing with a small number of reporters that cover your topic.

To plan and conduct an effective press conference, follow these steps:

1. Clarify your purpose and the key messages you wish to convey at the press conference. Use those guidelines to shape what the speakers will say.

2. Prepare a media list of the reporters and media outlets you wish to invite to the press conference.

3. Set the date, time, and place of the press conference. The best days of the week are Tuesday through Thursday; to increase attendance, try not to schedule a media event on a Monday or Friday, and definitely avoid the weekend. The best time to hold the press conference is in the mid-morning, between 9:30 a.m. and 11:00 a.m., to leave enough time for the reporters to make their deadlines for the day. The event should be held in a site that is convenient for reporters to get to and has appropriate accommodations for the needs of the press. There must be sufficient room and lighting to set up television cameras. If you can provide wireless Internet access, you will increase the chances of live coverage of your event via tools such as Twitter or blogs. You can use your organization's conference room, a local hotel or conference facility, a community center, or a visually interesting and related outdoor location such as in front of the state capitol building.

4. Select two to three speakers. They should be articulate, knowledgeable, and comfortable dealing with the media. In addition to your organization's spokesperson, you might wish to include an expert on the topic to provide technical explanations, such as statistics and medical information, or a person from the community who is affected by the problem. Limit each person's comments to 5 minutes or less, and roughly script what each will say to avoid duplication among the speakers.

5. Send out a media advisory to everyone on your media list. If you have time, send it out a week in advance. If the press conference was called on short notice, then fax the advisory. In either case, follow up with a telephone call the day before or the morning of the event to encourage attendance and to get an idea of who will be there. Make sure that the wire services include your advisory on their daybooks the day before and the day of your event.

6. Before the press conference begins, set up the room. Place a table and chairs at the front with a name card in front of each speaker (facing the audience). Chairs for the reporters should be arranged theater style. You probably will need a podium with a microphone for your speakers. To make it easier for the reporters to record the proceedings without placing their own microphones on the podium, you can rent a "mult-box" that they can plug into. Make sure you have signs directing people to the room, and have a sign-in table where you can greet the reporters and give each of them a press kit.

7. Keep the total length of the press conference to between 30 and 45 minutes. Leave time at the end for a question-and-answer period. Work with the speakers in advance to anticipate possible questions and how best to answer them. Reporters might wish to set up individual interviews with the speakers after the event.

8. Follow up with the media outlets that were not represented to see whether they are interested in receiving a press kit from the event and in interviewing the speakers. If you did not receive the turnout you expected, it might have been because another breaking news story was happening at the same time.

HOW WILL YOU RESPOND WHEN THE MEDIA CALL YOU?

Even if you do not actively seek them out, the media might come to you for information or your reaction to a news story. When this happens, do not panic. Your internal readiness plan should designate a contact who is comfortable talking to the media and has the authority to speak for the organization. If that person is not available, then the person answering the phone should know to ask the deadline for a response for all media calls and find someone else to call back. Otherwise, your organization might miss an important opportunity to provide comments, respond to allegations, counter misinformation, or build a positive relationship with a reporter. Often, there are no second chances.

When speaking to a reporter, always be honest. If you fudge an answer, then it might come back to haunt you and will damage your credibility. When you do not know the answer to a question, just say so. Find out the reporter's deadline and either call back with the answer or make a referral to other sources who could speak on that point.

Make yourself as understandable as possible. Speak in plain English, without jargon or acronyms; not everyone knows that CAPTA is the Child Abuse Prevention and Treatment Act or that the word *lacerations* refers to cuts on the skin. Avoid mumbling or speaking too fast when talking to a reporter, especially if you are being recorded for radio or television. Broadcast media require actualities—taped quotes from interviewees—interspersed with the narration throughout their stories. If your portion of the interview is not clear, then you might be cut from the story.

Know the main message you want to get across and repeat it in several different ways throughout the interview. Keep the sentences to short "sound bites" to make them more usable as actualities. As you answer the reporter's questions, do not limit yourself to the questions at hand; integrate your key points into the answers as well. The better able you are to articulate the main messages throughout the interview, the more likely they will come through in the final story.

Assembling Your Press Kit

A press kit should contain all the information a media professional needs to put together a story about your issue or organization. Provide press kits to the media at a press conference or media briefing or when you pitch a story.

A good press kit might contain the following, placed in a folder with pockets and labeled with your organization's name on the outside:

- Current press release
- Fact sheet providing statistics and information on the issue
- Backgrounder explaining what has happened to date on the issue or technical details
- Literature about your organization
- Photographs or camera-ready charts, graphs, or other materials to help illustrate the issue
- Copies of past articles on your organization or issue
- List of experts or people affected by the issue who are willing to be interviewed by the media
- Biographies of your key spokespersons
- Statements of support from your partner organizations

These items should also be available on your website in a section titled "Media Kit" or "Press Room."

WORKSHEET 17: IMPLEMENTATION PLANNING WORKSHEET

I. Deployment Plan

Deployment Checklist

Date to Be Completed by

Partners chosen to participate in dissemination of materials _____

Correct quantities of materials ordered _____

Materials ready to be distributed _____

Materials distributed to partner organizations _____

Partners received instructions on how to distribute materials _____

Materials available to target audience _____

Media materials distributed to media outlets _____

Inventory tracking system in place _____

Materials reordering system in place _____

Environmental changes in place _____

Partner Distribution Plan

Organization Disseminating Materials	Contact Name/Phone/E-mail	Item 1 Quantity	Item 2 Quantity	Item 3 Quantity
1.				
2.				
3.				
4.				

II. Internal Readiness Plan

    1. Program spokesperson: _____

    2. Backup spokesperson: _____

(Continued)

(Continued)

3. Key talking points about social marketing program:

a. _____

_____

b. _____

_____

c. _____

_____

d. _____

_____

e. _____

_____

4. Procedure for dealing with comments or complaints about the social marketing campaign:

_____

_____

_____

_____

5. Other people/organizations to refer reporters to for more information on topic:

Name	Organization	Phone Number	Type of Information
_____	_____	_____	_____
_____	_____	_____	_____
_____	_____	_____	_____
_____	_____	_____	_____

6. Partner roles:

Partner Organization	Contact Name/Phone/E-mail	Role(s) in Campaign
1.		
2.		
3.		
4.		

III. Media Buy Plan

1. Broadcast Media Buys

Flight dates:

_____ to _____

_____ to _____

_____ to _____

Station	Contact Name/ Phone Number	Rank for Target Audience	Ad Rate	Number of Ads	Total Cost

2. Print Media Buys

Ad publication dates:

_____   _____

_____   _____

_____   _____

_____   _____

_____   _____

Publication	Contact Name/ Phone Number	Ad Size	Ad Rate	Number of Ads	Total Cost

3. Out-of-Home Media Buys

Type of out-of-home media: _____

Posting dates: _____ to _____

(Continued)

(Continued)

Out-of-Home Company	Contact Name/ Phone Number	Ad Size	Ad Rate	Gross Rating Point Showing	Total Cost

IV. Public Relations Plan

1. What is your purpose in seeking media attention?

   _____

   _____

   _____

2. What is your "news"?

   _____

   _____

   _____

3. What type of media coverage will you seek? (check all that apply)

   ❑ News

   ❑ Feature

   ❑ Editorial

   ❑ Entertainment

   ❑ Public service

   ❑ Other _____

4. Which specific formats will you use (e.g., talk show, op-ed, letter to the editor)?

   _____

   _____

   _____

5. How will you seek media coverage to kick off or promote the campaign?

   ❑ Press release

   ❑ Press conference

   ❑ Media briefing

   ❑ Other media event: _____

6. What items will you include in your media kit?

_____

_____

_____

_____

_____

V. Social Media Engagement Plan

1. Who will coordinate the social media activities for the program?

_____

_____

_____

2. Who else will be authorized to engage in social media interactions on behalf of the program?

_____

_____

_____

3. Which social media sites do you need to set up (e.g., open account, design template, upload picture, etc.)?

_____

_____

_____

4. Will you create an editorial calendar to guide content creation?

❏ Yes   ❏ No

5. Do you have a social media policy in place?

❏ Yes   ❏ No, but will create one   ❏ No, don't need one

6. What keywords will you follow in your social media monitoring system?

_____

_____

_____

7. What types of social media sites will you monitor for your keywords? (check all that apply)

❏ Blogs   ❏ Twitter   ❏ Social networks   ❏ Discussion boards

❏ Videos ❏ Photos   ❏ Wikis   ❏ Consumer reviews

❏ Social news/bookmarking

8. What criteria will you use to determine when to respond or join in a social media conversation? (check all that apply)

❑ Respond to all relevant if time permits

❑ Geographical/audience limitation: _____

❑ Respond to organization or campaign-specific posts only

❑ Answer question on topic

❑ Correct misinformation on topic

❑ Provide additional context or useful resources on topic

CHAPTER 21

Monitoring Implementation

Before implementation even begins, put monitoring mechanisms in place to retrieve feedback on the program and to catch any problems in their early stages. Although you might not be able to anticipate every type of problem you will encounter, a monitoring system will at least help to identify problems as they arise during implementation. Most problems can be easily solved if you detect them early enough, but left unchecked, they can mean the difference between success and failure.

Tracking the progress of your program helps you to accomplish the following:

- Ensure that the elements of the program are being carried out as planned

- Ensure quality

- Address any potential problems that arise

- Alter the course of the program (if necessary)

- Keep staff and partners energized

- Know when you might be running out of materials for restocking

- Assess the results of your program

Monitoring may be as simple as asking callers how they found out about your program, tracking participation on your social media accounts, or making sure that your partners are doing what they promised. If you find that most of your referrals are coming from just a couple of partners, then follow up with the other partners to learn why they are not referring more people to you. Or, if the website traffic in response to your ads suddenly slows down to a trickle, make sure that the radio station did not stop running the commercials too early. Effective monitoring involves staying on top of trends in your program's activities and ensuring that implementation is on the right path toward accomplishing program goals.

PROCESS EVALUATION

Process evaluation activities monitor the day-to-day operations of your program so that you can say with relative certainty what comprised the actual intervention. You can evaluate the effects and contributions of each piece of the program to change or remove elements that are not working as intended. By keeping your finger on the pulse of the program, you will be able to adapt and make necessary adjustments along the way.

Before putting monitoring mechanisms in place, determine your process evaluation objectives. What measures will tell you whether your program is on track? You should not necessarily measure something just because you can; measure it only if it will help you in your assessments of program success. Identify the pieces of your program that will provide an indication of whether the campaign is progressing as planned.

Internally, determine how closely the program is meeting the projected timeline and budget as well as whether staff members understand and perform their roles correctly. Externally, assess the effectiveness of each of your partners in disseminating campaign materials or making referrals to your program. Make sure that media buys are implemented as directed. Track the online interactions with your organization as a result of the campaign and how they were handled. The specifics of your program will determine the elements that are included in your process evaluation.

The information that a process evaluation provides can help with improving the program during implementation itself rather than waiting until the campaign is over to assess whether the program went as planned. Tracking activities during implementation helps to answer the following questions:

- How many people were reached through the media with your advertisements or public service announcements? How many were target audience members?

- How many target audience members and other people participated in your program activities?

- What quantity and quality of interactions related to the campaign occurred via social media both with your social media accounts and among others talking about it?

- How many responses (e.g., phone calls, e-mails, website visitors, new appointments) did you get as a result of the program? How do these compare to those in the months leading up to the campaign and the same months the previous year(s)?

- How did your program respond to the inquiries that were received? Was appropriate action taken in each case?

- How many materials were handed or sent out to the target audience by your organization? How many materials were posted or displayed to be picked up? How many page views occurred on your website, and which pages were most popular?

- How many media "hits" (or news stories) appeared as a result of your public relations efforts? How many mentions in social media as a result of blogger relations and other online outreach?

- How many materials were each of your partners given? How many were disseminated by these partners?

- Were staff and partners adequately trained to effectively carry out their roles in the program? Did they perform their roles correctly?

- Were all activities carried out on budget and according to the timeline? If not, why not?

- Did all paid media ads run as scheduled? Did social media online community growth and participation occur as anticipated?

■ Are there any current events or pieces of legislation pending that might affect the program?

TRACKING MECHANISMS

The mechanisms you can use to track the progress of program implementation range from simple counts of phone calls and materials to complex analyses of management practices. Monitor closely all aspects of your program throughout the course of the implementation period rather than waiting until the end to look at the results. Some items will need to be assessed once a week or month, whereas others should be tracked on a daily basis. Following are the primary categories for monitoring during implementation, with a brief description and suggested list of methods.

Outreach Activities

Purpose: To evaluate whether communications were distributed or accessed in the manner and quantities planned

Tracking methods:

■ *Materials inventory.* Use tracking forms to keep an accurate count of how many of each type of material goes out and whether materials need to be reordered.

■ *Distribution list.* Create a list to track which organizations help to distribute the materials and follow up with phone calls to ensure receipt and dissemination.

■ *Materials placement audit.* Physically visit partner organizations or outreach locations to check whether posters are up, brochures are placed where people can pick them up, and other materials are being used correctly.

■ *Digital materials distribution tracking.* Keep track of how and where digital versions of materials are being distributed and how many times they were downloaded or e-mailed.

Target Audience Response

Purpose: To assess the number of target audience members responding to and participating in the program as a result of the campaign

Tracking methods:

■ *Response tracking sheets.* Categorize the incoming phone calls or mail to tally important items such as the type of request and the answers to the question, "How did you find out about us?" The same sheet can be used to track a day's or week's worth of responses. Use different e-mails or URLs to track the source of the interaction with the target audience.

■ *Activity reports.* Determine the number of people participating in program activities through sign-up sheets or attendance records.

- *Online metrics.* Track traffic to your website using an online analytics program (e.g., Google Analytics) to monitor volume of visitors, referral sources, pages viewed, location of visitors, and other information. Also gather information about participation on your social media accounts, including number of fans/followers/subscribers and their characteristics.

- *Public "diaries" or graffiti sheets.* Place blank journals or hang blank pieces of butcher paper up in places such as clinic waiting rooms, community recreation centers, and program events to collect feedback from target audience members about the program and their feelings about an issue.

Media Exposure

Purpose: To determine whether paid media ran as scheduled, whether and when media ran public service announcements, and whether your public relations activities yielded media coverage as well as the number of target audience members reached through all these methods

Tracking methods:

- *Television and radio logs.* If you purchased media time, you will receive a list of exactly when each ad ran including (usually) any extra spots the station provided as public service announcements. If you did not purchase spots, then the station may or may not provide this information.

- *Tear sheets.* When you purchase ad space in newspapers or magazines, each publication will provide you with a copy of the page on which your ad appeared.

- *News hits.* In most cases, coverage of your campaign by a news outlet can be found online using services such as Google Alerts or other search engines. For more comprehensive scanning, you can hire a clipping service to scan metropolitan and local community newspapers, television and radio news, and news wire services to provide you with clippings or transcripts of all stories mentioning your organization, a specific event, or topics of interest. Hire a clipping service before you begin your campaign because most cannot locate articles retroactively. You can analyze the media coverage of your campaign to assess whether your main messages got through and whether it was generally positive, negative, or neutral coverage.

- *Bounceback cards.* Enclose a postage-paid postcard printed with a few quick questions when you submit your public service announcement for the public service director to fill out and send back to you. You might be able to get an idea of which stations intend to use the public service announcement, although busy individuals might ignore the cards. You could also create a quick online survey or request feedback via e-mail.

Online "Buzz"

Purpose: To track the quantity and quality of conversations and mentions of the campaign online, as well as to identify potential problems early

Tracking methods:

- *Social media monitoring system.* Aggregate RSS feeds tracking search results for relevant keywords such as the name of your campaign, your organization, or topic. These may be via Google Alerts, Twitter Search, and other search engines for blogs, discussion boards, and social networks. Most of these can be set up for free, or you can contract with providers such as Radian6 or Scout Labs to monitor for you.

- *Content analysis.* In addition to just collecting mentions, you can analyze the content to determine common questions, general sentiment toward the campaign, misinformation being spread, and situations in which alterations to the campaign and/or a response beyond ongoing interactions may be necessary.

- *Online community interactions.* When building an online community of people interested in the campaign and issue, whether in a proprietary social network or spread across existing sites, tracking the rate of growth and level of participation of members can help indicate success.

Management Effectiveness/Efficiency

Purpose: To assess whether the program was managed well from the standpoint of staff, partners, timeline, and budget

Tracking methods:

- *Staff survey or focus groups.* Either anonymously survey staff involved in program implementation or conduct focus groups to determine ways in which program management or other processes are going smoothly or could be improved.

- *Partner feedback.* Elicit input from program partners regarding the effectiveness of program processes and communication through phone calls or surveys.

- *Timeline and budget assessment.* Compare the original program timeline and budget with the actual outcome and assess what could be done differently the next time to comply better with each (if necessary).

Issue Monitoring

Purpose: To stay on top of trends and developments in the field by tracking changes and events that have strategic implications for the social marketing program

Tracking methods:

- *News and information searches.* Use Google Alerts to track whenever keywords related to your issue appear somewhere online. In addition, subscribing to a daily source of news and information will notify you of any new developments or news in the field that might affect how the target audience responds to your program or how you present the program. Reading a major newspaper daily or monitoring news over the Internet also can help keep you informed.

■ *Legislative tracking systems.* Track what is happening with relevant legislation through free federal services such as THOMAS (http://thomas.loc.gov/) or paid services such as Congressional Quarterly's tracking alerts that notify you of any legislative actions on the topics of your choice. Most states have their own online tracking systems as well.

■ *Attitude surveys.* Polling organizations such as the Gallup Organization, Harris Interactive, and the Pew Research Center regularly conduct national surveys to assess general attitudes on social issue topics. Knowing the results of any polls taken on topics relating to your program may assist you in adjusting your program during implementation.

CASE STUDY

Implementation Case Study: Donate Life California

When Donate Life California launched the state's first online organ donor registry, the campaign carefully planned all the pieces of the implementation strategy.[1] It first focused on increasing public awareness of the importance of organ donation, then called on people to act by signing up for the registry. The program brought together two large meetings of people interested in the issue—one in Northern California and one in Southern California—with the dual purposes of attracting the collaboration and commitment of local leaders and to generate campaign ideas. Attendees included hospital and transplant center representatives, community thought leaders, clergy, and politicians. These discussions led to the campaign creating specific messages and execution strategies geared toward the needs of each group (see Table 21.1). Weekly conference calls kept the program on track for launching the registry to coincide with National Donate Life Month.

Activities were organized according to three tiers, each of which had task forces coordinating the pieces of the campaign. The first tier was media advocacy, which included activities that would help to reframe media coverage of the organ donation issue from a personal problem affecting individuals and families to a public health issue affecting all Californians. The campaign created media kits to distribute to news outlets to inspire compelling stories and provide up-to-date information about organ donation and the registry. The media kits were also posted online prior to the launch. The team sent out media releases about the campaign and public service announcements that could be read on live radio. In addition to the media releases, the campaign issued a press conference advisory detailing the 12 different locations around the state where media could attend a simultaneous news conference. These news conferences required months of planning to ensure that the key spokespeople, local celebrities, organ donors and recipients, people on the waiting list, and others would be in place at the right day and time. Following the launch, Donate Life California submitted op-eds and conducted in-person briefings for major metro newspapers.

The second tier focused on community outreach through a series of registry drives and partnerships to continue the momentum of the media advocacy. Communities throughout California held drives to encourage people to sign up for the registry, including competitions between cities and universities. Partnerships with key community leaders, such as clergy and political leaders, helped to get the word out. The team created tools to help the faith-based leadership promote the registry, including church bulletins, announcements, and sermon topics to use with their congregations. The campaign offered these types of partner-specific tools to many different types of organizations.

The third tier focused on people who did not have access to the Internet. By partnering with public libraries, Donate Life California was able to reach the people who use free computer access there. The campaign created signs to place around the computers and trained librarians to help library patrons register online. Eventually the registry was linked to the Department of Motor Vehicles, which made it easy for people who did not have Internet access to register as well.

[1]Allrich, H., Dougall, E., & Heneghan, D. (2007, June). Donate Life California: A campaign launch case study. *Cases in Public Health Communication & Marketing.* http://www.casesjournal.org/volume1/peer-reviewed/cases_1_05.cfm

Process evaluation and campaign monitoring was set up from the beginning before implementation began. They tracked every visit to the registry website, including number of people who registered, number of visitors, links selected, and more. The web-based registration form also included the question, "How did you hear about us?" with the drop-down responses changing based on the promotions that were happening at a given time. The team also tracked the number of news stories that ran about the program, both at the launch and over the course of the campaign. Feedback they received from these monitoring activities was used to refine the program, such as learning that the second most common way people heard about the campaign was through family and friends. This spurred more of a focus on word-of-mouth-based activities.

From the evaluation results, the Donate Life California campaign was successful in meeting and exceeding its initial objectives. The original campaign goal was to sign up 15,000 potential donors to the registry; they exceeded this by 160,000 people. Six months after the registry was linked to the Department of Motor Vehicles, the number of registrants exceeded one million. Much of the success of the campaign was due to the careful planning and partnership development that occurred prior to implementation.

Table 21.1   Planning for Implementation

Audience	Description	Messages	Execution
Public	~ Donor/families ~ General public	~ You can save a life. ~ Go online to sign up for the registry.	~ News media coverage ~ Registry drives ~ Posters, flyers ~ Sponsorships
Transplant Centers	~ 27 hospitals in California that perform organ transplants	~ New online registry will help ease your job in fulfilling patients' wishes. ~ Help us spread the word.	~ Letters to transplant centers ~ Invitation to workshop
Hospitals	~ Hundreds of hospitals throughout California that speak with families about organ donation	~ Support legislation to bring the registry to the DMV. ~ Help us spread the word.	~ Letters to hospitals ~ Personal conversations with those who work in transplantation ~ Invitation to workshop
Community Leaders	~ Consists of influential "movers and shakers" in the community: local celebrities, athletes, etc.	~ Register on the new online registry. ~ Use influence to help spread the word.	~ Personal calls ~ Letters to community leaders ~ Invitation to workshop
Clergy	~ Religious leaders who can clarify that organ donation is not against the tenets of their religion	~ Explain religious beliefs about organ donation. ~ Encourage congregation to register online.	~ Face-to-face meetings ~ Religious toolkits ~ Invitation to workshop
Medical Associations	~ Other medical associations like the National Kidney Foundation that would benefit from organ donation	~ Partner with us to help us spread the message.	~ Letter-writing campaign ~ Direct conversations with leaders ~ Invitation to workshop
Political Leaders	~ Government leaders who will influence vital legislation regarding organ donation	~ Online registry is important. ~ We need the DMV to host the website and collect data.	~ Letter-writing campaign ~ Invitation to workshop

WORKSHEET 18: IMPLEMENTATION TRACKING WORKSHEET

1. What are the key process evaluation objectives for your program? (Remember to make them SMART objectives.)

    a. _____

    _____

    b. _____

    _____

    c. _____

    _____

    d. _____

    _____

    e. _____

    _____

2. What types of mechanisms will you use to track progress of your implementation?

    a. Outreach activities:

    ❑ Materials inventory

    ❑ Distribution list

    ❑ Materials placement audit

    ❑ Digital materials distribution tracking

    ❑ Other: _____

    b. Target audience response:

    ❑ Response tracking sheets

    ❑ Activity reports

    ❑ Online metrics

    ❑ Diaries/graffiti sheets

    ❑ Other: _____

c. Media exposure:

❑ Television and radio logs

❑ Tear sheets

❑ News hits

❑ Bounceback cards

❑ Other: _____

d. Online "buzz":

❑ Social media monitoring system

❑ Content analysis

❑ Online community interactions

❑ Other: _____

e. Management effectiveness/efficiency:

❑ Staff survey

❑ Staff focus groups

❑ Partner feedback

❑ Timeline and budget assessment

❑ Other: _____

f. Issue monitoring:

❑ News and information searches

❑ Legislative tracking systems

❑ Attitude surveys

❑ Other: _____

Section VII

Step 6
Evaluation and Feedback

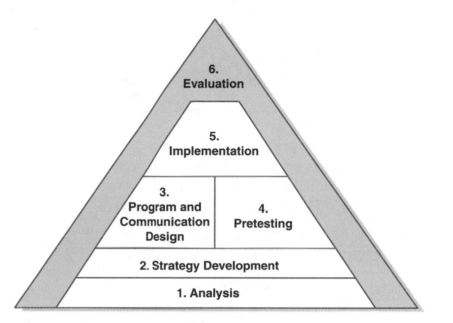

SECTION OVERVIEW

What if we never evaluated what we did in our daily lives? We might continually take the longest, most inefficient route home from work. We might lose a friend or spouse because we were unable to assess and correct the things that we did wrong in that relationship. Or, we might not realize that the medicine we were taking for an illness was ineffective and that we needed to try a different treatment. Just as we constantly evaluate our own actions based on their results, a social marketer must assess the effects that the program is having and make adjustments based on that information.

Although listed as the final step of the process, forms of evaluation and feedback occur throughout the life of a social marketing program. They are addressed here last because until you implement the program, you cannot assess whether it was successful in actually changing the behavior of your target audience and in meeting other objectives. To avoid a last-minute evaluation tacked on at the end of your campaign, build evaluation into the social marketing process from the very beginning.

This section consists of the following chapters:

- Chapter 22: Evaluation Basics

- Chapter 23: Evaluation Design

- Chapter 24: Evaluation Methods

- Chapter 25: Using Feedback to Improve Your Program

Evaluation Basics

The word *evaluation* often strikes fear in the hearts of program planners. However, with an understanding of why it is necessary and what it entails, you soon will see evaluation as an indispensable and not so daunting piece of a well-planned social marketing program.

WHY DO EVALUATION?

Increasingly, funders require that their grantees include an evaluation component in their programs. If this is your situation, then think of evaluation as something that you are doing for yourself rather than for your funders because you will benefit much more than they will. Even if you do not have an outside organization telling you to evaluate your program, it still is good social marketing practice.

Evaluation creates accountability. For this reason, many people are wary of having their programs evaluated and would prefer to rely on anecdotal evidence of success rather than actual data that may or may not reflect well on them. Do not be intimidated by evaluation; instead, see it as an opportunity to prove that your program has made a difference. Positive results also might assist you in securing additional funding in the future.

If done well, your evaluation activities also will help to improve your program while it is being implemented as well as in later incarnations. By identifying what does and does not work, you will be able to focus your resources on the most effective parts of the program and eliminate or reduce other components. A good evaluation is one that provides useful information, not just interesting statistics. Design your evaluation activities around the questions you need answered to improve your program. Remember the concept of "backward research"? This is the same idea.

Your evaluation need not be conducted by an outside evaluator, although if you lack research expertise on your staff or wish to ensure a totally objective assessment, you will find a consultant quite useful. You can carry out most types of evaluation methods yourself or with volunteers, if necessary. Social marketing research does not have to be the type of research you learned about in school with randomized treatment and control groups, complicated statistics, and primarily academic questions. There is a place for this type of research in social marketing, but for the most part, you can use relatively simple methods to get the type of information you need.

TYPES OF EVALUATION

When you begin to consider evaluation of your social marketing campaign, you might focus primarily on the question "Did the program work?" But evaluation entails more than this broad question. Several types of evaluation help to assess different aspects of program success throughout the life of the project, as depicted in Figure 22.1. Balch and Sutton[1] aptly pose three simple questions pertaining to each level of evaluation research:

■ What should we do?

■ How are we doing?

■ Did we do it?

The first question "What should we do?" is answered through formative evaluation. Formative research is done to shape the program strategy and pretest the materials prior to implementation. You are already familiar with formative evaluation through your activities in the first four steps of the social marketing process: analysis, strategy development, program and communication design, and pretesting. This is the research you used to determine the messages, media, and overall marketing mix that might work best for the target audience and then to narrow down the choices through pretesting.

During implementation, the second question "How are we doing?" assesses whether the program is executed as planned. Process evaluation, discussed in Chapter 21, determines

FIGURE 22.1 Evaluation in the Social Marketing Process

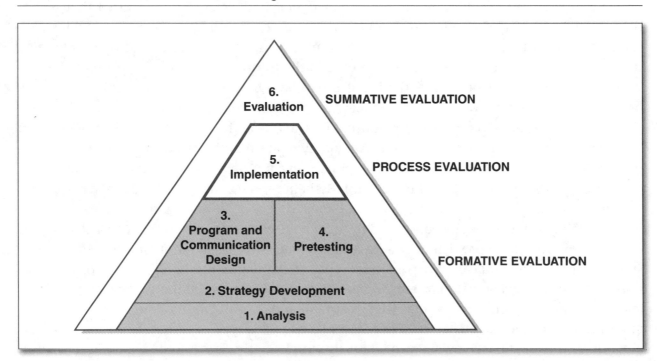

[1]Balch, G., & Sutton, S. (1997). Keep me posted: A plea for practical evaluation. In M. Goldberg, M. Fishbein, & S. Middlestadt (Eds.), *Social marketing: Theoretical and practical perspectives* (pp. 62–74). Mahwah, NJ: Lawrence Erlbaum.

what information or services were delivered as a result of the program and to whom. Understanding what actually happened during the course of implementation, as opposed to what was supposed to occur, can help identify why certain elements of the program were or were not effective. Process evaluation is especially useful for determining how to adjust the program in midstream or to improve implementation for the next time.

Answering the third question "Did we do it?" involves summative evaluation. This type of research investigates the effect that your program had on factors related to the problem or issue it was designed to address, and it is the focus of this chapter. Summative evaluation can be further separated into two different components: outcome evaluation and impact evaluation.[2] Outcome evaluation occurs at the end of program implementation or periodically over the life of a campaign. Identifying the extent of attitude and behavior change in the target audience and correlating it with individual exposure to the campaign is an important measure of the program's effectiveness. Outcome measures are commonly used in summative evaluation to link achievement of the program's objectives to campaign activities. Pre- and post-

> ## Ethical Evaluation
>
> Kotler and Roberto[a] propose another type of evaluation for social marketing programs ethical evaluation. Whenever we strive to change people's behavior, we must do so responsibly and be accountable to the target audience members. Although in the end the results of the program are the final measure of success, the means to that end are just as important. Ethical issues should be considered at each stage of program development to ensure the integrity of target audience research and that the program itself does not encourage behavior change in an unethical way.
>
> People never should be coerced into a behavior, even though it might be "for their own good." Making offers that the target audience members cannot refuse, such as large amounts of money, might be ethically suspect and counterproductive to long-term behavior change. Excessive incentives might encourage materialism and a disinclination for people to help themselves without an extrinsic reward.
>
> Social marketing programs might have side effects or unintended consequences that are harmful in the long run. For example, a program intended to empower low-income women to use condoms resulted in beatings by several male partners who perceived the women's insistence on using condoms as an insult. Whenever possible, potential negative effects of the program should be identified and explored with the target audience during the initial formative research. Implementation of the program should be monitored to ensure that it "does no harm" so that changes can be made midstream (if necessary).
>
> ---
>
> a. Kotler, P., & Roberto, E. (1989). *Social marketing: Strategies for changing public behavior.* New York: Free Press, 1989.

campaign knowledge, attitudes, and behavior surveys to assess related changes are the most common type of outcome evaluation method.

Impact evaluation makes the leap from behavior change to health or social outcomes. This type of evaluation determines whether the people who adopt the behavior promoted by the social marketing program experience a subsequent reduction in morbidity or mortality (or improvement in quality of life) related to the overall goal of the program. The actual impact of the campaign often is difficult to assess accurately. Because many of the problems that are tackled by social marketers will not appear until many years after the campaign (e.g., heart disease, cancer), it might be impossible to determine the effect of a particular social marketing program

---

[2]Depending on your academic background, you might have learned different names for each type of evaluation. This book follows the standard used in the field of social marketing. The names are not as important as the concepts, so do not worry if you use a different set of labels to distinguish each type of evaluation.

on overall trends. Long-term prospective studies following participants over time often are necessary to assess the program's effects on these types of issues. However, for other outcomes that change relatively quickly (e.g., HIV status, pregnancy), it is possible to track rates before and after implementation of the program.

EVALUATION CHALLENGES

The anxiety often felt by new social marketers about evaluation is not entirely without basis. Done correctly, an evaluation can provide valuable data and feedback. Done poorly, an ineffective campaign might receive a glowing review, or the positive effects of a well-constructed program might go undetected. This is due to a variety of challenges to conducting a sound evaluation. These hurdles can best be overcome by recognizing and planning for them from the start.

The main challenges you might face in your evaluation include the following:

Unrealistic expectations. Communications alone can go only so far in bringing about reductions in morbidity and mortality, particularly for chronic diseases. Your social marketing program, in all likelihood, will not dramatically alter these rates in your community overnight or even after 1 or 2 years. When evaluating your communications activities, be realistic in what you can expect for your results. Awareness, knowledge, attitudes, intentions, and behavior all can be measured and linked to your program. Whether that behavior change actually affects the problem it is designed to address might be out of your control. An incorrect theory of causation of the problem (whether biomedical or psychosocial), additional campaigns being done by other programs, and delayed effects of the intervention that might not be evident for decades are among the factors that can conceal or confound the related morbidity and mortality data.

Limited resources. The most imposing barrier to conducting an evaluation can be lack of resources, whether in the form of funds, staff time, or expertise. Often, social marketing projects barely have enough money for formative research and materials production, so summative evaluation gets short shrift. There are, however, ways in which to stretch your project funds and use low-cost methods to ensure at least some evaluation of whether your program met its objectives. Universities can provide a wealth of evaluation expertise as well as potential free or low-cost labor in the form of a professor interested in combining his or her research with your campaign or a health education or research methods graduate student looking for a class project. Using secondary data from other sources, such as annual surveys or epidemiological surveillance systems already in place, is another way in which to minimize the costs involved with data collection.

Reliance on a single method. Just like the six blind men feeling various parts of a pachyderm and coming to vastly different conclusions about what an elephant looks like—a snake (trunk), a tree (leg), a wall (side), a rope (tail), a fan (ear), or a spear (tusk) from each of their perspectives—you might find diverse results depending on the research methods you use in your evaluation. To avoid getting just one possibly skewed description of your program's effects, use several different methods whenever possible to round out the picture. Combining the results of more than one research method can compensate for the weaknesses of each technique; this is called triangulation.

Using the wrong model. Social marketing is not hard science. Although rigorous standards still apply to the research we do, the "A causes B" type of model that is found in the biomedical sciences is not as clear-cut in the behavioral sciences. Human behavior cannot be put into a vacuum to test the effects of various messages; external and internal factors always are at work, and controlling for them is not easy. For this reason, the experimental model so often used in clinical trials does not always yield accurate results for communications-based programs. The type of evaluation done by those in the advertising and marketing fields to assess the effectiveness of their communications is more appropriate for a social marketing program than that of the medical world. Scientists would be aghast at social marketers using preliminary evaluation data to adjust the program in midstream. Remember that you are not testing various hypotheses of behavior change theory. Your mission is not to produce pristine data but rather to implement the most effective campaign possible.

Asking the wrong questions. Maybe it would be nice to know the height, weight, and nutritional habits of all the respondents to your survey, but if you are assessing the results of a breast cancer screening campaign, do you really need to know that? Avoid the temptation to learn as much about the participants as possible while you have their attention and cooperation; do not take advantage of the situation to ask 20 additional questions that are irrelevant to your evaluation. Questions should focus on whether you achieved the program objectives as laid out in the planning phase. Always ask yourself, "What will I learn from this question, and how will I use the responses?"

Technical problems. Even when you structure the evaluation research correctly, other issues can arise that make your results invalid. Statistics software, for example, can make data analysis much easier; however, when someone who does not fully understand the meanings and limitations of various statistical tests runs the analysis on that software, the results might be misinterpreted or meaningless. Other problems might affect the evaluation process outside of imperfect procedural techniques such as a small target audience making it difficult to find people to interview, a low response rate to your survey, and inexperienced interviewers. Seeking advice from an expert evaluator, or at least someone in your field who has conducted evaluation research previously, can help you to identify potential problems and to pose solutions.

Resistance from program staff or participants. Staff often feel threatened by evaluations. Members of the target audience might not see any benefit to themselves in giving you information on their private lives. This can wreak havoc with collecting evaluation data. Your staff and others working on the program might need assurances that their jobs or reputations will not be put in jeopardy by negative evaluation results. Process evaluation examining project management can be done anonymously. Any data collection done by frontline staff should be as unobtrusive to their normal responsibilities as possible to avoid their balking at additional work. Target audience members might need incentives (monetary or otherwise), as well as a guarantee of confidentiality, to get them to participate.

Waiting until the program is over to start evaluation. Do not get all the way through implementation of your program before starting to think about evaluation. Ideally, you should collect baseline data at some point before implementation begins to be able to compare factors such as attitudes and behaviors before and after the campaign. Process, outcome, and impact evaluation need to be designed into the program to have meaningful results at the end. In addition, ongoing evaluation provides real-time feedback to help you adjust and improve the program while it still can make a difference.

Failure to use evaluation results. There is an epidemic among program managers (social marketing and otherwise) of the "put it on a shelf" syndrome. Every year, thousands of evaluation reports that were sweated over for months end up on bookshelves, never to be touched again. Do not let this happen to your evaluation. If designed well, your evaluation results should provide you with recommendations for how to improve the next phase of your campaign. The feedback also can assist you with designing and implementing social marketing programs on other issues, based on what you learned about the process and target audience. Make the evaluation report a living document rather than just a pile of dead tree pulp on the shelf.

CHAPTER 23

Evaluation Design

With any research method you choose, you first will decide how to structure your evaluation design. This will determine where you find your data, at what points you take measurements, and whether you will use comparison groups. The design you use to carry out the evaluation will depend in part on your resources and the length of time the program is implemented. An evaluation design can be either cross-sectional (i.e., administered to people randomly chosen at particular points in time) or prospective (i.e., following the same individuals over time). Prospective studies involve more intensive recruitment and follow-up but can yield more detailed data.

In your summative evaluation, the ultimate goal is to determine the effects of your program on the target audience. How accurately you do this relates to whether or not you use an experimental approach. A true experimental design allows you to state with relative certainty that it was your campaign, rather than other outside influences, that caused any differences you find. By randomly assigning people or communities either to participate in the social marketing program or to serve as a comparison group that is not exposed, you can eliminate much of the "noise" that obscures the program's effects. Because true experimental research can be very costly and requires a high level of expertise, it is not practical to expect from most small-scale social marketing programs. You can, however, structure your evaluation to increase your chances of obtaining valid results even if you do not use the most rigorous design.

Before you decide the actual method you will use, such as a survey, observations, or qualitative techniques, determine the points at which you will collect the data and how complex the evaluation design will be. The following four sections discuss the most commonly used approaches.

DATA FROM EXISTING RECORDS

You do not always need to create an elaborate questionnaire to find information that is useful for your evaluation. Use data that are already being collected, either by your organization or by secondary sources, to compare relevant measurements before and after the social marketing program. These measurements could be statistics your program collects routinely such as the monthly numbers of visitors to your website or mammograms done by your program. Or, you might be able to obtain data from other public or private organizations such as frequencies of diagnoses from a local disease or emergency room registry, condom sales from local

Elements of an Evaluation Design

An evaluation design consists of the following elements:

1. Program goals and objectives. The goals and objectives you set during the planning phase will be used to assess whether the program achieved what it set out to do.

2. Data to be collected. You must specify exactly what information will be collected in the evaluation to measure attainment of the goals and objectives.

3. Methodology. The research methods that you will use to collect the data should be laid out clearly. This includes how you will recruit research participants or find the data to be used, the sample size needed, when the research will take place, and exactly how the research will be conducted.

4. Data collection instruments. The survey questionnaire, focus group topic guide, or other research instrument should be developed and pretested before using it in the actual evaluation.

5. Data processing and analysis. Before collecting any data, determine how they will be converted into a usable format and analyzed. This will assist you in designing a data collection instrument that will facilitate these processes before it comes time to input the data.

6. Evaluation report. To be most useful, write up the resulting data analysis into an evaluation report that relays the key findings and recommendations for changes in the program.

drug stores, and state morbidity and mortality statistics. The Behavioral Risk Factor Surveillance System (BRFSS), a telephone survey conducted by all states, might be a useful source of data on knowledge and behaviors for your purposes.

The advantage of using existing data is clear: You do not have to start from scratch by conducting new research. If you can find data that answer your evaluation questions, then by all means, use them. In cases where the exact information you need is not available or easily measurable, consider using proxy measures, that is, variables that often occur along with or are caused by the phenomenon you wish to measure. For example, you can get an idea of changes in behaviors related to HIV risk by looking at trends in the rates of hepatitis B, which is transmitted in a similar way and is reportable in all states.

Disadvantages of this design are common to all approaches that measure changes only in the population that is exposed to the campaign. There is no way in which to tell whether changes in your evaluation indicators were the result of your program. Other factors occurring simultaneously with your campaign, such as a major news story about your issue, a splashy new advertising blitz by another organization, and changing demographic trends, might be the impetus for the changes you see. For example, the 2009 appearance of the H1N1 flu virus (aka "swine flu") did more to raise people's awareness of pandemic flu than years of pandemic preparedness interventions. Your environmental analysis during the planning phase, as well as issue monitoring throughout implementation, will help you to identify any possible factors that might obscure the effects of your program in the evaluation.

SAME-GROUP PRETEST-POSTTEST

For small-scale social marketing programs, the most common evaluation design is to take measurements of the target audience before and after implementation (and sometimes at additional midpoints for long-term programs). This generally is the least expensive method of collecting valid data if you are conducting primary research. For example, if you wish to test changes in knowledge, attitudes, and behaviors, you can conduct a survey during the planning phase and then administer the same survey with additional questions to assess exposure to the campaign after implementation. Because your media communications likely will be seen throughout your whole community or geographic area, it might be difficult to find a control group that has not been exposed to the campaign. As discussed earlier, the disadvantage of following only the exposed group is that you might not be able to attribute changes in outcomes specifically to the campaign.

COMPARISON TO A STANDARD

If you cannot use a control group in your design but wish to have an external standard with which to compare your results, you might be able to find state or national data for the same time period that will give an indication of overall trends. Look for a large-scale survey being conducted with a similar population, such as the BRFSS or the Youth Risk Behavior Surveillance System (which includes national, state, and local school-based surveys of adolescents), and use the same questions in your own questionnaire. If the survey you are using as the standard is done annually or more frequently, then you can compare the differences you find in your population to those of the larger population over the same time period. National surveys of this type, however, might not analyze their results quickly enough for your purposes, or you might not be able to find an analogous standard for the type of research you wish to do.

If your target audience is significantly different in key ways from the population used

Behavioral Risk Factor Surveillance System

The U.S. Centers for Disease Control and Prevention (CDC) sponsors several large-scale, health-related surveys that you can use to follow trends over time or as a comparison for your own survey results. One ongoing survey that you can use to analyze changes in your state is the Behavioral Risk Factor Surveillance System (BRFSS). You might be able to work with your state's behavior risk factor coordinator to add questions on your issue or to get a copy of the questionnaire for your own use.

The BRFSS is the primary source of state-based information on risk behaviors among adult populations. Questions elicit information from adults on their knowledge, attitudes, and behaviors related to issues such as health status and access to care, tobacco and alcohol use, dietary patterns, leisure-time physical activities, injury control, women's health issues, use of preventive services (e.g., immunization; screening for breast, cervical, and colorectal cancer), and HIV/AIDS.

Every month, states select random samples of adults for telephone interviews. The questionnaires have three parts:

- Core questions used by all states
- Standard sets of questions on selected topics that states may choose to add
- Questions developed by individual states on issues of special interest (e.g., prostate cancer, bicycle helmet use)

Information on age, gender, racial/ethnic background, education, and other demographic factors is gathered so that estimates can be made for specific population groups. The CDC edits and processes data from each state's monthly interviews and then returns prevalence information and selected reports to all states for their use.

For more information or to locate your state behavior risk factor coordinator, go to the BRFSS website: http://www.cdc.gov/brfss/.

to determine the standard, then this design will not yield accurate results. For example, your community might have a better high school health curriculum than do most districts in your state, which would make adolescents in your target audience more knowledgeable about health issues from the start. Or, the death from steroid use of a well-known local athlete during the course of your campaign might increase awareness of the issue in your community but not within the larger population being used as a comparison. For this reason, this research design should be used only when the target audience is very similar to the standard's population.

USING CONTROL GROUPS

To be the most certain that your evaluation results truly reflect the effects of your social marketing program, use a control group that has not been exposed to the campaign for comparison. This more complex and costly evaluation design is not often used by community-based programs that have fewer fiscal and professional resources, but it is the most rigorous type of research. In an experimental design, you randomly assign the research participants either to be exposed to the campaign or to serve in the control group. Because it can be difficult to do this when using mass media throughout the community, an experimental design works best when you are able to control exposure to the program's elements such as with one-on-one counseling or in a classroom setting.

A "quasi-experimental" design might be more appropriate for a program using mass media in one or more communities. Your control group could be a community or population that is similar demographically to the target audience but is not exposed to the campaign. The comparison might be, for example, with those who fit the target audience definition in another similar community outside of the range of the mass media channels you use in the target community. A college-based alcohol abuse prevention program could use another college with similar demographics and alcohol use rates as a control. A statewide immunization program could randomly select some of its clinics to participate in the campaign in their communities, with the rest serving as controls.

If both the exposed and control groups are similar to each other in key ways, then you can assume that any changes you detect between the beginning of the program and after implementation are a result of your campaign. This is the basis of the experimental design; any differences in the people selected for the exposed or control group will be taken care of through randomization. In the quasi-experimental design, however, you take a risk that the control group might differ from the exposed group in an important but unforeseen way. Administering both a pretest and a posttest will help to assess the similarity between the groups on key variables such as knowledge, attitudes, and behaviors. With an experimental design, however, you may assume a similar starting-off point for both groups and collect only postimplementation data (although a pretest still will be useful as a check).

EVALUATION INDICATORS

Changes in the evaluation indicators, or key outcomes to be measured, will tell you whether you have achieved your social marketing objectives. By carefully selecting the indicators you track, you will be able to identify where your program has been most successful or where it needs more work. Indicators should be linked to the program objectives you set at the beginning and must be measurable. You can use indicators occurring at either the individual or community level.

Individual-level indicators consist of data for particular individuals, which are then aggregated and analyzed. Surveys are the most common method used to collect this type of information. Individual-level indicators encompass measures such as the following:

- Knowledge

- Attitudes

- Beliefs

- Behaviors

- Stage of change

- Demographics

The advantage of using individuals as the base of analysis is that you can directly measure changes in the factors your program seeks to influence. You also can examine the characteristics of those who adopted the behavior versus those who did not. Collecting the data you need from a large number of individuals, however, can be expensive and time-consuming and, therefore, is not always feasible.

For this reason, community-level indicators might be more appropriate to use when you have limited resources. Community-level data cannot provide firsthand information about items such as knowledge, attitudes, and behaviors linked to individual attributes; rather, they show trends occurring on a larger scale. Data come from organizations, public agencies, providers, and businesses rather than from the individuals who are your primary target audience. Unobtrusive observations of relevant factors in the community or of people's behavior are a key method of tracking community-based indicators. Instead of asking people directly whether they smoke, you could work with local stores to obtain sales data for cigarettes, observe the number of people smoking in a particular location, track enrollment in smoking cessation programs, or look at surveillance data for smoking rates in your community.

Community-based indicators can be related to the following:

- *Environmental change* (e.g., number of streets in the community with a bike lane, availability of fresh fruit at convenience stores)

- *Policy and regulation* (e.g., number of companies with recycling policies, whether local school districts have an effective AIDS education curriculum)

- *Information accessibility* (e.g., percentage of health care providers that routinely counsel their patients to quit smoking, extent of local media coverage about your issue)

- *Behavioral outcomes* (e.g., tobacco sales to minors, proportion of shelf space devoted to low-fat foods in grocery stores)

Because you are collecting data from a relatively small number of organizations rather than from many individuals, community-based indicators can be less expensive and time-consuming to track. It might be difficult, however, to identify indicators of this type that are relevant to your program. Also, if you did not actively work to address the indicators you choose to assess, then you would be hard-pressed to link any changes back to your program.

FIGURE 23.1 Examples of Community-Level Indicators

The following community-level indicators are among those generated by participants in a project to evaluate community-based cardiovascular disease programs sponsored and organized by the U.S. Centers for Disease Control and Prevention.[a]

Tobacco Use

Policy and regulation:

- Clean air laws for public buildings, restaurants, worksites, and so on
- Vending machine regulations in communities
- Enforcement of "no sales to minors" ordinances throughout the community

Information accessibility:

- Materials for screening and cessation in use by health professionals
- Signs telling of environmental tobacco smoke

Environmental change:

- Percentage of restaurant seats in no-smoking sections
- Percentage of worksites with no-smoking areas
- Presence of vending machines in restaurants

Behavioral outcomes:

- Surveillance data on tobacco sales to minors
- Disappearance of tobacco products (store inventory)
- Observations of behavior in no-smoking areas

Physical Activity

Policy and regulation:

- Presence of local policy to include physical education in K–12 curriculum
- Amount/percentage of local budget per capita devoted to physical activity or recreation
- Presence of policies promoting inclusion of recreation facilities with new construction

Information accessibility:

- Percentage of health care providers that routinely advise patients to exercise more
- Availability of materials at worksites linking physical activity to cardiovascular disease

Environmental change:

- Miles of walking trails per capita
- Number of physical activity facilities per capita in schools
- Availability of exercise facilities to community members

Behavioral outcomes:

- Observations of use (e.g., in malls, on trails)
- Membership in physical activity organizations (e.g., YMCAs, YWCAs, health clubs)
- Sales of selected physical activity items (e.g., sports equipment, exercise videos)

Diet and Nutrition

Policy and regulation:

- Percentage of schools with lunch options congruent with dietary guidelines
- Presence of low-fat foods in commodity food programs
- Policy to monitor nutrition claims made by local food retailers

Information accessibility:

- "Point of purchase" information provided (e.g., cafeterias)
- Presence of food pyramid charts in learning environments

Environmental change:

- Presence of healthy food in vending machines in schools
- Healthy menus in schools, at worksites, and at other locations
- Number of low-fat items in restaurants (menu analysis)

Behavioral outcomes:

- Barcode sales data
- Inventory control data for food use (e.g., school and worksite cafeterias)
- Proportion of low-fat items in stores (via use of marker items such as low-fat milk)

a. Sterling, T., Cheadle, A., & Schmid, T. (1997). *Report from a CDC-sponsored project to develop community-level indicators for evaluating cardiovascular health promotion programs.* Unpublished manuscript, Centers for Disease Control and Prevention, Division of Chronic Disease Control and Community Intervention, Atlanta, GA.

Evaluation Methods

Collect the evaluation data using a variety of research methods, both quantitative and qualitative, for the broadest view of the effects of your social marketing program and areas that need improvement. The methods you use will be determined in part by the evaluation design and indicators you select. For example, focus groups will not yield data on the rate of adoption of the target behavior but can provide important feedback on how the campaign was received among target audience members and how they used the information and materials. The most common research methods used in evaluation are discussed in this chapter.

SURVEYS

Surveys are by far the most widely used method to assess the success of a social marketing program. Quantitative data, preferably those that can be compared to the same measurements before the campaign was implemented, are the only way in which to really demonstrate behavior change and other effects to funders or critics of your program. If you conducted a knowledge, attitudes, and behaviors survey in the planning phase of your program, then use the same questions in the evaluation questionnaire and the same methodology to assess overall changes in responses. You also can add questions to assess whether the respondents were exposed to the campaign and what actions they might have taken as a result.

Many methods of collecting survey data exist, each with its own advantages and disadvantages, including the following:

Mailed questionnaires. The survey questionnaires are sent by mail to randomly selected respondents along with cover letters and stamped return envelopes. This is a low-effort way of distributing and collecting the questionnaires. The problem is that the response rate generally is low as well. Providing an incentive to return the questionnaires, such as a chance for winning a prize in a drawing of all the respondents or a gift certificate in exchange for participation, will help to increase the number of responses you get back. Mailed questionnaires also offer the respondents anonymity and more time to consider their answers.

Telephone interviews. Trained interviewers call potential respondents, either by randomly dialing or by using a prescreened list of numbers, and ask the survey questions by telephone. This method is more labor intensive, but having a live person to persuade the individual to participate can increase the response rate dramatically. With the rise of telemarketers, people are more wary of phone calls from strangers asking them questions, but a good interviewer or an introductory letter telling them they will be receiving a phone call can dispel those concerns. Telephone interviews might not be appropriate for asking questions on sensitive or very personal topics because respondents might not be comfortable or truthful. Although this method excludes anyone who does not have a telephone, you might be able to reach more people over the phone than in person. But you are also more likely to miss those who only use a mobile phone, unless they have opted in to receiving phone calls from your program.

In-person interviews. Trained interviewers meet with the survey respondents, whether chosen randomly or through a preselection process, in person to administer the questionnaire. This type of survey can take up a significant amount of the interviewers' time, especially if the interviews take place at different locations, and the interviews often run longer than telephone interviews. Interviewing someone in person means that you can ask questions that involve audiovisual components or can conduct observations during the same session. You also can establish rapport with participants to enlist their cooperation more readily and to be able to ask sensitive questions. This method, unlike the previously described designs, requires interviewers who are geographically near the people participating in the survey.

Computerized surveys. Surveys can be administered by computer, either in person or online. If you are collecting responses on-site, participants read each question on the computer screen and directly input their responses using a touchscreen, keyboard, or mouse. Laptop or tablet computers make it easy to collect data quickly anywhere and have the information immediately available for data analysis, skipping the data input step. Or a link to an online survey can be sent out via e-mail to make it easy for people to quickly click through and respond. Wording of questions can be personalized based on previous responses, and the users need not worry about skipping inapplicable questions. Respondents might be more comfortable providing answers to sensitive questions directly into the computer, particularly if they are familiar with the technology. For certain populations that are not used to working with computers, however, this technique might be intimidating.

OBSERVATION

As Yogi Berra once said, "You can observe a lot just by watchin'." Observation is a technique you can use to measure people's actual behavior in a given situation or to assess whether they have the skills needed to perform a particular task. Research that relies on self-reports of behavior runs the risk of obtaining answers that the respondents think reflect best on themselves, whether accurate or not. Observing people in a natural setting without their awareness of you watching them can provide a better indication of what they actually do. Of course, this technique might not always be appropriate, but for behaviors such as wearing a bicycle helmet or looking at nutrition labels in the supermarket, observation is very effective (see Figure 24.1). Observation also can assess whether a particular skill promoted by the campaign, such as mixing an oral rehydration solution in the proper proportions or lifting heavy boxes with the knees rather than with the back, is being done correctly (with or without the individual's knowledge of participation in the research). In some situations, researchers have ethical concerns related

FIGURE 24.1 Sample Observation Checklist

This is a sample of an observation checklist used to track bicycle helmet use in one community.

Date: _____ Time: From _____ a.m./p.m. to _____ a.m./p.m.

Location: _____

Weather: _____

Observer: _____

For each person observed riding a bicycle, circle the appropriate mark:

Observation	Sex	Age (years)			Group/Alone		Helmeted?		Child on Board?		Child Helmeted?	
1	M F	<12	12–18	>18	G	A	Y	N	Y	N	Y	N
2	M F	<12	12–18	>18	G	A	Y	N	Y	N	Y	N
3	M F	<12	12–18	>18	G	A	Y	N	Y	N	Y	N
4	M F	<12	12–18	>18	G	A	Y	N	Y	N	Y	N
5	M F	<12	12–18	>18	G	A	Y	N	Y	N	Y	N
6	M F	<12	12–18	>18	G	A	Y	N	Y	N	Y	N
7	M F	<12	12–18	>18	G	A	Y	N	Y	N	Y	N
8	M F	<12	12–18	>18	G	A	Y	N	Y	N	Y	N
9	M F	<12	12–18	>18	G	A	Y	N	Y	N	Y	N
10	M F	<12	12–18	>18	G	A	Y	N	Y	N	Y	N
11	M F	<12	12–18	>18	G	A	Y	N	Y	N	Y	N
12	M F	<12	12–18	>18	G	A	Y	N	Y	N	Y	N
13	M F	<12	12–18	>18	G	A	Y	N	Y	N	Y	N
14	M F	<12	12–18	>18	G	A	Y	N	Y	N	Y	N
15	M F	<12	12–18	>18	G	A	Y	N	Y	N	Y	N
16	M F	<12	12–18	>18	G	A	Y	N	Y	N	Y	N
17	M F	<12	12–18	>18	G	A	Y	N	Y	N	Y	N
18	M F	<12	12–18	>18	G	A	Y	N	Y	N	Y	N
19	M F	<12	12–18	>18	G	A	Y	N	Y	N	Y	N
20	M F	<12	12–18	>18	G	A	Y	N	Y	N	Y	N

Note: M = male; F = female; G = group; A = alone; Y = yes; N = no.

to observing people without their consent, so consider whether you need to address privacy or informed consent issues in your research plan.

Although it sounds very simple, observation requires a systematic approach to ensure valid research results. You create a protocol for the observers to follow that tells them where and when to conduct the research, what behaviors to look for, and how to code their observations. The categories must be clearly delineated and often are coded by the observer using a checklist or tally sheet. To verify the reliability of the research, you might wish to have two people code the same situations and compare their results. Making observations on different days of the week and times of day also can help to increase the validity of the results. Every Tuesday at noon, the bicycle safety club might take its weekly ride through the neighborhood; multiple observations will help you identify the unusual number of helmet wearers at that time and take it into account in your pre- and postcampaign research design. Another source of bias may come from the influence of the observer on the research participants. People often will behave differently when they know that they are being watched, so observations should be carried out as unobtrusively as possible.

In addition to conducting observations of people's behavior directly, you can measure the evidence of their actions. Percentage of supermarket shelf space, for example, is a good indicator of the types of food that neighborhood shoppers buy; the proportions of low-fat and skim milk compared to all milk on the shelf will be similar to the proportions of people who purchase them. The number of fitness center memberships in a community can give an indication of the extent of awareness about the benefits of exercise (if not how frequently people use the facilities). The quantity of cigarette butts in and around the ashtray outside an office building can provide evidence of the number of smokers working there. Make sure, however, that the things you are observing truly do reflect the behaviors you wish to measure.

QUALITATIVE METHODS

Just as you used qualitative methods to flesh out your exploratory research while planning your program, so too can these methods help you to better understand the effects of your campaign from another perspective. Although you generally cannot validly compare the results of qualitative research before and after the campaign, the data gathered using these methods will give a good indication of which elements were effective from the target audience's perspective and how the campaign could be improved for the next phase. For qualitative evaluation research, the most useful type of person to recruit as a participant is someone who has been at least moderately exposed to the campaign messages or materials. If you talk to people who do not have any knowledge of the campaign, then the results might be very similar to those of your exploratory research.

The questions you ask using qualitative methods will be somewhat different from those in a survey because you can draw out more detail and context. Although you still will be looking for evidence of changes made as a result of your social marketing program, you will find it couched in the experience and viewpoint of individuals rather than as general trends in a population. Questions you might wish to explore include the following:

- What elements of the campaign have you seen or heard?

- Where have you seen or heard the campaign?

- Do you think that many of your peers saw or heard the campaign? If so, how do you know?

- What do you think about the campaign?

- What do you particularly like about the campaign?

- What do you dislike about the campaign? What would you change?

- Why do you think the campaign was successful or unsuccessful?

■ How could we reach more people like you with the campaign?

■ Do you have any questions that the campaign materials left unanswered?

■ What changes have you made as a result of the campaign?

Qualitative methods for gathering evaluative data include the following:

In-depth interviews. A trained interviewer meets one-on-one with individuals who have been exposed to the campaign. Through these interviews, the researcher can learn about the context in which the program's messages and materials were received and how they were interpreted by the participants. This method might be appropriate when the subject of the campaign is sensitive or when you wish to delve more deeply into individuals' experiences.

Focus groups. You can bring together either formal or informal groups of people to discuss the campaign and its effects. As discussed in Chapter 7, the groups should be composed of people similar to each other in key ways related to the campaign (e.g., separate men/women or adopter/nonadopter groups). The group setting is ideal for eliciting information on the campaign's influences in peer groups and for generating ideas on how to improve the program.

Anecdotal feedback mechanisms. The stories of individual people can be quite powerful as a way of demonstrating the program's effects at a personal level. By themselves, anecdotes do not prove anything about the program, but they can be used to bring to life the people behind the statistics. In addition to collecting stories and comments through in-depth interviews and focus groups, you can use other mechanisms to accumulate feedback from your target audience members. For example, blank journals with a message on the front cover inviting comments on particular issues can be placed in waiting rooms. Request comments on your blog or e-mailed feedback from people who participated in your program. You can personally invite people to submit testimonials describing what the social marketing program did for them. These types of stories are effective to use when seeking additional funding, media attention, or volunteers to assist with your program.

CHAPTER 25

Using Feedback to Improve Your Program

The ultimate purpose of each of your evaluation activities should be to learn how to improve your current and subsequent social marketing programs. The results will do no good to anyone if they are not acted on or are immediately retired to a shelf.

REAL-TIME FEEDBACK

Ideally, the feedback function should not wait until the end of the program when summative evaluation activities are complete. Responding to relevant information in real time—as events actually occur—allows you to improve your program when it counts rather than retrospectively realizing what you should have done. Effectively using feedback is an interactive, as well as iterative, process in which the elements of your program constantly are adjusted in relation to other components based on new information.

You can make your evaluation results more practical and actionable by considering the following strategies:

- Involve key decision makers and stakeholders in the design of program objectives and evaluation planning.

- Keep in mind the technique of backward research to ensure that all the data you collect drive your programmatic decisions rather than sitting around unused.

- Focus on strategic, rather than exploratory, formative research to answer questions about the target audience and development of the program.

- Use pretesting results to build a strong communication strategy and to explain and justify the executions to stakeholders who are not part of the target audience.

- Use your process evaluation to go beyond bean counting and toward more diagnostic qualitative research that can uncover problems or opportunities for your program during implementation.

- Use social media to tap into the pulse of your audience on what it is saying (or—even worse—what it's not saying) about your program and campaign so you can make changes if necessary.

- Conduct preliminary evaluations before the program's completion to identify potential improvements and highlight program successes.

- Stay flexible enough to make changes in the program or evaluation based on the feedback you receive in the evaluation process.

- Use summative research to make future program decisions as part of a process rather than as just an end point.

IMPROVEMENTS FOR THE FUTURE

Whether you will continue with additional phases of implementation of the same campaign or design future social marketing programs on other topics, you can learn and apply the lessons gleaned from the outcomes of this program. These lessons might include the following:

- How to make the social marketing process run more smoothly
- Which elements of the campaign worked and which did not
- Which objectives require additional effort or a new approach
- Which distribution channels were most effective
- How to realistically budget your time and funds for the next phase
- What types of challenges to anticipate and how to overcome them

Writing an Evaluation Report

The following information should be included in your evaluation report.

Program background:

- History of the program
- Description of the program
- Goals and objectives

Evaluation methodology:

- Evaluation design
- Research participants
- Research protocols
- Research instruments

Evaluation findings:

- Research results
- Strengths and weaknesses of the program

Recommendations:

- Elements of the program that should be kept or enhanced
- Elements of the program that should be changed or eliminated
- Future opportunities

In addition to considering the elements you would change or eliminate from your program, think about what you might add. Are there any new developments in the issue you addressed that should be included in future campaigns? Or, has anything changed about the target audience, the community, or your organization that necessitates creating new goals and objectives?

Summarize these guidelines in a written evaluation report so that a record exists for others to read in the future, in case you leave your position or for those in other organizations who might wish to replicate your program. This report should be user-friendly—no longer than necessary, easy to read, and providing clear action items.

Compile all the documentation from the development and evaluation of the campaign as an appendix for easy reference. Share your results with all those involved in the development of the program including staff, partners, and funders.

If you feel that others could learn from your efforts, then take the time to write up a synopsis of your project for publication as either a journal article or a brief program note. You also could submit your program's results as a conference presentation or poster session to get the word out further. Use what you learned from the experience to continually improve your program. That is what social marketing is all about.

CASE STUDY

Evaluation Case Study: Road Crew Project

The Wisconsin Department of Transportation, with funding from the National Highway Traffic Safety Administration, led a statewide team to create a community-based approach to reduce drunk driving and alcohol-related crashes involving young male drivers.[1] The year-long Road Crew demonstration project conducted extensive formative research to identify the best way to provide and promote alternative transportation services designed to separate drivers from their vehicles before they started drinking. Three Wisconsin communities piloted the project, which featured limousines and older luxury cars that would provide rides to and from bars, obviating the need for bar patrons to drive at all. The Road Crew was promoted as a fun, convenient, hassle-free way to enjoy a night out.

After the project had been implemented for a year, several evaluation methods were used to assess its effects. First, a random phone survey in each of the three communities assessed awareness, knowledge, and attitudes about the program. The 10-minute survey sampled both the general population and the target audience of 21- to 34-year-olds, with approximately 400 respondents in each category (which overlap) in each community. Another set of more intensive interviews was done with members of the community leader population ($n = 25$) and the bar owner and wait staff population ($n = 25$) in each of the three demonstration communities to determine their awareness and attitudes toward the program.

The evaluation also included tracking the number of rides provided through the program in the ride logs. Each community kept a log of all rides given, as well as the age and gender of the rider, and the origin, destination, date, and time of each ride. This allowed them to track how many potentially impaired drivers were kept off the road and to estimate the number of crashes avoided.

The crux of the evaluation was a pre- and posttest survey in treatment and control communities to learn the general level of driving after excessive drinking by bar patrons. This research was conducted in the three demonstration communities (treatment) as well as in several communities where there would not be a ride program (control). Surveys were conducted in the month prior to the onset of the program and during the last month of the demonstration in both the test and the control communities. Because they were asking about whether respondents had engaged in an illegal activity (drinking and driving), the survey was constructed to increase confidentiality and anonymity by using a computerized phone and data collection service.

Bar patrons were given coupon cards by the bars' wait staff. They were told to read the coupon the next morning and then call the toll-free number on the coupon. Patrons were offered a $7 voucher for future nonalcoholic purchases at the tavern where they received the coupon, which would be activated after calling the number and answering a few questions. Upon calling, a computerized female voice asked the questions, to which the patron only needed to push a number on the phone keypad in order to respond. Upon completion, the patron was given a validation code that activated the coupon for use.

(Continued)

[1]Rothschild, M. (2003). *Road Crew research report.* http://www.roadcrewonline.org/research

(Continued)

The survey included questions about how patrons got home on the night they received the coupon, how much they drank that night, and how often they drove after excessive drinking during a typical 2-week period.

Over the year of the program, Road Crew provided 19,757 rides, with most going from bar to bar or from bar to home (8% home to bar, 52% bar to bar, and 41% from bar to home). Within the first year, awareness of the program rose to over 80% of bar patrons and close to 70% in the general community. According to the bar coupon surveys, the amount of drinking somewhat increased in the treatment communities as compared to the controls, as did the number of bars visited. In the community phone survey, 19% of the target audience responded that they had used the ride service, compared to 7% of the general population. And the bar coupon survey found that 58% of respondents in the treatment group had used the ride service, compared to 28% of the control group. Of those who most closely matched the project's target audience—21- to 34-year-old men who spent time in bars—76% reported that they used the ride service at least once during the demonstration year.

On the basis of the evaluation results, the program estimated that these rides prevented 15 alcohol-related crashes on area roads during the 1-year study, a 17% reduction. A cost-benefit analysis showed an estimated total savings of $610,000 to the communities by avoiding those crashes. While these calculations are, by necessity, imprecise, they give a general estimate of the impact of the Road Crew project.

WORKSHEET 19: EVALUATION PLANNING WORKSHEET

1. At what points in the program will you collect evaluation data?

   ❑ Pre- and postcampaign

   ❑ Postcampaign only

   ❑ Periodic monitoring at specified intervals

   ❑ Other

2. From where will you collect your evaluation data?

   ❑ Existing records:

   _____

   _____

   ❑ One group exposed to the campaign

   ❑ Comparison to a standard: _____

   ❑ Comparison to a control group: _____

3. Which evaluation indicators will you use to assess the effectiveness of the program?

Individual-level indicators:

   ❑ Knowledge:

   _____

   _____

   ❑ Attitudes:

   _____

   _____

   ❑ Behaviors:

   _____

   _____

   ❑ Other

   _____

   _____

Community-level indicators:

   ❑ Environmental change:

   _____

   _____

(Continued)

(Continued)

❑ Policy and regulation:

_____

_____

❑ Information accessibility:

_____

_____

❑ Behavioral outcomes:

_____

_____

❑ Other _____

4. Which evaluation methods will you use?

   ❑ Knowledge, attitudes, and behaviors survey:

      ❑ Mail

      ❑ Telephone

      ❑ In-person interviews

      ❑ Online

      ❑ Other _____

   ❑ Observation

   ❑ In-depth interviews

   ❑ Focus groups

   ❑ Anecdotal feedback mechanisms

   ❑ Other _____

5. Do you or your staff members have the necessary skills to conduct and analyze the evaluation?

   ❑ Yes. We have the expertise on staff.

   ❑ Possibly. We need some additional training.

   ❑ No. We need to hire outside assistance.

If more training or outside assistance is needed:

    a. What is your available budget? $_____

    b. What aspects of the evaluation do you need assistance with?

    _____

    _____

    _____

    c. From which companies or consultants will you solicit bids?

    _____

    _____

    _____

If evaluation will be done in-house:

6. What is your available budget? $_____

7. Who will be responsible for coordinating the evaluation activities?

_____

8. Who will assist in the evaluation activities?

Name	Role
_____	_____
_____	_____
_____	_____

9. Evaluation timeline:

Activity	Date to Be Completed
Put evaluation team in place	_____
Design evaluation plan	_____
Develop questionnaires or other research instruments	_____
Test and finalize evaluation instruments	_____
Train people who will be conducting the research	_____
Recruit research participants	_____
Conduct research	_____
Input or organize data	_____
Analyze data	_____
Create evaluation report	_____

(Continued)

(Continued)

10. How will you use the results of your evaluation?

_____

_____

_____

_____

_____

Appendix A

Social Marketing Resource List

The online resources in the following list are up-to-date as of the printing of this book. Because website addresses change frequently, you can find updated links to all the addresses listed here, as well as downloadable copies of the worksheets and other new resources that become available, at the author's website, http://www.social-marketing.com/booklinks.html.

Print

Andreasen, A. (1995). *Marketing social change: Changing behavior to promote health, social development, and the environment.* San Francisco: Jossey-Bass.

Andreasen, A. (Ed.). (2001). *Ethics in social marketing.* Washington, DC: Georgetown University Press.

Andreasen, A. (2001). *Marketing research that won't break the bank: A practical guide to getting the information you need* (2nd ed.). San Francisco: Jossey-Bass.

Andreasen, A. (2006). *Social marketing in the 21st century.* Thousand Oaks, CA: Sage.

Andresen, K. (2006). *Robin Hood marketing: Stealing corporate savvy to sell just causes.* San Francisco: Jossey-Bass.

Backer, T., Rogers, E., & Sopory, P. (1992). *Designing health communication campaigns: What works?* Newbury Park, CA: Sage.

Basil, D. Z., & Wimer, W. W. (2007). *Social marketing advances in research & theory.* Binghamton, NY: Haworth.

Cheng, H., Kotler, P., & Lee, N. (2011). *Social marketing for public health: Global trends and success stories.* Sudbury, MA: Jones and Bartlett.

Donovan, R., & Henley, N. (2003). *Social marketing principles and practice.* Victoria, Australia: IP Communications.

Glanz, K., Rimer, B., & Lewis, M. L. (2002). *Health behavior and health education: Theory, research and practice.* San Francisco: Jossey-Bass.

Goldberg, M., Fishbein, M., & Middlestadt, S. (Eds.). (1997). *Social marketing: Theoretical and practical perspectives.* Mahwah, NJ: Lawrence Erlbaum.

Hastings, G. (2007). *Social marketing: Why should the devil have all the best tunes?* Oxford, England: Butterworth-Heinemann.

Heath, C., & Heath, D. (2007). *Made to stick: Why some ideas survive and others die.* New York: Random House.

Heath, C., & Heath, D. (2010). *Switch: How to change things when change is hard.* New York: Random House.

Kline, M. V., & Huff, R. M. (2007). *Health promotion in multicultural populations: A handbook for practitioners and students* (2nd ed.). Thousand Oaks, CA: Sage.

Kotler, P., & Lee, N. (2008). *Social marketing: Influencing behaviors for good* (3rd ed.). Thousand Oaks, CA: Sage.

Kotler, P., & Lee, N. (2009). *Up and out of poverty: The social marketing solution*. Upper Saddle River, NJ: Wharton School Publishing.

Krueger, R. A., & Casey, M. A. (2000). *Focus groups: A practical guide for applied research* (3rd ed.). Thousand Oaks, CA: Sage.

Prochaska, J. O., Norcross, J., & DiClemente, C. (1995). *Changing for good: A revolutionary six-stage program for overcoming bad habits and moving your life positively forward*. New York: HarperCollins.

Siegel, M., & Lotenburg, L. D. (1998). *Marketing public health: Strategies to promote social change* (2nd ed.). Boston: Jones & Bartlett.

Thaler, R. H., & Sunstein, C. R. (2008). *Nudge: Improving decisions about health, wealth and happiness*. New York: Penguin.

von Oech, R. (2008). *A whack on the side of the head: How you can be more creative* (25th Anniversary Edition). New York: Business Plus.

SOCIAL MARKETING-RELATED JOURNALS

American Journal of Health Behavior
American Academy of Health Behavior
http://www.ajhb.org/

Cases in Public Health Communication and Marketing
George Washington University School of Public Health and Health Services
http://www.casesjournal.org

Health Education & Behavior
Society for Public Health Education
http://www.sph.umich.edu/hbhe/heb

International Journal of Nonprofit & Voluntary Sector Marketing
http://www3.interscience.wiley.com/journal/110481870/home

Journal of Health Communication
http://www.tandf.co.uk/journals/titles/10810730.asp

Social Marketing Quarterly
Academy for Educational Development
http://www.socialmarketingquarterly.com

ONLINE RESOURCES

Beth's Blog: How Nonprofit Organizations Can Use Social Media to Power Social Networks for Change
http://beth.typepad.com/beths_blog/

CDCynergy-Social Marketing Edition online
http://www.orau.gov/cdcynergy/soc2web/default.htm

Community-Based Social Marketing
http://www.cbsm.com

Georgetown Social Marketing Listserv
To subscribe, send an e-mail message to LISTPROC@LISTPROC.GEORGETOWN.EDU. In the body of the message write "SUBSCRIBE SOC-MKTG yourname" (with your actual name in place of "your-name").

Health and Risk Communication Network
http://hrcnetwork.groupsite.com/

On Social Marketing and Social Change
http://socialmarketing.blogs.com

Osocio
http://www.osocio.org

Path of the Blue Eye
http://www.pathoftheblueeye.com/

Pulse and Signal
http://www.pulseandsignal.com

SocialButterfly
http://www.fly4change.com

Social Marketers Global Network
http://socialmarketers.net

Social Marketing Links (bookmarked by Nedra on an ongoing basis)
http://delicious.com/weinreich

Social Marketing Panorama
http://www.socialmarketingpanorama.com

Social Marketing Wiki
http://socialmarketing.wetpaint.com/

Spare Change Blog
http://www.social-marketing.com/blog/

Stephan Dahl's Blog: The Social Side of Marketing
http://stephan.dahl.at/

Tools of Change
http://www.toolsofchange.com

Turning Point Social Marketing National Excellence Collaborative
http://socialmarketingcollaborative.org/smc/

We Are Media
http://www.wearemedia.org/

Weinreich Communications, Social-Marketing.com
http://www.social-marketing.com

Appendix B

Sample Knowledge, Attitudes, and Behaviors Survey

Phone: _____ Date: _____ Time: _____ Initials: _____

Call disposition: _____ Residence, person answered

               _____ No answer/answering machine/busy signal

               Callback 1 date/time/initials: _____

               Callback 2 date/time/initials: _____

A. When Someone Answers "Hello"

Hello, I'm calling with a research firm called Weinreich Communications. We are doing a survey on health issues to help us develop a health education program. We have selected your phone number from a random sample. We are not selling anything, and the survey will take only about 5 minutes. All responses are completely confidential.

A1. May I ask how many people between 18 and 24 years of age live in your household? _____

     If none: Thank you for your time. *[Terminate interview.]*

     If 1: May I speak with [him or her]?

     _____ Yes *[Go to Section B.]*

     _____ Not available *[Go to Question A2.]*

     _____ Refuses interview *[Go to Question A3.]*

     If 2 or more: May I speak with one of them?

     _____ Yes *[Go to Section B.]*

     _____ Not available *[Go to Question A2.]*

     _____ Refuses interview *[Go to Question A3.]*

     If not home or cannot come to phone:

A2. When would be a good time to call back? _____

     Who should we ask for? _____

     If person answering phone refuses interview:

A3. The interview will take only about 5 minutes and is completely confidential. Our research results will be more accurate if we can speak with everyone who we have randomly selected. May I ask you to reconsider?

_____ Yes *[Go to Section B.]*

_____ No *Say:* Thank you for your time.

[Terminate interview.]

B. When You Have the Person 18 to 24 Years of Age on the Phone

[If different person from who answered phone:]

I'm working with a research firm called Weinreich Communications. We are conducting a random survey with men and women between 18 and 24 years of age. The information will help us to develop a health education program. The survey will take only about 5 minutes, and your responses are completely confidential.

B1. Would you mind taking 5 minutes to answer some questions for us?

If yes: Thank you. *[Go to Question C1.]*

If no: Are there any concerns you have that I can answer for you? This will take only a short time, and your answers will not be able to be traced back to you. Our research results will be more accurate if we can interview everyone who we have randomly selected. Can I ask you to reconsider, or can we call you back at another time?

If no: Thank you for your time.

[Terminate interview.]

_____ Check if interview terminated at this point.

C. Initial Demographics

C1. How old are you as of your last birthday? _____

C2. Just for the record, I need to ask you if you are male or female?

1. Male

2. Female

C3. Are you:

1. Single *[Go to Question C4.]*

2. Married *[Go to Question C5.]*

3. Separated or divorced *[Go to Question C5.]*

If single:

C4. Would you describe yourself as:

1. Not dating anyone right now

2. Dating, but with no steady [boyfriend/girlfriend]

3. Dating a steady [boyfriend/girlfriend] or engaged

C5. Do you have any children?

    1. Yes *[Go to Question C6.]*

    2. No *[Go to Question D1.]*

If yes:

C6. How many? _____

D. Information Seeking

  D1. If you had questions about sexual health or birth control issues, how would you get the answers? *[Do not read answers. Code first two responses.]*

    1. Friends

    2. Parents

    3. Brother or sister

    4. Doctor

    5. Internet

    6. Other _____

    7. Butte Family Planning *[Go to Question E.]*

If does not list Butte Family Planning:

  D2. Are there any organizations you would call?

    1. Butte Family Planning

    2. Other _____

    3. No

If does not answer Butte Family Planning:

  D3. Have you ever heard of an organization called Butte Family Planning?

    1. Yes

    2. No

    3. Not sure

E. Attitudes

I'm going to make some statements, and I want you to tell me for each whether you agree or disagree with it. The possible answers are strongly agree, agree, no opinion, disagree, and strongly disagree. *[Circle number corresponding to response.]*

	Strongly Agree	Agree	No Opinion	Disagree	Strongly Disagree
E1. Caring for a baby at my age would be difficult.	1	2	3	4	5
E2. I will not have a baby until I am financially secure.	1	2	3	4	5

(Continued)

(Continued)

	Strongly Agree	Agree	No Opinion	Disagree	Strongly Disagree
E3. Using condoms is a way to show you care about the other person.	1	2	3	4	5
E4. A parent should talk to his or her child about sex and birth control.	1	2	3	4	5
E5. Using condoms is a way to take care of yourself.	1	2	3	4	5
E6. You cannot get pregnant the first time you have sex.	1	2	3	4	5
E7. If no birth control is available, then you should not have sex.	1	2	3	4	5
E8. Men should take responsibility for birth control during sex.	1	2	3	4	5
E9. Sexual encounters should happen the way they are shown on television.	1	2	3	4	5

F. Knowledge About Birth Control Pills and Unintended Pregnancies

F1. Now I would like to ask you what good things you have heard the birth control pill can do besides preventing pregnancy. Please name as many as you can.

[Do not read answers. Code all responses.]

1. Prevents cancer of the ovaries
2. Prevents cancer of the uterus
3. Prevents some types of cancer
4. Relieves premenstrual syndrome (PMS)
5. Relieves menstrual cramps
6. Strengthens bones
7. Protects against some forms of arthritis
8. Helps clear up skin
9. Other _____
10. No good effects
11. Do not know

F2. What are the bad things you have heard that the birth control pill causes? Please name as many as you can.

[Do not read answers. Code all responses.]

1. Acne
2. Blood clots
3. Breast tenderness and/or enlargement
4. Cancer
5. Emotional swings or depression

6. Headaches

7. Heart attack

8. High blood pressure

9. Nausea

10. Stroke

11. Weight gain

12. Other _____

13. No bad effects

14. Do not know

F3. What percentage of all pregnancies do you think happen by accident? _____ %

F4. If 10 young women have sex without birth control a few times a month, how many of them do you think will become pregnant within a year? _____

G. Campaign Exposure

G1. In the past 2 months, have you heard any radio commercials about birth control, condoms, or other sexual issues on KAAR-FM or Y-95?

1. Yes

2. No

3. Not sure

G2. In the past 2 months, have you seen any newspaper advertisements in the *Montana Standard* about birth control, condoms, or other sexual issues?

1. Yes

2. No

3. Not sure

G3. In the past 2 months, have you seen any posters or drink coasters with the slogan "Don't Kid Yourself" in locations around Butte?

1. Yes

2. No

3. Not sure

[If answered yes to any of G1, G2, or G3:]

G4. After you [heard/saw] the [radio ads/newspaper ads/posters/drink coasters], did you do any of the following? Please answer yes or no.

[Read each answer and circle if answer is yes.]

1. Think about the message?

2. Talk about the ads with your friends or family?

3. Talk about the ads with your partner?

4. Call the phone number?

5. Make an appointment with a health professional to discuss sexual issues or to get birth control?

6. Use birth control more often?

7. Use condoms more often?

H. Sexual Behavior

Now I'm just going to ask you for some information we need for our statistics.

H1. Have you had sex in the last 6 months?

1. Yes *[Go to Question H2.]*

2. No *[Go to Question H4.]*

[If yes:]

H2. I would like you to think back to the last time you had sex. Did you use birth control?

1. Yes *[Go to Question H3.]*

2. No *[Go to Question H4.]*

[If yes:]

H3. What type of birth control did you or your partner use?

[Do not read answers. Code all responses.]

a. Birth control pill

b. Norplant

c. Depo-Provera (the shot)

d. Condom

e. Spermicide

f. Diaphragm/cervical cap

g. Intrauterine device

h. Withdrawal/pulling out/coitus interruptus

i. Rhythm method/natural family planning

j. Other _____

H4. Have you ever [become pregnant/gotten someone else pregnant] when you did not intend for that to happen?

1. Yes

2. No

3. Rather not say

I. Income Level

I1.   My last questions are about your annual income. I am going to list ranges of incomes, and I want you to stop me when I reach the range that includes your income:

1. $0 to $20,000

2. $20,001 to $30,000

3. More than $30,000

I2.   Do you live with your parents or receive financial support from them?

1. Yes

2. No

Thank you very much for your time. We appreciate your participation.

Appendix C

Sample Focus Group Recruitment Questionnaire

When someone calls in response to focus group recruitment advertisements, determine whether she is eligible through the following questions.

To determine whether you fit the particular characteristics of the women we need for our focus groups, I need to ask you some quick questions.

Screening Questions

1. How old are you? _____ [If not 18 to 24 years, then thank caller and terminate call.]

2. Do you have any children? ❑ Yes   ❑ No

   If yes: Is your yearly income more than or less than $20,000?

   ❑ More ❑ Less

   If no: Is your yearly income more than or less than $15,000?

   ❑ More ❑ Less

   [If answer is "more," then thank caller and terminate call.]

3. Are you currently sexually active? ❑ Yes   ❑ No

   [If answer is no, then thank caller and terminate call.]

Focus Group Assignment Questions

4. When you have sex, how often do you use a method of birth control (either prescription or from the drug store)?

   ❑ Always

   ❑ Most of the time

   ❑ Half of the time

   ❑ Rarely or never

5. Have you ever become pregnant when you did not want to be? ❑ Yes   ❑ No

   Assigned to the following focus group:

   ❑ Group 1: Contraception always or most of the time

   ❑ Group 2: Contraception half the time, rarely, or never

   ❑ Group 3: Had unintended pregnancy

Group 1	Group 2	Group 3
❑ Thursday 10–12	❑ Thursday 2–4	❑ Thursday 6–8
❑ Friday 6–8	❑ Friday 10–12	❑ Friday 2–4

Mark "1" for first choice, "2" if can attend other time also.

Tell the person that we will call to confirm which time and date she is assigned to. If she cannot attend the time and date for his or her group, then put her on the list for future focus groups.

Name _____ Phone _____

Appendix D

Sample Focus Group Topic Guide

INTRODUCTION

Welcome and thank you for coming to our session today. My name is Nedra Weinreich, and I am an independent consultant working with Planned Parenthood of Utah. Assisting me is Jane Smith from Planned Parenthood of Utah.

We are developing a statewide campaign to prevent unintended pregnancies, and we have chosen Salt Lake City as one of the locations we are developing the campaign in first. These focus groups are a research method that will help us to develop the campaign. They are like an opinion survey, but rather than asking questions of one person at a time, we bring a group of people together to discuss a particular topic.

We have invited you to this focus group to find out what you think about birth control and family planning services. There are no right or wrong answers, just differing points of view. Please feel free to disagree with one another; we would like to have many points of view. Keep in mind that we are just as interested in negative comments as in positive comments; sometimes, the negative comments are the most helpful. Also, I want you to know that I do not work for Planned Parenthood, so you will not hurt my feelings if you make any negative comments about the organization.

Before we begin, let me explain the ground rules. We are recording the discussion because I do not want to miss any of your comments. All of your comments are confidential and will be used for research purposes only. We will be on a first-name basis today, and in our later reports, there will not be any names attached to comments. I want this to be a group discussion, so you do not need to wait for me to call on you. But please speak one at a time so that the audio recorder can pick up everything.

We have a lot of ground to cover, so I might change the subject or move ahead. Please stop me if you want to add something. Our discussion will last about 1 hour and 45 minutes, and then we have a short questionnaire we would like you to fill out. When you turn in your questionnaire, you will receive your $50 honorarium.

First of all, let's just go around the room and introduce ourselves. Please give us your first name; what you do; and whether you are single, are married, or have any children. Also, how about telling us your favorite thing to do on a Saturday night? I will start . . .

GENERAL CONTRACEPTIVE KNOWLEDGE/INFORMATION SEEKING

1. Where do you get your information about birth control? Who do you trust to give you that information? What about information about sex?

2. Do you have any worries or concerns about using birth control pills, condoms, or other contraceptives? Are these worries or concerns based on things you have heard or on your own experience? Are there things you need more information about?

ATTITUDES/MOTIVATIONS

1. When I mention the words *birth control,* what is the first thing that comes to your mind? What type of person uses birth control?

2. I am going to name some birth control methods. I want you to tell me what you think of each: what you like and what you do not like about it. *[Name: the pill, condoms, diaphragm, Norplant, spermicide, Depo-Provera, the morning-after pill]*

3. What affects your decision to use birth control or not? *[Probe: partner, situation, friends, time of month, concern about pregnancy, media]*

4. Do your friends use birth control? Pretend that I am a friend of yours considering whether or not to start using birth control. What advice would you give me?

ATTITUDES TOWARD PREGNANCY

1. I would like you to think back to the last time you had sex. Did you plan for it to happen, or did it just happen? In general, which way do you think it should be? Why?

2. What about having a baby? Do you think that it should be planned, or should it just happen when it happens? What is the ideal time or situation to have a baby?

3. What do you think your odds are of becoming pregnant in the next year or so? What are you basing that on?

4. What do you think would happen if you became pregnant? Do you ever think about that as a possibility when you do not use birth control? Are there good things about becoming pregnant?

MEDIA AND LEISURE HABITS

Now I am going to shift gears a little bit and ask you some questions to help us plan how to get our message out.

1. Where do you and your friends tend to hang out?

2. What types of entertainment do you and your friends prefer? Television? Radio? Where and when do you listen to the radio? Which stations/shows? Do you read a newspaper? Magazines? What websites or social networks do you spend time on online?

3. If we wanted to reach a lot of people similar to you in our campaign, where should we place our ads or messages? Do not worry about whether it is feasible. Where and when do you think you would be most receptive to messages promoting the use of birth control?

Appendix E

Readability Testing Formula

The SMOG Readability Formula is one of the most common and easiest to use readability tests. Use it to check the reading level needed to understand your printed materials. In general, the sixth- to eighth-grade level will be appropriate for most general audiences, but consider the educational attainment of your target audience to determine the correct readability level. You can also easily test the readability of a web page or document using online tools such as http://read ability.info.

To determine the approximate reading level of a publication, use the following steps:

1. Mark off 10 consecutive sentences each at the beginning, middle, and end of the piece.

   - A sentence is a string of words that ends with a period (.), a question mark (?), or an exclamation point (!).

2. Count the total number of words containing three or more syllables (polysyllabic), including repetitions, in those 30 sentences.

   - Hyphenated words count as one word.

   - Numbers and abbreviations should be pronounced to count the number of syllables.

   - Proper nouns should be counted as well if they are polysyllabic.

3. Use the conversion chart below to determine the approximate reading level.

   - Keep in mind that some polysyllabic words (e.g., exercise) are the simplest and clearest way in which to say something. In other cases, a one- or two-syllable word (e.g., larynx) might be more difficult. Use your judgment, and try to write as simply as possible.

SMOG Conversion Chart	
Polysyllabic Word Count	Grade Level
0–2	4
3–6	5
7–12	6
13–20	7
21–30	8
31–42	9
43–56	10
57–72	11
73–90	12
91–110	13
111–132	14
133–156	15
157–182	16
183–210	17
211–240	18

Source: Center for Substance Abuse Prevention. (1994). *You can prepare easy-to-read materials.* Rockville, MD: U.S. Department of Health and Human Services.

Note: Grade level predicts the grade-level difficulty ± 1.5 grades.

Index

About the Author

Nedra Kline Weinreich is President of Weinreich Communications, a consulting firm that works with nonprofits and government agencies to help them bring about health and social change. Since 1992, she has developed social marketing and social media programs for clients such as the U.S. Centers for Disease Control and Prevention, U.S. Substance Abuse and Mental Health Services Administration, National Institute for Child Health and Human Development, National Minority AIDS Council, Population Services International, Loyola University of Chicago, and many others. Prior to her work with Weinreich Communications, Nedra designed health education and communication programs for public and private organizations. She earned her master's degree in health and social behavior from the Harvard School of Public Health and teaches a course on social marketing at the UCLA School of Public Health. She offers in-person and online trainings via her Social Marketing University program, as well as customized workshops. Nedra lives in Los Angeles, California, with her husband Gil and children Ariel and Leora. Nedra would love to hear from you with your thoughts about the book. You can reach her at:

E-mail: weinreich@social-marketing.com

Web: www.social-marketing.com

Spare Change Blog: www.social-marketing.com/blog/

Twitter: www.twitter.com/Nedra